18.00

||| ||| |||||| || ||||| ||||||||||||||||||| ||| ||||

☑ **W9-BRL-012**

PLATO FOR THE MODERN AGE

Plato for the Modern Age

ROBERT S. BRUMBAUGH

GREENWOOD PRESS, PUBLISHERS
WESTPORT, CONNECTICUT

Library of Congress Cataloging in Publication Data

Brumbaugh, Robert Sherrick, 1918-
    Plato for the modern age.

        Reprint of the ed. published by Crowell-Collier
    Press, New York.
        Includes bibliographies and index.
        1. Plato. I. Title.
    B395.B77 1978   184   78-13271
    ISBN 0-313-20630-9

Copyright © 1962 by The Crowell-Collier Publishing Company

Reprinted with the permission of Robert S. Brumbaugh.

Reprinted in 1979 by Greenwood Press, Inc.
51 Riverside Avenue, Westport, CT 06880

Printed in the United States of America

10 9 8 7 6 5 4 3 2

Preface

A BOOK ABOUT Plato is not easy for a Platonist to write. Since, as I will show, part of Plato's own practice was to make his dialogues themselves concrete examples of the problems they discuss, a consistent Platonic book about Plato's philosophy must also be a philosophic contribution to contemporary Platonism. Further, since Platonists distrust lectures and didactic presentations, any such book, even if it both is and is about Platonic philosophy, will misrepresent it unless it can suggest the form of a conversation in which the reader shares ideas and investigations with the author as we talk to Plato.

This present book is an attempt to meet these difficult demands. It seems to me that only through sharing such a conversation will the reader be shown what to expect from Plato's works themselves. Those works are not only beautiful, but they illustrate a philosophic program that is good, and contain many insights that both were and still are true.

Three twentieth-century achievements make a new introduction of the present sort both necessary and possible. There is the continued advance of Plato scholarship, giving us more and more exact information about the world in which Plato wrote, exactly what his original text said, and the way in which modern analysis shows his ideas and arguments hold together. We can get a better picture than ever before of Plato as the great historical figure who culminates Greek philosophy. From the philosophy of A. N. Whitehead, the great modern Platonist (as opposed to Plato scholar), we see how Plato's central insights and ideas can be adapted and applied to our modern world. Third, recent work in literary criticism, applied to the dialogues, shows that Plato does in fact make his writings examples of the themes and methods discussed in each. This third point still seems dubiously imaginative to most British and American philologists and historians working on Plato, though an increasing number of detailed studies have shown that it is so. I have taken advantage of this self-illustrating character and explained it wherever it has been shown conclusively that it appears.

Notes, an annotated bibliography, and the book itself should help us to keep clear the differences of the two ways of looking at Plato that are combined here in a stereoscopic picture. On the one hand, we want as precise an account as can be had of the historical master of the Academy; on the other hand, we are dealing with a writer whose work sells widely because it is such good contemporary philosophy, and it would be un-Platonic not to recognize Plato as a major contemporary philosopher.

No matter how evident the need for a book like this one, I could never have written it at all without the assistance of my wife. She has discussed the organization and the central ideas with me, proposed many necessary changes in style, and firmly remanded for rewriting drafts that were tangles of obscurity. It is a pleasure to conclude my Preface with this acknowledgment, and with my thanks for her help.

CONTENTS

PART FIVE: HISTORY

PART SIX: AN APPRAISAL: THE ACADEMY'S PROGRAMS AND IDEAS, 2500 YEARS LATER

ERRATA

Page 154, line 23, should be *later tradition says that he passed the period of his retirement from political life as a*

Page 200, line 11, the date *1889* should be *1915*

Page 241, number 42, the words *Bk. V* should be *Bk. III*

Page 243, number 67, line 5, the words *13 vols.* should be *12 vols.*

Page 251, number 136, the date *1889* should be *1915*

Page 253, the word *Eryimachus* should be *Eryximachus*

To Bob, Susan, Eric, Katy, and Joanna
good Platonists all
within the limits of their powers of recollection

Introduction

PLATO IS GENERALLY regarded as the most brilliant speculative mind the West has produced. Some philosophers have
preferred the greater patience and methodical procedure of
Aristotle, Aquinas, or more recent analytic philosophy; others
have argued that the Platonic vision did not do justice to our
intuitions of duration and existence; but no one will ever deny
the continuing inspiration that Western philosophy has gained
from Plato.

A recent study of the teaching of philosophy in the United
States showed something else about Plato that may surprise
the reader who thinks of classical Greek philosophy as something cultural and beautiful, but remote and long past. For
Plato was found to be the most widely read contemporary
writer on philosophy in America (in various English translations) by a margin of two to one. In 1960, I casually picked
up twenty-five new English and American editions of translations of dialogues, individually or in sets, and I am sure that
there were more. The reason is not only that Plato was unique
in his ability to present philosophy in a dialogue form which
draws his reader into the inquiry and makes it vital, but also
that one has the feeling of a remarkable vision, addressed
for the most part to problems that are central in our lives
today.

Even in translation, we are aware of a brilliant logical
and aesthetic coherence; there is no fine detail of any authentic dialogue, except perhaps a few minutiae of the model
municipal legal code, that does not have a reason which makes
it logically and aesthetically just right. But with this flawless
sense of form, Plato combined a restless, engaged programmatic imagination; each new idea suggests to him a new proposal for research or a new project for human welfare. In

some cases, the projected work was rapidly accomplished: twenty years intervened between Plato's remark that someone ought to invent solid geometry, and its actual invention. In other cases, twenty-five hundred years have not been time enough to execute or disprove the feasibility of Platonic programs, such as the construction of an axiomatic-deductive science of society, the development of a universal theory of value, and the achievement of the unity of science. We must, to appreciate Plato, share this sense of speculative adventure, and be aware that our problems of the present often continue a conversation or contain a suggestion from the Hellenic past.

As an admirer of Plato, I agree with him that philosophy should be shared inquiry, and that the meaning of a dialogue depends to some extent on its setting and the character of the speakers. What is of permanent value to us is our heritage of Platonic writings; but it is peculiarly true of these that we cannot fully appreciate what Plato said without enough biographical background to feel acquainted with the man who said it. And since Plato was dependent on the science and culture of his own time for illustrations and for his notions of how close the ideal could come to the actual, it helps us to see what some of the immediate issues were when Plato wrote and what the things were that everyone took for granted. In a number of cases, particularly when we deal with practical applications of philosophy, we will find that history and science have gone beyond what Plato's time imagined possible, so that his specific proposals—e.g., for treatment of slaves in a good Greek colonial town of his time—give the modern reader exactly the wrong notion of the principles at work unless we recognize these historical limitations. This does not, however, deny the point made above, that when it comes to principles—to broad issues and basic questions— Plato's programs and proposals still go beyond what the Western world has been able either to prove impossible or to carry out.

Plato's life, like his works, divides roughly into three major periods: a youthful commitment to philosophical inquiry and its defense, a mature systematic vision, and a final careful criticism and application of the system he had envisaged. For each of these main periods, this book first introduces Plato at different stages of his career. Throughout, we find a life of intellectual adventure while administration, political experiment, and travel give some contrast to this life of speculation, and perhaps we have to thank such episodes as his imprisonment in Syracuse, or seeing his favorite nephew enlist in a hazardous military campaign, as well as the general Greek flamboyance of the age, for the fact that Plato's university work is seldom a retreat from reality into an ivory tower.

Plato's philosophy is reflected in the form as well as in the content of his writings; and our appreciation of the philosophic ideas depends on an appreciation of the way in which the dialogue's literary form is essential to the meaning of the abstract issues its characters discuss. For each major period of Plato's life, I will give some account of the dialogues he wrote: the characters who enact these dramatic intellectual conversations and confrontations, the theme they explore with its major variations, and I will also note some internal evidence that our biographical notions are correct in assumptions such as that a visit to Tarentum would have led to new confidence in mathematics, one to Syracuse to less confidence in unprincipled dictatorship.

The central interest of our conversation with Plato is, of course, philosophical. We will want to see what new philosophic ideas make their first appearance in Western thought in his writings. More important, however, is the question of whether this philosophy is true, and whether it gives us valid contemporary insights into the world and ourselves. It seems important, in a world where we wonder whether it is realistic to try to act on the basis of principles and ideals, as opposed to expediency and immediate interest, to consider one of Plato's central and repeated arguments: that the ideal is in fact a component of the actual, and that it is unrealistic to set aside principles or ideals in favor of living in a more "realistic" way. In our world today we find a sharp opposition between fact and value, science claiming to describe fact objectively, value being treated somehow intuitively and humanistically with more dogmatism than discipline. Plato challenges us to consider a second major argument, namely, that values and value judgments are presupposed by all existence and description alike, so that a supposed opposition of fact and value is an illusion resulting from unclear thinking. It seems particularly vital where, as on the contemporary scene, philosophy stresses literal and objective analysis—with technical concerns limited to a small set of problems—to see once more what a Platonic dialogue can offer us as a model of philosophy more directly concerned with life, wider in range of inquiry, and implicitly committed to the proposition that only living conversation can be adequate for any communication of analysis or meaning. We will end our conversation with Plato by asking him about these themes; from his own character, and the relevant statements he has left us, we should be able to appreciate his answers, and to see where we must go next in carrying forward our own philosophic discussions.

All of my interpretations are responsible, though they stress the speculative and imaginative dimension of Plato's thought, but some are unconventional. An annotated bibliography of editions, standard works, and alternative approaches may help the interested reader to check and appraise the argument presented here against other interpretations, including his own. Footnotes have been used to treat a few particularly technical problems of idea, text, translation, or historical documentation.

In general, the text itself centers its interest on the presentation of Plato's life, works, and philosophy, and the notes and bibliography are used to treat scholarly problems that are involved in getting the philosophy clear. The one exception to this may be a section on the history of Plato's text, as it was copied, preserved, altered, and handed down. I know that some non-specialists are fascinated by the factual detective work of textual history, and that others are not; but it seemed to me so interesting that I could not resist a brief outline of the route by which we have received our copies of the works of Plato. I offer no apology for including a discussion of writings of doubtful authenticity that appeared in the Academy's manuscripts of Plato's works for these are relevant to our interpretation of the emphasis and development of Plato's philosophy.

PART ONE

Philosophy and Inquiry

CHAPTER I

Young Plato in Athens

IN 423 B.C., when Plato was four years old, an explosive collision of new ideas and conservative resistance to them was represented on the Athenian stage in *The Clouds,* a brilliant comedy by Aristophanes. The comic poet, a reactionary looking back to days when Athens was a happy, 100 per cent Greek town, attacked the new "atheistic science" and new "shyster legal training" that were "ruining young men." He mistrusted eggheads and progressive educators, and expressed that distrust with an unmatchable, if libellous, humor.[1]

As the second scene of the play opened, the audience saw a snub-nosed young scientist, master and proprietor of "the small idea-works," sitting above the orchestra in a basket, having had himself hoisted up "to think better about higher things." Both mask and name identified him as "Socrates," a man who in real life had attained a certain notoriety in Athens for his scientific interests. This villain taught that "the gods are only folklore, as physics has discovered," and that "a proper training in legal trickery can teach even a stupid man to evade his just debts." The sense of freedom these teachings brought with them became apparent in a later scene, where one of the young students rushed home from the "idea-works" to beat his father.[2]

Two things in particular should be noted about this play; the first is that the ideas and techniques it attacked were intrinsically interesting, and the second that in Athens at that date these ideals and techniques were relatively new. This puts Athens a century and half behind the Greek cities of

Ionia, in Asia Minor, where "science" had been in business
since about 585 B.C., and perhaps forty years behind Sicilian
developments of rhetoric and the applications of it to politics and law.

In 415 B.C., when Plato was twelve, another play, Euripides'
tragedy, *The Trojan Women,* attacked a change in Athenian
policy in the conduct of her long-extended hot-and-cold war
with Sparta which had begun some twenty years before. In the
war, the island of Melos desired to remain neutral; the Athenians
decided to discourage such neutralism by executing, in an act
of unprovoked aggression, all the Melian men and enslaving
the women and children. Euripides' play dramatized a parallel
situation in the story of the fall of Troy, to protest against
the brutality of misused power and the unjustifiable suffering
of captive women and children whose husbands and fathers
had died nobly in defense of their city. Athens, which had
taken pride in the equity and justice of her dealings with
smaller allies, rejected any claim to such ideals by her action
in the Melian affair, a piece of arrogant barbarity which
marked the beginning of a downturn of Athenian fortunes in
the war.[3]

This was a long way from the Athens Plato had heard of
in stories told him by his mother Perictione, and Pyrilampes,
his stepfather. His ancestors were all of important and aristocratic Athenian families, and surely repeated with pride the
story of the defeat of the great Persian invasion less than a
century before; Platea, Thermopylae, Salamis were among
the moments of Greek gallantry and glory in their victory
against overwhelming odds. Then, as his older relatives could
remember at first hand, there was the history of the rise of
Athens to leadership; her naval power and growing commercial activity made the city a natural leader and center of
prosperity and expansion. Under the leadership of Pericles,
the great statesman whom Plato's stepfather had known,
Athens, leader of a league of smaller allies, advanced in
trade and industry; and a financial surplus (accumulated from
contributions paid by the other league members) was spent
on public works for the capital. The greatest artists of the

time were commissioned by the Athenians; public taste rose to a level that could appreciate unsurpassed sculpture, tragedy, and comedy, delicate die-engraving of coinage, as well as the fascinating gadgetry of a new type of sundial installed near the market-place.[4] The only jarring note in this great story was that the Athenian expansion had collided with the interests of Sparta and her allies, and their collision of interests had led to the Peloponnesian War, during which Plato grew up, and which was not ended until he was twenty-one.

Part of Pericles' program of building Athens as the center of culture, and a part which Socrates, who was a friend of Plato's family, must have talked about often, was Pericles' invitation to Anaxagoras, a leading scientist and philosopher of Asia Minor, to come to Athens as consultant and companion. Anaxagoras brought with him from the Greek frontiers the results of a hundred years of research in physics, logic, mathematics, and medicine. We will discuss, presently, what some of these ideas were; for the moment, we will only note that although conservative opposition forced Anaxagoras to leave Athens, the new ideas that he had brought were come to stay. And of course we can be fairly certain that young Plato knew of the adventures of the small scientific circle that remained active in Athens, debating such questions as whether the earth was flat or round, whether we thought with the brain or the blood, since two academic generations later, a leading figure in this circle was Socrates himself.[5]

In this way, then, young Plato grew in an Athens filled with memories of victory, power, and glory. Everywhere about him he could see what we still admire as the characteristic of Athenian culture of that period: recognition of the importance of the ideal in the realm of the actual. From the bravery of the soldiers at Marathon, through the brilliant art and architecture of Pericles' program, to the everyday spoons and pottery around him, his world repeated the same lesson: beauty and nobility were possible, but could only be won by loyalty to an ideal form. After the loss of the long war to Sparta, much remained; new statesmen might once more restore the Athens of the past; or, failing that, might at least encourage her to hold her cultural leadership of Greece, which defeat in battle had not taken from her. Perhaps a new constitution or new administration could rebuild better than ever; perhaps Plato himself could play some part in the rebuilding. With such thoughts in mind, and with a family tradition of political activity behind him, young Plato had decided at the age of twenty that politics was to be his career.[6]

However, as we are reminded by the attacks on the "lawyers" when we think back to Aristophanes' play, the "traditional" order that Athenian aristocrats admired was not without opponents; the scientists were not the only active critics of aristocratic values. After the Persian War, other Greek cities grew as Athens had in increasing prosperity, creating new leaders from the upper middle class, and also moved toward increased democracy and class mobility (trends against which Aristophanes directed another play). In this new dynamic period, training in law and in speaking in Assemblies became essential tools for the young man eager to get ahead. To meet this need, the Sophists, expensive professional teachers of manners, law, and political tactics, appeared on the scene. Looking back, some Greeks (Plato among them) saw in Sophistic education the same "realism" that the Athenians had shown in their treatment of the Melians. The Sophists themselves, at least the older generation of them, were "gentlemen," rather like a modern college faculty. But here the resemblance, I hope, ends. For the lesson they taught their students was that prestige and property were the measures of success, and that right techniques would make it possible to win these in the game of life. Perhaps one could not, as Stephen Potter's "Lifeman" could, "win in the game of life without actually cheating"; but even so, the crucial thing was to win. "Justice" and "nobility" were somehow set aside, as mere simple-minded loyalty to arbitrary convention; whereas what was natural, beyond conventions, was the contest for personal advantage and survival. There is much to be said in favor of the Sophists' challenge to "tradition" as identical with "morality"; sharp practice in contract cases, which so annoyed Aristophanes, hardly seems "worse" than the traditional mistreatment of slaves and insolence to tradesmen that figured among the old feudal values to which the comedian wanted to return. Yet on balance, the Sophistic appeal to voracity and flamboyance, at the expense of beauty and nobility, was not a better influence than Aristophanes' unreconstructed ridicule of innovation. The Sophists were successful in the sense that they made great fortunes, but they did not win over everyone as friends. The older families, challenged by the rising middle class, disliked them; and the proletariat, envious of the effectiveness of their higher education but unable to afford it, resented them. Socrates, who admired many of their new ideas and shared their enthusiasm for inquiry, remained fundamentally against them; and young Plato did not have the advantages of this liberating "progressive education." We must remember that in the foreground of our picture of Athens there are frequent entrances and exits of these expensive and eloquent educators, suggesting, as they come on stage, that we take the actual and forget about the ideal. It was quite unfair of Aristophanes to muddle together Sophists, scientists, and anarchists in the composite caricature of "Socrates" in his play.[7]

We have seen that it was in this setting of science, Sophistry, beauty, past military glory and defeat, that Plato's determination to be a politician was formed; it had its first chance of realization in 404 B.C. In that year, with tacit approval (or at least non-intervention) of the victorious Spartans, a conservative interim government of oligarchic Athenians drove out the most active democratic faction; then, pending what was supposed to be a constitutional revision, a Committee of Thirty assumed control. Plato's uncle, Charmides, was one of "The Thirty," and his relative, Critias, a leader of it. They invited Plato to join the group. But before the young man could decide, "The Thirty" had begun to tighten their hold on dictatorial power—opposition was met by assassination, criticism by intimidation, treasury deficits by arbitrary execution of wealthy citizens for treason (since the property of executed traitors was confiscated by the state). "In short, I saw," Plato wrote of this period much later, "that the injustices of these men made the Athenians look back upon the war as a happy time." And the young aristocratic idealist refused to join them.[8]

Within two years, the extreme democratic faction which had been driven out of Athens returned in force, and overthrew "The Thirty." The restored democratic government recognized that continuing old feuds and battles would have destroyed the city entirely, and wisely passed a law that the past be forgotten—no political crimes prior to their restoration could be prosecuted by the democracy's courts. At this point, again, young Plato felt that a chance to begin his career might have arrived. A son of an old and influential Athenian family, who had refused to share in the work of "The Thirty," and who looked forward to a compromise of the differences between extremes, could reasonably feel there was an opportunity for him to work with this new government. Once more, however, he waited to see what the democratic leaders would do; and when, in 399 B.C., they executed Socrates, he saw that he could not join them either, and for the time he put aside his ambition for an Athenian political career.

Background: Science and Philosophy

What most distressed Aristophanes about the new ideas that came to Athens was that they included the scientific attitude which we still share today. That is, there was an assumption that nature was an ordered system, predictable and lawlike in behavior; and that such things as lightning, planetary motion, or meteorites were to be explained by reference to laws of nature, not by some whimsical intervention of demons, gods, or dryads. In fact, the scientists doubted whether "gods,"—in the traditional sense, beings with human bodies who lived forever—existed at all. But even if they did, such unpredictable and unobservable agents had no place in scientific theory.[9]

We will trace two lines of development of Greek thought which had gone on before Athens became a center of science and philosophy. From the work of engineers in Asia Minor, there developed the notion that physics, the study of laws governing matter in motion, was able to answer questions about the ultimate nature of things. This attitude moved from the rather simple first theory, that of Thales of Miletus, that reality was matter in a fluid state, to the final elaboration of a classical atomic theory. It was this "materialistic" tendency that Aristophanes particularly distrusted—his title and the songs of the "Chorus of Clouds" in the play are a parody of the scientific theory that everything real is a condensed or rarefied state of "air," so that "Zeus is no more, the whirlwind rules instead." But asides in the play, for example a brief story of how "Socrates" took an enormous compass as if to draw a circle, but slyly used its sharp point to hook some meat from a neighbor's altar across the wall, reflect a different line of thought. For, in the West of the Greek world, we find pure mathematicians and logicians who were less concerned with the material of things than with their structure. Pythagoras and his school could, in fact, take credit for the invention of pure geometry, and for an enthusiasm for mathematics as a tool of research that led to their slogan, "things are numbers." And in the city of Elea, formal logic came into being, as a tool that could be used critically against common-sense, Ionian materialism, or against Pythagorean mathematics, or to reveal a paradox inherent in the nature of thought itself.[10]

Thus by 423 B.C., Greek thought faced two important problems. The first was that of combining materialism with formalism: to find some way to use the insights both of the physicists, who thought of reality as matter, and the formalists—mathematicians and logicians—who thought that what was most real was structure. The second problem was that of reconciling science and human value; the Sophists, who favored discarding science in favor of studies with more human interest, held one radical position, the scientists, who thought their techniques of objective description could account for all phenomena, held another. The collision of science and Sophistry directed immediate attention to the gap between a world of value and a world of neutral fact, though there is not much evidence that either the scientists or the Sophists saw this opposition clearly until Socrates and Plato were able to show what the difference between these two ways of thinking involved. (See note 10, which gives a compressed outline of the two traditions—materialism and formalism—that had developed in Greek scientific and philosophic thought.) All these controversies were in the air when Anaxagoras accepted Pericles' invitation. As we have seen, Anaxagoras scandalized conservative Athenians with his new scientific explanation of the sun, moon, and stars; they were, he argued, heated stones, kept in place by the speed of their revolution around the earth. The seasons, rains, and wind, were the result of natural causes, not special dispensations of Zeus, or Zephyrus, or Boreas. To find that the stars were not gods and the weather was not a matter of direct divine operation was shocking enough; but when Anaxagoras added that *"Nous"* (reason or mind) was the moving force and ordering principle of the universe, and that this Mind *had no body,* this seemed to many "sheer atheism."[11] The idea that there are infinite worlds, "and they have men on them, and a sun and moon, and canals and houses," attracted rather less attention. When Pericles' prestige weakened, the first move of the opposition against him was to bring an accusation of "impiety" (which could carry a death penalty) against Anaxagoras; and, with Pericles' help, the philosopher left Athens without standing trial.

But the damage the conservatives feared had already been done. An intellectual curiosity was awakened that continued to animate the city until the pagan philosophic schools were closed in 529 A.D. A "research center" of sorts, devoted to the new science, operated by Archelaus of Athens, survived Anaxagoras' departure; and presently a leading role in its work seems to have taken by an enthusiastic young scientist named Socrates, whose influence was so decisive in the career and on the thought of his young admirer, Plato.

Where Ionian science had concentrated on the objective world, on phenomena men could observe, to the relative neglect of the observer, the new Sophistic movement shifted emphasis to the other extreme, from nature as observed to man as its observer. Knowledge was to have human value, or it was worthless. A second Sophistic characteristic was the unwillingness to accept conventional standards as necessarily right, or as laws of nature. What seemed "natural" they argued, was that every man try to get ahead in the world; it was only because of "custom" that nations agreed on legal and ethical systems, and imposed mutual obligations on their citizens. This scepticism extended to traditional religion; many of the traditional stories about the gods seemed silly, and while civic religious festivals might be socially desirable, no clever man would be likely to take religious myths dogmatically or literally.

The Sophists were influenced by a number of factors: an apparent speculative dead-end in philosophy and science, a new set of facts pointing out the great diversity of human cultures, a new self-consciousness about the role and importance of language, and a new confidence that men could achieve self-realization through skills which gave them control of society and commodities. The new skills the Sophists taught met a real demand, for the Athenians did not allow their excellent taste and loyalty to ideals on appropriate occasions to interfere with some cutthroat practices in their rather vivid daily lives. One authority has estimated that the average Athenian businessman could expect to appear in court for one breach of contract suit a year; and, under the local laws, he had to present his own case. A small group of petty operators made a living from threatening lawsuits with nuisance value against important citizens, and settling out of court. Charges of treason or impiety were brought on occasion as political maneuvers. Not only success, but sometimes effective survival, made skill in law something to be desired. The Town Meeting was much the same: a man who could not talk persuasively was· at a serious disadvantage; not only would he be unlikely to hold elective office, but he might end up with a special contribution to the navy or the theater assessed against him.

The new humanism and new skills were needed; but as we

have seen, the Sophists' ideas were too superficial to be satis-
fying to serious inquirers. In claiming to make men happy or
better, the Sophists seemed only to be offering tools—techniques for winning lawsuits and influencing voters—with no
warning that such tools could be used in ways disastrous to
the happiness of their owners. Much as it may have annoyed
Socrates to find himself agreeing in the criticisms of the "progressive education" of the day, he had to admit the inadequacy of the amoralism, subjectivism, and open instrumental-
ism of the Sophistic training.

CHAPTER II

Plato and Socrates

The Trial of Socrates

YOUNG PLATO FINALLY decided to give up his political ambitions when the restored democracy tried and executed his
dear older friend, Socrates, "who was, of all the men I have
known, the most just." Plato set about defending Socrates'
memory and carrying on his mission, and in his *Apology*
recreated the defense Socrates offered at his trial. Why did
Anytus, the leader of the democratic .group, persuade two
other Athenians, Meletus and Lycon, to join him in prose-
cuting a well-known scientist and moralist, by this time an
elderly man? (Socrates was then seventy.) This seems particularly puzzling when we remember that this same statesman
had passed the law prohibiting prosecution of political crimes
committed before "The Thirty" were driven out after their
reign of terror. It cannot have been for co-operation with "The
Thirty," for as a matter of fact the democratic restoration
saved Socrates from assassination at their hands. It seems most
unlikely that mere personal animosity could have been the motive. But the only other thing Socrates had done was to ask questions about virtue and government. "The Thirty" had not been
able to quiet him, and under the democracy he continued his
investigations. To nineteenth-century readers and scholars,
living in an atmosphere that took freedom of speech for
granted, the whole case was a mystery. But Plato suggests the
answer clearly enough in passages that give us some idea of
what Socrates' questions were, and what Anytus' reaction to

them was. Socrates no doubt persisted in suggesting that democracy was an unsound form of government: just as a city that decided questions of public health by popular vote would do better to consult a doctor, wouldn't one suppose that questions of public policy could be better decided by expert opinion than by popular referendum? And yet, had Athens ever produced a leader able to teach virtue to its citizens? Or was the fact that a national hero like Pericles was finally repudiated by the public not proof that his administration had failed to make men better? These questions challenged both the theory of democrary and the success of its practice, at just the time when Athens was still defenseless against possible Spartan interference, and the restored democratic government was in a very precarious position. In effect, Anytus must have seen Socrates as a "clear and present danger"; and those of us who have lived in the twentieth rather than the nineteenth century can very readily see why he might have done so. Where Anytus would much have preferred uncritical patriotism and conformity as the order of the day, Socrates was insisting on giving young people ideas that at least implicitly were critical of the government, hence un-Athenian. By his own account at the trial, Socrates had deflated a good many politicians in debate by asking simple questions, and had stirred up a number of young men to imitate his example.

And so we see that there was an obvious motive, not mysterious or hidden, for the action Anytus took in accusing Socrates of "impiety and corrupting the youth." We must realize, too, that although this charge could carry the death penalty, it was almost certainly intended only to frighten Socrates so that he would leave the town, as Anaxagoras had many years before. To show that the accusation represented general opinion, Anytus chose as his associates a conservative religious man, Meletus, and an orator—about whom nothing else is known—Lycon. However, they had miscalculated: Socrates stayed in Athens, stood trial, and forced the issue.

We have mentioned Socrates several times in passing, and what we have said fairly summarizes what many members of the jury knew about him. Socrates had been the central character of a comedy in which he was attacked as a dangerous intellectual innovator; he was a student of the new science, which was suspected of atheistic tendencies; he was insistent in the kind of cross-examination that the Sophists had perfected in their new legal training, though he differed from them in asking questions about human excellence and the self rather than questions about "success." He had been very indiscriminate in his associations: members of "The Thirty," visiting lawyers, foreign mathematicians had all been his hosts and partners in conversation on occasion. Thus public opinion was against him as the trial began.

But the Socrates that Plato re-creates for us is very different from this public image based on Aristophanes' hero. Socrates was in fact one of the young men enthusiastic about Ionian science; but after a time, he realized that scientific explanation of the Ionian type could not answer the most important questions that he had in mind. For example, his science could not answer "What is human life?" "What am I?" or even "What good is science itself?" The Sophistic answers were not satisfactory, either; the human self must be something more remarkable and complex than the Sophistic "bundle of greedy appetite" or the scientific "current of dry air"; it obviously must be so, or it would never ask the question, "What, then, am I, and what ought I to be?" Here was a pressing and practical problem; neither science, law, nor society could be properly organized and used until one had some answer. Socrates had seen this much: that man can be sensitive to ideals, that inner integrity is more dignified than physical comfort, and that excellence and knowledge go together—though exactly how, we will never know if we don't inquire. Justice and honesty have, for Socrates, intrinsic value; they are not merely means to some other end, but give human dignity and value to their possessor. He is certain of this, and will never do an act that would make him a worse person simply to gain property, status, or even longevity. But his fellow Athenians remained indifferent to this tremendous discovery and curiosity; rather than seeing the importance of

self-knowledge and the demand it made for a new concept
of "virtue," the ideal of human excellence, they spent their
lives concerned with currant futures and district political
clubs. Socrates felt passionately that he must show them their
mistake, their ignorance and indifference to the question of
greatest moment; and this he had set out to do. In spite of
our advances in science and law, a twentieth-century teacher
suddenly awakened by this realization might do the same.

What, then, was Socrates to do about the accusation brought
against him? If he ran away, this would show either that he
didn't really prefer personal integrity to saving his own skin,
or that he admitted his inquiry had been an undesirable social
enterprise and that he was guilty as charged. But he did really
believe what he had said, and he did not think he had committed any injustice; on the contrary, if the Athenians only
would see it, he had been doing them good, not harm.

And so Socrates stayed for the trial. Plato's *Apology* is
probably fairly a curate as a report, but probably also edited
and polished to bring out the philosophic issues that the
situation held. Socrates asks the jury to forget old prejudices
they may have against him based on *The Clouds*, and explains
that he inquires because he has a "divine mission." The
Oracle of Apollo at Delphi, asked by a friend, "whether any
man was wiser than Socrates?" had answered "None." Socrates knew he was not wise, and tried to find the real meaning
of this answer; for Oracles were always or at least ordinarily
ambiguous in what they said. So he set about trying to find
a wiser man; he questioned the statesmen, poets, and artisans
of Athens. To his surprise, however, Socrates found he had
one advantage over all he met: about important things (for
mere craftsmanship could not count as the highest "wisdom"),
the men he talked to knew nothing, but were absolutely sure
that they did know; he, at least, realizing his own ignorance,
was that much wiser. The real "clear and present danger"
seemed to be the men who had complete power, confidence,
and ignorance, who spoke of "justice" but with no knowledge
of its meaning, who made laws for national security with
excellent intention and uncritical stupidity. (It is characteris-

tic of Socrates that he says he wanted to find a wiser man as "an excuse for going back and cross-examining the Oracle"; given that excuse, even Apollo would not be immune to Socrates' questioning!)

How true this is becomes clear as Socrates briefly questions Meletus, the prosecutor. Meletus has charged Socrates with impiety; in response to a question, he says this means atheism; and presently he explains to the jury that what he really means is "that Socrates is an atheist who worships strange gods." How far can we trust Meletus' judgment, in spite of his sureness that he knows about religion and piety, if he cannot see that atheism and worship of gods (however strange) don't go together? Again, when questioned, Meletus says that "Socrates is the only Athenian who deliberately makes young fellow citizens worse and more unjust, and does this knowing that the worse they become, the more harm they will do him." Is this a possible explanation of the charge of "corrupting the youth"?

Socrates turns now to the balance of his defense. His speech is interesting, because it follows the topics of other defendants' speeches in establishing Socrates' character and citizenship, then, unlike any other such defense, rejects this evidence as irrelevant to the point at issue. Socrates has done all of the things a good man and good citizen should: he has a family, an excellent military record, he was not intimidated by "The Thirty" into complicity in their crimes, though his resistance risked his life. If he had stopped there, he could surely have gained an acquittal. But what was really on trial, he reminded the jury, was the social value or danger of his inquiries; and other considerations should be set aside. To deny the importance of his mission, to admit he should be punished for it, or even to agree that he will now stop it, are not open to him, he tells the jury; all would be unjust, and he has always been motivated by a love of justice.

At this point, a first ballot is taken of the jury, to decide Socrates' guilt or innocence; if guilty, he can propose a counter-penalty to the prosecution's recommendation, and a second jury vote will decide which penalty to impose. When he is

found guilty, Socrates says that in all honesty, since he has
been a public benefactor, he thinks what he deserves at the
hands of the Athenians is permanent board and lodging at
public expense; but, since he puts no value on money anyway,
it would not be a punishment or admission of guilt to give a
token of money as a penalty. The prosecution has proposed
the death penalty, and the jury votes for it—by a larger
margin than the first vote for condemnation.

In a further speech to the jury, Socrates sums up his decision. Human life, to be valuable, must be directed by intelligence; intelligence involves self-knowledge and a correct esti-
mate of what things have intrinsic, what merely instrumental
value. He has concluded that "a life immune to questioning
is not worth living."

Plato's Biography of Socrates
(*Apology, Crito,* and *Phaedo*)

The most powerful, yet classically restrained, writing in
Western literature is Plato's account, in his dialogue the
Phaedo, of the final conversation on immortality and of the
death of Socrates.

We have indicated Plato's interpretation of Socrates' re-
fusal to leave Athens and of his conduct at his trial. That
many Athenians needed such an interpretation is clear from
the bewilderment of Xenophon, Plato's contemporary and
another admirer of Socrates; the latter finally decided that
Socrates had provoked his execution deliberately as a means
of avoiding suicide, yet escaping the infirmities of old age.
Plato's alternative interpretation seems better; here we have a
man of principle, who had done no injustice, and who does
not intend to act in any way that could seem a tacit admission of guilt. Socrates believed that man's only hope for excellence or happiness lay in attaining self-knowledge through
critical inquiry; and "knowledge" to him meant both abstract recognition and concrete awareness of value, so that
no man who "knew" justice to be better than injustice, in
Socrates' sense of "knowing," would ever act unjustly. So-

ciety and law were more important than the individual, yet ultimately owed their value to the fact that they were essential means to the end of individual virtue and happiness; so that a court order prohibiting education or free inquiry, even such an order by a duly constituted court, would be a contradiction of the very purpose of court and law.

But Plato and Socrates were neither anarchists nor anti-social individualists: both recognized the claims of society upon the individual. In a Greek city-state, these claims were much more personal and intense than they are today—the account of the *polis* in Kitto's book, *The Greeks,* makes this feeling and its intensity clear. A just man had to observe the principle of *respect for law*—this is the necessary condition for human association, and such association is the necessary condition for nurture and education which make man truly human. Could Socrates justify his claim that he was just, if by his actions he set a precedent which would overturn all law and justice in a state were others to follow it? This is the theme of the second dialogue in Plato's trilogy of the trial and death of Socrates, the *Crito.* (Crito was a wealthy friend of Socrates, who had offered at his trial to pay a large fine if the court would accept it as the alternative to the death penalty. Socrates, we recall, holding money to be of no value, had himself offered to pay any fine he could afford, because this would not be a punishment for him and would not amount to any admission that he deserved a penalty for acts of in-justice.) Crito came to Socrates in prison with the news that he could arrange for Socrates' escape. The jailer could be bribed to help, and there would likely be little risk to him or Crito for arranging the escape; probably Anytus and his sup-porters would not be unhappy to have Socrates leave Athens unharmed; this was probably what they had intended in the first place. But they must act at once: the voyage of the sacred ship, during which no executions could be performed, would soon be over—the ship had been sighted at sea. Socrates, before he decided to act, must first inquire with Crito whether this would be right—and he stated the issue in the form of an imaginary conversation between himself and the Laws of

Athens. As an Athenian, Socrates was under an obligation to the Laws, and he had been tried and sentenced by their due process. ("But unjustly," urged Crito.) Whether the sentence was just or unjust, said the Laws, will not change the fact that due process was observed and the sentence was a legal decision. The Laws said to Socrates that if he were to run away, he would be committing an act of cowardice and of injustice, and would indeed be guilty of the charges brought against him. It might have been within his rights to disobey a court injunction, but only if he was then willing to stand trial for that disobedience before the court. He owed the principle of respect for law his allegiance, and he was not released from his implicit contract with Athenian law just because he found it personally unpleasant. The Laws told him it would be wrong to escape; and Socrates remained.

In the final dialogue of this trilogy, the *Phaedo,* which seems to have been written considerably later than its two companion pieces, Socrates talks, on the afternoon set for his execution, with fellow philosophers. They discuss the nature of the soul, and its immortality. "Not even a comic poet," remarks Socrates dryly at one point, "could say I am now idly babbling about matters that are none of my concern!" Calmly as ever, still questioning, he encourages his friends to refute, if they can, his beliefs that the human self has some power in it to reach beyond a short physical career in space and time; that there are objective ideals our souls can know; and that Socrates' own "idealistic" behavior in standing trial and remaining in prison is right, not merely perversity or error.

It appears that, on the level of physics, as part of a cosmic "vital force," the soul has a kind of immortality (though not a kind that would justify Socrates' beliefs; rather a kind that even an Ionian physicist would acknowledge). But one level higher, Simmias, a young Pythagorean, urged to speak his mind, suggests that the human soul is a "harmony"—an accompaniment or overtone of the mechanical operations of the body, as music springs from the vibrating strings of a tuned lyre. (This is indeed a Pythagorean way of putting the case;

it brings together the Pythagorean notions that harmony is a key to nature, and that health is *isonomia,* a kind of tuned equilibrium. Simmias' idea recurs in modern philosophy, where the position is given the technical name of "epiphenomenalism".) This "harmony" view gives us a much more human *psyche* than some indeterminate cosmic vital force, and one which would correspond much better to the kind of "soul" Socrates believes to be immortal, *except* that the harmony ceases with the destruction of the lyre. Since on this analogy the soul would cease with dissolution of the body, Socrates' hopes and ideals seem groundless.

Socrates replies to this analogy with a brief autobiography to illustrate how he himself came to discover where it is in error. The fact is, in spite of any contrary supposition by science, that the soul directs and causes the behavior of the body it inhabits, rather than passively reflecting it. It is as if someone, asked why Socrates is sitting here in prison, were to answer that Socrates is made of bones and muscles, and the bones have joints at which they are bent—"omitting to state what is the true cause, namely that the Athenians thought it best to condemn me, and I that it was better . . . and more just . . . to remain. For, by the Dog!" Socrates continues, with a side reference to the "scientific" and Sophistic postulate of a natural instinct for self-preservation, "these old bones and sinews would have been in Boeotia or Megara, under the impression that this was best . . . if I had not thought it better . . . to await my execution." He goes on, "One would speak truly if he were to say that I could not do as I am *without* bones and muscles . . . but this does not mean I do it *because* of them . . . for a necessary condition is different from a cause." He himself, as a young man, had been enthusiastic in the study of science, and had wondered about many questions—the shape of the earth and why it stays in the center of the universe, the nature of the human body, and "whether we think with the blood, or air, or fire? Or perhaps none of these, but in the brain." Then he "heard someone reading from a book he said was by Anaxagoras, that '. . . mind is the orderer and the cause of all things.'"

This gave him a whole new set of ideas, and he hurried to buy a copy of the book (which could not have been a very long one, since it retailed for one drachma). He had great expectations, for if reason ordered all things, it would surely order them in the way that is best; and "I expected the book to tell me whether the earth is round or flat . . . and then to show me why this is better." But the young philosopher was disappointed: Anaxagoras used Mind in his system only to set the world in motion, then reverted to the Ionian accounts via "conditions," not "true causes." But Socrates, from this time on, turned his main attention from questions of fact to questions of value.

As against any "harmony of the body" hypothesis, we must recognize that a soul (1) directs the body; (2) is able to know truths that are unchanging; (3) feels the attraction of "ideals"—it has some "divination" or "vision" of wisdom, courage, and justice as qualities that have intrinsic value; (4) realizes, reflecting on this, that its true identity as a human soul lies in the unchanging realm of ideals and ideas; these are the causes, not merely the conditions, of a good human life. Seen in this way, the soul is different in kind from any physical process, and its nature must reach beyond the immediate adventures of its body; and insofar as a man's true identity is an unchanging ideal goal, he can claim immortality.

But what sort of thing happens to the individual soul after death? We do not *know*, yet a myth can give a vivid picture of the sort of thing that we might expect. And Socrates proceeds to tell an imaginative story, in which the earth is in the center of the universe, and the latest details of Greek science (astronomy, geography, chemistry, and geology) are harmonized into a *good* cosmic order. He thus leaves his friends with a concrete example of the sort of philosophy he had hoped Anaxagoras' book would offer: a synthesis of scientific detail resting on the postulate that the cosmos has a good over-all order and plan. In such a cosmos, justice must have intrinsic value, and the human soul, with its vision of eternity and desire for it, ought to be immortal.[1]

As evening approaches, Socrates calmly drinks the hemlock which his weeping jailer has prepared. He lies down, and his body begins to grow numb and to stiffen. Suddenly, he speaks to Crito: "Crito, I owe a cock to Aesculapius. Will you pay this debt?" "The debt shall be paid." These are Socrates' last words; shortly thereafter, he is dead. Aesculapius is the god of medicine and healing; Socrates, about to be free of the body's pains and pleasures, and confident that no harm can await him, is remembering that he should offer payment for treatment rendered—that is, for the poison—to the god of healing. Plato concludes, "So died our friend, of all men I have known the most just."[2]

As we go on to discuss Plato's career and his other works, we will find him extending his defense of Socrates, and trying to carry forward the mission of inquiry. The good man must know himself, and, like the good scientist, he must be careful to avoid confusing *conditions* and *causes*, either in ethics or astronomy.

Over the centuries, readers have debated whether the arguments in the *Phaedo* do or do not prove the independence of soul and body, personal immortality, or an immortality of one's ideal self which is his true identity. The arguments may or may not be "conclusive"; but what the *Phaedo* does establish beautifully and convincingly is, I believe, the immortality of Socrates. On this last afternoon of his life, all worldly ties behind him, he is already separated from bodily concerns, and has become an incarnation of the eternal ideal.[3]

We will return presently to some of the more profound philosophic themes that Plato's account of this last conversation introduces. But first, since Plato intended to show that Socrates was indeed "just" and the charges against him unfounded, we will turn to the dialogues that answer charges that Socrates was irreligious, that he corrupted young men, and that he was "just another Sophist" sharing their amoral opportunism and naive relativism. We will want to note some cases where Plato's Socrates proposes some wholly new ideas for Western thought—ideas that remain relevant down to the present day.

The Charge of Impiety
(*Euthyphro*)

The *Euthyphro* shows Socrates in action, talking with a religious extremist on the subject of piety. Euthyphro and Socrates meet outside the court; Socrates is to be tried on the following day, on a charge of "impiety." Euthyphro is about to bring a charge of a similar sort against his own father; he is so certain of the intentions of the gods that he feels no hesitation. The case in question is so complex that its justice or injustice require the most astute legal analysis to determine. Euthyphro's father had an employee who murdered a slave, and, intending to bring him to the city, left him tied up overnight. The man died of exposure. Euthyphro proposed to prosecute his father for murder; the case therefore brings out the remarkable nature of Euthyphro's complete assurance that he is right. Socrates asks Euthyphro to instruct him, so that he will know whether his own indictment for impiety is correct, and what to say in his defense.[4]

As the conversation goes on, however, it turns out that Euthyphro can't say what piety is; his statements keep running in a circle. At first, he tries to establish piety as a kind of barter and exchange between men and the gods; we trade sacrifices for favors. Socrates wonders whether gods really stand in need of sacrifices for their food and drink, since they are good and immortal. Euthyphro reconsiders a bit, and now thinks that piety is giving praise and honor to the gods in return for which they give us favors. Socrates still wonders whether beings who are immortal and perfect would either need or be much impressed by the honors men paid them. Euthyphro tries to explain piety now in another way: piety is "what is dear to the gods." But the gods in the religious books Euthyphro relies on often disagree, don't they? Euthyphro would like to make a speech on the subject, but Socrates holds him to the argument; yes, they do. And probably, since even men don't disagree in cases where measure or counting will settle a dispute, these disagreements are about the very things most relevant to Euthyphro and Socrates in their present situation: justice and the like. But perhaps another question will help: there must be some reason why things are dear to the gods, for surely we don't want to accuse them of sheer irrationality; Euthyphro would agree to that. Then what sorts of things are these? Euthyphro thinks the answer is "pious ones"; but he must leave now, and the discussion ends. (From the abrupt way he leaves, we could suspect, though we are never told, that Euthyphro may no longer be on his way to accuse his father.)

It is surely no mistake to see Plato's intention to defend Socrates in this conversation. Euthyphro is a religious conservative, a dogmatist who claims to be an authority on piety, and who therefore represents the most conservative Athenian opinion and tradition. Of the two, as Socrates' questions challenge the simple assumptions that religion is a subdivision of barter and exchange, or that gods act without motivation, or that if we have textbooks on piety we don't need reason, it seems quite clear that Socrates is the man of higher religious sensitivity and piety.

The dialogue is an excellent example of Plato's early work. The problem under discussion is one in which both the participants are personally and immediately involved. The argument is inconclusive, but tied in directly with the concrete situation: at least we know that at his trial Socrates will not be able to defend himself by saying that he has now been taught the nature of piety by an eminent man, and knowing better, has reformed. And we suspect that Euthyphro will want to reconsider his dogmatic certainty that faith requires him to bring a suit that may be unreasonable or lacking in filial piety.

Corrupting the Youth
(*Lysis, Laches,* and *Charmides*)

Young Plato, according to one traditional report, had seriously considered making his career poetry, as well as politics. There is certainly evidence of a first-magnitude literary talent shown in the dialogues with which he opened his defense of Socrates. In addition to his account in the *Apology, Crito,* and *Phaedo* of the trial, imprisonment, and execution of Socrates, and the defense against the charge of "impiety" offered in the *Euthyphro,* Plato wrote three short, brilliant dialogues which show the error of charging Socrates with "corrupting the youth" of Athens.

The *Lysis, Charmides,* and *Laches* depict Socrates in action as an educator. He talks, respectively, with Lysis and Menexenus, two boys of eleven; with a young man of sixteen or so (Plato's uncle Charmides, ward of and dominated by Critias); and with Laches and Nicias, two of his former commanding generals, men of middle age. Socrates is critical of the answers given by each group to his questions (which concern the natures of friendship, temperance, and courage), but he does not himself advance any final constructive conclusions. At least in the *Charmides,* Plato shows Socrates associating with men who were remembered in Athens for their part in the tyranny of "The Thirty." If a hasty critic merely noted these facts, he might see superficial grounds for blaming Plato's Socrates either for teaching scepticism, or for teaching students who turned out badly, or for both. But before deciding on Socrates' merits as educator, it is necessary to see what really are the effects of these conversations on their participants.

The *Lysis* has a central cast of five characters, who represent all combinations of likeness and difference in age and temperament, and in friendship or its lack. Lysis and Menexenus, the main respondents, are boys of eleven; they are friends. Lysis is shy and gentle, young Menexenus the opposite. The occasion of the talk is Socrates' meeting with two young men in their late teens, Hippothales, who is gentle, and his aggressive companion, Ctesippus (whose ridicule suggests that there is at least a temporary lack of friendship here). Socrates begins a discussion of friendship with the two young friends. Friendship, they agree, requires two persons; a mere strong one-way emotive feeling is not enough. However, contrary to the opinion of "some sages—these are the men who talk and write about nature and the whole," we cannot reduce friendship to an automatic operation of some law of natural attraction, either between persons who are opposite or persons who are alike. (In fact, as we have noted, the varied relations among the five characters of the dialogue already show that neither likeness nor difference in temperament or in age will automatically make friends. See Fig. I.)

Figure I: THE LYSIS: IS FRIENDSHIP AUTOMATIC BETWEEN LIKE AND LIKE OR LIKE AND UNLIKE?

Characters: Socrates, Hippothales, Ctesippus, Lysis, Menexenus.

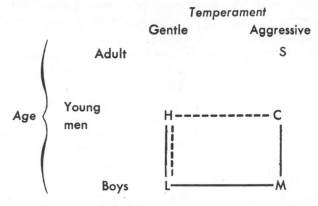

Relations at beginning of dialogue:

—— Friends at beginning

– – – – *Not friends at beginning*

═══ Different feelings between the two at the beginning

If "like to like" always held, then (1) the pairs "alike" in age, LM and HC, should be friends; this fails for HC; or (2) the pairs "alike" in temperament should be friends; this fails for HL. If "opposites attract" is a universal law, then (1) the pairs "unlike" in age, CM and HL, should be friends; this fails for HL; or (2) the pairs "unlike" in temperament, LM and HC, should be friends; this fails for HC. The relations of HM and CL are ambiguous; we assume S is neutral at the outset, friendly to *all* at the end.

Nor can we agree to say simply that friendship is a matter of self-interested usefulness (as the Sophists probably would). Grant that friends are dear to us because they are or procure something intrinsically good (which, Socrates convinces his hearers, is the only cause of anything being "dear to us"), the boys can neither say what this is, nor how friends do it. At the end of their talk, no positive conclusion has been reached in the inquiry; but the participants *have* become friends. This use of the concrete situation to illustrate the abstract discussion—and often to indicate constructive results where the argument has failed to do so—is beautifully handled. There is no doubt that the boys are both better and better friends as a result of this conversation; they have a better knowledge of friendship both concretely and abstractly. No one could possibly think that they were "corrupted," or in any way the worse for their encounter with Socrates.

Perhaps, however, Socrates' effect *was* bad on older boys—particularly those with an oligarchic background; may he not have been partly responsible, for example, for the career of Plato's uncle, Charmides? In the *Charmides,* Plato gives an answer, by way of a conversation about temperance between Socrates, Charmides, and Critias, the latter's guardian. *Sophrosyne,* "temperance," is the virtue of self-control and moderation. Charmides lacks a proper idea of it, because, apparently, he has confused "nothing too much" with "nothing too energetic"; he is shy and backward. Critias, on the other hand, is dogmatically certain of his answer, that temperance is an application of "know thyself" (here Socrates would agree), which means, Critias thinks, that temperance is "a science which has itself as subject," or "a knowledge of what is knowledge" (here Socrates differs entirely; temperance for him is self-knowledge by a human knower, not Critias' abstract and formal self-reference within a "science of science"). Critias is irritable and inconsistent; he does not enjoy Socrates' repeated requests for explanation. But Socrates (with Charmides listening) can't help pointing out that (1) no other art or science has just itself for its subject-matter, (2) that this definition is so formal and abstract that he cannot see "what good such a thing would be," let alone how it would be a "virtue." During their conversation, Charmides and (to a lesser degree) Critias actually become more temperate, though the argument ends with temperance still undefined; and Charmides for once does his own thinking to the extent of questioning what Critias has told him. The intemperance of "The Thirty," we conclude, was in no sense the result of their listening to Socrates, but if anything the result of their not listening more carefully and oftener.

Finally, in the *Laches,* courage is the immediate theme (in the context of the broader problem of proper education for young men); at first, the two generals become annoyed at Socrates' cross-examination—for they feel sure they know what education will corrupt and what improve young Athenians—but as the dialogue ends, Socrates and two elderly fathers who had initiated the discussion agree, in spite of the irritation of the generals, that it would show lack of courage on their part to give up further inquiry.

The subtle changes in the characters of the respondents as they talk with Socrates, and the beautiful interplay of concrete situation and abstract argument, make these dialogues literature at its best.[5]

The defense on this count can rest. Socrates did not make young boys, youths, or responsible older men, worse by his shared inquiries with them; on the contrary, recognizing their own need to know and sharing the inquiry in each case makes them better.

Admirers of the current existentialist thesis that man's peculiarity is to ask questions about his own nature, questions to which there is no determinate answer except that man by nature asks these questions, will find these three early dialogues very congenial and contemporary in tone, though Socrates is more positive about the existence of some final objective and intrinsic standard of value than they themselves would be.

The New Notion of the "Soul" and Its Care

On the temple at Delphi three sayings were inscribed, which in some ways are what they claimed to be, a capsule picture of Greek attitudes and wisdom. The first was "KNOW

THYSELF," the second "NOTHING TOO MUCH," and the third "GIVE A PLEDGE AND DISASTER IS AT HAND." The third of these, advice against second mortgages and collateral loans, seems to us to belong to commercial rather than philosophical speculation; but to the Greeks it seemed one of the fruits of experience that young men should know. Originally, "know thyself" may well have meant "know your place," that is, your social station and its duties; but the wider questions of self-knowledge it suggested went far beyond any aristocratic notion of social adaptation. The second saying probably reminded men that "pride"—setting oneself as "equal in measure to the gods"—brought the sort of nemesis that is reflected in Greek history and tragedy. But it, too, admitted extension into a rule of behavior and psychology much more philosophical.

The entire course and quality of Greek thought were changed by Socrates' interest in and interpretation of the injunction, "know thyself." What is a self, and how can one find out? It may be absolutely certain that I exist—but what this existent "I" is may be harder to discover. Three notions of the "self" in Greek thought preceded Socrates' investigation.

Homer's heroes had a *psyche,* a "soul" (evidently not a "soul" in our modern sense), which at death left the body and went to Hades as a breath, a powerless shade. Apart from this, what interested Homer about a man was what he looked like and what he did; Homer was a poet, and his passages often show a poet's sensitivity, but they do not provoke him to question his opinions as to the operation of Fate or the insubstantial nature of the *psyche.*

In Ionian science, the *psyche* was construed as a sort of natural force: a dry breath, a spark of a cosmic moving principle, a source of magnetism. Human conduct would, in principle, be only a predictable special case of the new universal laws of physics which were just being discovered. Friendship, for example, might be the operation of a natural law that like attracts like; and anything that set itself in motion could be thought to have a *psyche* (thus Thales reportedly said "the magnet has a soul," because it moved iron). Insofar as nature's laws were unchanging, human behavior would be predictable and determined; a "vital fire" would behave much as physical fire. Thus a fatalism and a tendency to view men from the outside as typical parts of nature were part of the mind-set both of conservative cultural mentality (still reflected in the role of Fate in the tragedians) and the radical new science.

Sophistry, with its revolt against tradition and speculation, might have been expected to do somewhat better. It was true that the Sophists stressed the uniqueness of individual experience, and took an extreme subjectivism for granted; but it was also true that the "subject" as they saw him was a being whose goal in life was to "succeed" by achieving wealth, prestige, pleasure, and power. This seemed an adequate characterization of "human nature" to these teachers—and to their pupils; other habits and standards were lumped together as "custom." Not that custom was unimportant; a successful man should "know himself" in the old sense of knowing his, and other people's, proper stations, and the etiquette suitable for young gentlemen. The successful man would not fear fates or gods (that would be superstition) but he would do well to follow "nothing too much" as a way to get along in society. And he had better avoid second mortgages until he had his "degree" in contract law and could evade them.

Socrates' contribution was to point out the inadequacy of these viewpoints to explain the subjective experience and outer behavior of human beings. In one of Plato's earliest dialogues, we see Socrates pointing out to Lysis and his friends that "friendship" involves something more than automatic natural attraction, of like for like (Empedocles), or unlike for unlike (Anaxagoras); there is an element of choice, of desire for good, of goals that may be shared, to be explained. (If the naturalistic theories were right, our "natures" would predetermine our friendships, and we could predict reactions infallibly by matching similarities on an IBM machine.) Presently, we find him asking whether the Sophists' "self" is really simply the bundle of desire they make it, or whether instead things are not desired as instruments to the attaining of "the good." All men desire the good; they have an inner direction toward a goal that will have intrinsic, not merely instrumental value. This goal that is desired is "virtue:" full human excellence that is worth having in its own right. But then why are men ever bad? Socrates believes it is because they are ignorant; they accept something as good without close examination, and thus mistake appearance for reality, instrument for end, transitory for permanent satisfaction. No one would choose what he knew to be only an apparent good in preference to a real one; and so Socrates could argue that "no one does wrong voluntarily." If we include in knowledge the value element of what is known, the further point follows that "virtue is knowledge"—the man who knows what human excellence really is will choose it; the man whose choice is not based on knowledge has no fixed principle and may often make mistakes.

This means that a human self is a strange and complex thing. (1) I evidently have freedom to act on the basis of incomplete or incorrect belief; (2) I have a natural desire to attain something intrinsically good; (3) I am surrounded by appearances that seem good yet are not really so; (4) I am able, if I put my mind to it, to discover at least some of the differences between appearance and reality—both as to what is "good" objectively and what is "good" for me.

What a distance such a self is from fire or fate or pure survival drives! And what a needless waste there is in snatching at apparent goods, without further inquiry! How foolish to spend all of your time thinking about ways to gather property, leaving no moment for an attempt to know and realize your self. And what an extraordinary self it must be that is waiting to be known; for there seems nothing quite like it in physics, politics, or epic poetry.[6]

The Dialogue: A New Philosophic Form

Plato's decision to write in dialogue form was not simply a matter of literary preference nor of rhetorical effectiveness but involved a philosophic conviction that this was the proper form in which to present ideas. "The" Platonic dialogue form undergoes various experimental modifications, but all of the dialogues have something in common. Plato distrusted textbooks heartily. When a young student wrote "a textbook of Platonism," Plato countered (in the *Seventh Letter*) with one of the most unfavorable "book reviews" on record. No one who understood his philosophy, he argued, would try to reduce it to textbook form. And Plato's Socrates resents written speeches which "are unable to ask and answer questions, but just go on repeating the same thing"; he has no use at all for the "current textbooks of rhetoric," which are mere lists of tricks and examples; he laughs at himself wryly when, in his last conversation with his friends, he finds that "I am talking like a textbook."[7]

Philosophy, as Plato understood it, is engaged inquiry. This means that the participants must feel the challenge of a problem which involves themselves; a disengaged, abstract discussion misses the point. The dialogue form makes it possible to present characters who are involved in this way in the argument—intemperate men, for example, whom Socrates made anxious to discover the nature of temperance. In a dialogue, the setting and character can show such an engagement, and the reader, too, can be counted in and made to join the inquiry.

And beyond this, dialogues prevent the dangers of a reader memorizing formulae he has not understood, and putting them forward "as though they were the key to sublime mysteries"; it does this just as effectively as it prevents another type of reader from "turning from the writing in contempt" on the ground that it is abstract and has nothing practical to do with him and his interests. These are the two main dangers which arise when ideas are "immobilized and nailed down in writing." But if "no man of sense commits his most profound thoughts to writing," why does Plato write the dialogues? And not only jot them down hastily, but expend real care and craftsmanship on them, as we can tell, for example, from the report that his effects included tablets with many different drafts of the opening sentence of the *Republic?* Perhaps we can answer this by noticing that whereas it would be futile to compile a set of doctrinal conclusions in fixed words, an inquiry shared (even though in writing) corrects the immobility and impersonality of the textbook; we are led to participate and think, and the words of dialogue are no longer mere formulae, but given life and motion.

A further reason for Plato's use of the dialogue is that it reflects his central concern in philosophy: the relation between a world of unchanging ideas or forms, and a concrete world of individuals on whom the forms act causally, who "see" the forms and "share" them, but remain apart. There is no danger in a dialogue of losing sight of the tension and relevance that holds between the concrete and the abstract; the persons and situation are individuals and concrete, the theme of discussion, when the dialogue is one with Socrates, is a world of meanings and ideas that lie behind and structure concrete appearance and flow.

Plato's dialogues have an interesting property when we take them all together as a single set. If, as we well might, we read them as an account of the development of Socrates, his character emerges with consistency as the ideal philosopher. At first, he is concerned with questions of science—we never meet him in this role, but hear a good deal about it— and of logic (he is shown in the *Parmenides* as a very young man, being shown the need for logical discipline). As he grows older, he becomes concerned with the analysis of words and meanings. But finally, as we see him at his trial, his interest has turned to human existence and concrete value. He is going to provoke men into thinking about themselves, with a feeling that this is a divine mission. On the other hand, if we arrange the dialogues not in terms of their dramatic dates, but in terms of their approximate dates of composition, we can read them as an account of the development of Plato as a philosopher. And Plato's concerns move from passionate exhortation through systematic speculative vision to a concern with the precise analysis by which speculation must be clarified and tested. The result is a counterpoint: the ideal philosopher must develop at the same time toward the passionate intensity of Socrates in the agora and the austere objectivity of Plato thinking alone in the garden of the Academy.[8]

C H A P T E R   I I I

Science and Sophistry

Socrates and the Experts
(*Gorgias, Protagoras, Ion, Menexenus, Euthydemus, Hippias Minor, Cratylus, Meno*)

THERE STILL REMAINED one part of Socrates' defense for Plato to present. Socrates had seemed to Aristophanes a typical Sophist; and evidently many Athenians continued—even up to his trial—to equate Socrates and Sophistry in their thinking. Plato now began to write a series of dialogues in which Socrates was shown talking with the leading Sophists of his day; it was to be clear both that he disagreed with them in theory, and that he differed totally in motivation and character. The issues to be raised were still the familiar themes of virtue and knowledge, to which rhetoric—the Sophists' stock in trade—was to be added. But these conversational antagonists were not so easily led or satisfied as the non-professionals who were respondents in Plato's Socrates-as-teacher dialogues. The arguments become more extended, character and dramatic form more complex, as Plato has his hero press the inquiry further. Some idea of the work Plato wrote in this period can be given by an itemized summary of the themes and characters of these duels between Socrates and the experts.

The *Gorgias*[1]
Socrates talks in turn with the famous orator, Gorgias, with the latter's impetuous student, Polus, and with their

"realistic" admirer, Callicles. Gorgias has come to teach "rhetoric," the art which wins cases in courts and persuades political parties; he does not, he says, claim to teach virtue or ethics. Socrates doubts if "rhetoric" so defined can be a kind of "knowledge" at all; how can we *know* what we are doing in a law case, for example, if we don't know the nature of justice? It would be like a man setting up medical practice with no knowledge of the criteria of disease or health, and no rules by which his "art" could operate. Gorgias concedes that, if one of his students should come to him ignorant of justice, he himself would have to teach him this, as well as law. Young Polus, however, urges that rhetoric is a morally neutral tool for attaining what one wishes; that is, he explains when questioned, what one *really* wishes; that is, it turns out, to be a better person. But in that case, Socrates concludes, rhetoric is not morally neutral, but when properly understood always on the side of justice and virtue—quite the opposite of Polus' initial thought. Callicles, finally, defines a good life, not in conventional terms of "nobility," but as unlimited cultivation and gratification of appetite and ambition. He poses as a realistic observer of the world, who has studied rhetoric, but has no patience with "philosophy" as an adult occupation. Socrates outrages Callicles by a series of examples and a Pythagorean myth, all showing that "unlimited desire and satisfaction" would be a very poor life. What satisfaction could be greater, or desire more intense (to take a modern example) than the wish for freedom from dentists when a hot drill hits a nerve? Callicles' notion of happiness obviously has omitted the inner conditions of harmony and integrity without which he could be neither a fully effective nor indeed a fully human self. Although he is infuriated when Socrates, none too gently, points this out, Callicles can find no counter-argument to offer. Of the four main characters in the *Gorgias*, Plato deftly makes Socrates, who knows the nature of justice, come off the best rhetorician.

The *Protagoras*[2]

Here is a set of portraits, for Protagoras is shown together with the philologist Prodicus and the polymathic Hippias. The central discussion is between Protagoras and Socrates, and again concerns the nature and teachability of virtue. Are there several components to human excellence; and is it an innate talent, or can it be taught? Plato does not here discuss Protagoras' "man is the measure of all things" thesis; that he reserves for the *Theaetetus,* a later dialogue; but, as the meaning each gives to "virtue" and "education" becomes clear, so that Socrates and Protagoras seem to reverse their initial positions during the conversation, the nature-convention distinction plays a central role.

The *Ion*

A short, simple conversation; a sample, perhaps, of Socrates' results when he interrogated poets and artists to see if they were wiser than he was. Ion is a rhapsode—a travelling reciter of Homer—inclined to think that Homer has all the answers to every question. But in that case, it is surprising that Ion's talents—for instance, as a general—have gone unrecognized; and when pressed, there seems to be *no* special field where Homer or Ion is more of an authority than a professional in that field would be. Ion, and Homer, do not, apparently, work from "science" or "knowledge"; they must therefore owe their effectiveness to the magnetic transmission of some "divine inspiration." It is a brief encounter, simply presented.

The *Menexenus*

Another treatment, this time by example rather than argument, of the theme of truth and rhetoric, probably written as companion case study to the *Gorgias.* The shade of Socrates returns to repeat a funeral oration he has learned from Pericles' mistress to his former friend, Menexenus. (Plato had evidently read Thucydides' version of the great Funeral Oration of Pericles.) A series of flat misrepresentations of historic fact occur in this oration, in the interests of patriotism, with the effect of making one wonder whether *any* of the speaker's claims are true, and how on earth one can tell? For the reader interested in history and ceremonial speeches, this Platonic parody is still of intrinsic interest, much as most of Plato's admirers have apologized for it. Consider, for example, the claim of the Athenian, "We have never lost a war to a foreign power, but defeated ourselves!" Compare this to the historical situation at the end of the war with Sparta, when Athens was occupied and required to demolish her harbor fortifications, and it seems clear that truth and patriotism create different views of history. One can go further, and say that in today's American partisan speech-making, history itself as distinct from fantasy is in some jeopardy; only a Socrates in a less playful mood than that of the *Menexenus* is likely to provoke the critical discussion that can rehabilitate the distinction.[3] Socrates' ghost knows events from his death to an Athenian treaty with Persia some twelve years later; this may have been the occasion that made Plato feel that a funeral speech was in order for the Athens that Socrates had known so well.

The *Euthydemus*[4]

Although this fits well with the present period in its experiments with tone and with the limits of philosophic dialogue form, the serious point of the farce anticipates ideas central in the late dialogues of Plato. Two brothers, formerly fighters in armor, have now taken up philosophy, that is, fighting with words. They have developed a "wonderful technique of refutation," which rests on the application of Eleatic logic; and Socrates, though he gets the floor for two exhibitions of the kind of discussion he would prefer to their "pranks," does not convert them. We will return to this later on. It may be significant that the two brothers come from Gorgias' part of Italy, and that their "arguments" often sound like a notorious speech by Gorgias in which he made fun of speculative philosophy.

The *Hippias Minor*[5]

The *Hippias Minor* is also known as the *Lesser Hippias,* since two dialogues featuring Hippias occurred in the Academy's collection of Plato's papers; this is the shorter; the other will be discussed later. A sharp skirmish in which Socrates insists, against the pompous Hippias, that "a man who lies deliberately is better than one who does so involuntarily." A question had arisen as to whether the temperamental Achilles or the wily Odysseus was a better man; Socrates' thesis would make Odysseus better, though Hippias preferred Achilles. But this thesis that Socrates puts forward seems itself to be a lie; and the intricate tangles of truth and falsehood between the concrete situation (is Socrates deliberately lying to Hippias?), the abstract argument (is it true, in general, that a deliberate liar is a better man than an inadvertent one?), and the case in point (is Achilles better than Odysseus?), are so brilliantly handled that it is hard to doubt, as some few critics have, that Plato is indeed the author.

The *Cratylus*

This is Plato's simultaneous summary of his ideas about language and his criticism of the philosophic doctrine that "all things flow." It will be discussed in more detail below.

The *Meno*

Here is a final summing-up of Socratic versus Sophistic education, as Socrates examines a pupil and admirer of Gorgias'. They consider the question of whether education can make men "better" or only "better informed" and "cleverer."

The *Meno* ends with an exchange between Socrates and Anytus, the statesman who later engineered Socrates' trial. Anytus is inclined to think Socrates lacking in patriotism: he should not be denying that the great past democratic leaders of Athens could teach anyone how to be good. Socrates wonders why, if Pericles knew how to be good, his sons turned out poorly, and the Athenian people whom he had led ended by repudiating him? It would almost seem, Socrates says, that under Pericles' administration (if indeed Pericles was a good man) his subjects had become worse instead of being educated to be better. (This reminds one of another Socratic comment, equally unlikely to amuse Anytus, that "Pericles had filled Athens so full of public works, he had left no room for temperance and justice"—a comment that sounds like a quotation from the historic Socrates.)

Summary[6]

During this period, Plato was travelling and experimenting with new insights and ideas. The dramatic form of the dialogues he wrote is on occasion much more extended, and various experiments are tried in emphasizing or dropping the "concrete self-reference" and "inconclusive inquiry" themes. The underlying intention is still that of completing the portrait and defense of Socrates; in a portraiture which attempts to fuse more tightly the "critical analyst" of the *Lysis* and its companion dialogues, and the "man of principle" of the *Apology* trilogy. The stress remains on shared inquiry, but new philosophical insights are seen to be presupposed by the faith that "we can become better men if we inquire." In particular, the program of these writings—Plato's in writing them, and Socrates' as he appears in them—is diametrically opposed to the Sophists' ideas of the aims and methods of "education."

An Experiment in Education: The *Meno*[7]

In the *Meno,* we find Socrates in a discussion with a young man educated by Gorgias; we can see the contrast here between Socratic and Sophistic methods and aims of education. Young Meno surely is "Sophisticated," but our question is whether this has made him a better person? Or is this a foolish thing to expect; for perhaps virtue can't be taught?

This is the question, addressed to Socrates, with which Meno opens their conversation. Socrates does not know the answer himself, nor has he met anyone that did. Meno thinks, however, that he has an answer, learned from Gorgias. "Virtue," proper human excellence, was different for every sex and social station—Meno repeats part of a book-of-etiquette catalogue he heard from his teacher. But what is there in common among all of these rules of behavior (tending to housework for women, not being noisy for children, etc.) that makes them all "virtuous"? Well, Gorgias had not said, so Meno doesn't know and cannot answer. In fact, it is only with some difficulty that Socrates makes him see the kind of answer that this question requires; Meno does not generalize easily.

In spite of Socrates' suggestion that the best procedure would be to find out first what virtue is, Meno persists in pressing Socrates to tell him, with a simple yes-or-no answer, whether it can be taught. Meno seems to have the idea that teaching and learning are simply the imparting and recalling of information: one can almost see what he wants is an "answer" that he can write in his notes: "Socrates the Athenian says that 'virtue can' (or 'virtue cannot') 'be taught.' " But Socrates can't answer the question, any more than Meno could say what the common character was of his "swarm of virtues." Meno becomes outraged; Socrates is the worst teacher he has ever known! Instead of helping him, Socrates has only confused Meno by his questions. Their situation, Meno thinks, is hopeless. How can a student learn about something that neither he nor his teacher knows? Even if they found the truth, they could not recognize it. (Meno seems to think of "recognizing" a truth in the way one recognizes birds, by matching them against illustrations in a handbook.)

Socrates answers with a myth, an experiment, and a general reflection on method, all of which show why Meno is wrong and deficient in wisdom, justice, and courage in his blaming Socrates and wanting to give up the discussion.

The myth is a story about "recollection." The human soul is immortal, and has seen all truths before its present life; knowledge is the recollection of truths it has seen, when something "reminds" it of them. Learning must be an effort on the part of the student himself to remember clearly what he already knows; external authority can never really teach him anything, but at best remind him. Now, possibly not all of the details of this myth are true; Socrates declines to commit himself on that point; but what he will fight for is the conclusion that "we will be better, braver, and less savage if we inquire than if we do not."[8] Inquiry makes us recollect truths we knew before, but this recollection comes about through our own effort, and *can* at least occur without "expert instruction," so that we escape Meno's dilemma.

Socrates offers an experiment to prove his point. He will have Meno's slave boy recollect the answer to a problem in geometry. This discussion, in which Socrates questions the boy, is famous in Western educational theory as the classic example of "the Socratic method of teaching." Yet as Meno sees it, Socrates is not "teaching" at all: for he is not telling the boy facts to be remembered.

Figure II: THE MENO EXPERIMENT

I. The boy knows what a square is, and that a square with sides two feet in length contains four square feet.

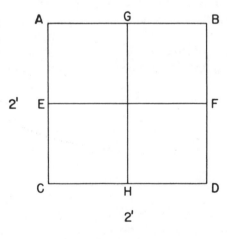

DIAGRAM 1

II. Now, what length of line will be the side of a square with double this area? The boy is positive it will be a line "twice the side," i.e., of four feet. His belief is tested by a diagram.
But the square is sixteen feet in area! (See Diagram 3, below.)

III. The required line must, therefore, lie somewhere between two and four feet; the boy is getting closer, and now believes "three feet" to be the right answer. He recognizes, however, that he does not know; and Socrates tests his new proposal by another diagram.

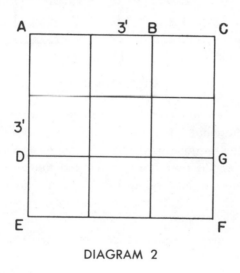

DIAGRAM 2

This time the square has an area of nine feet.

IV. Socrates returns to the figure of a sixteen-foot square, building it by adding four four-foot squares. If we draw the diagonals of these, each is cut in half (BFHD = ½ ACIG). What is the resulting area of the inscribed square? Eureka! Half of sixteen, which is what was wanted.

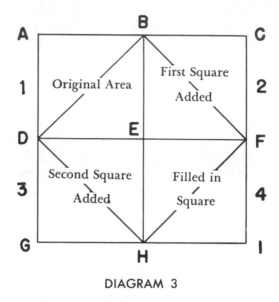

DIAGRAM 3

Then, since the line bisecting each square is what the learned call "the diagonal," has Meno's slave discovered that "the square on the diagonal is double the square on the side"? He has; and Meno is now partly convinced that one can learn something new without being told the exact answer.

Socrates draws a square four feet in area, with sides of two feet. Now what line will be the side of a square of just twice this area? "A line twice as long; a line of four feet," the boy answers promptly; but when they test this answer by drawing a diagram, the boy finds to his surprise that doubling the side does not double the square. The line they want is longer than two feet and less than four; "three feet!" decides the boy. Once more a test shows this answer fails; and the boy now finds that he just doesn't know! Going back to the sixteen-square-foot square, this will divide into four squares of four feet area; and the diagonals will cut each of these in half; the boy suddenly sees that the square on the diagonal gives the answer he was looking for. Meno is impressed: "incommensurables" had an air of "higher mathematics" about them, and Socrates certainly had not "taught" the boy his answer. Now it is time to inquire once more into virtue. Meno still holds out for asking whether it can be taught; but he is now willing to share the inquiry; he admits that he is better off for realizing his ignorance, and he no longer thinks Socrates a hopeless teacher. Suppose, Socrates suggests, that they use "the method of hypothesis." Given a problem, we first look to see what assumptions would solve it; then examine the consequences of each, in turn, to see whether they are consistent and true.[9] Socratic and Platonic method must always have the three stages of challenge, speculation, and confirmation; the three periods of Plato's own life can in fact be seen as moving through this same three-stage plan.

Figure III: THE "METHOD OF HYPOTHESIS"

(A. Benecke, Ueber die geometrische Hypothesis in Platons "Meno," Elbing, 1867)

The precise illustration of "the sort of thing a geometer would say" has caused a good deal of discussion. Apparently, three levels of meaning are involved: (1) the purely abstract method being illustrated; this could be described without an example at all, but the specific problem is offered to clarify the method for Meno and the reader; (2) a technical mathematical problem to which this method actually was being applied when Plato wrote (this, we may assume, is the reason he has Socrates pick the example); (3) a special case of the general problem, which can be illustrated by a simple figure that Meno and the reader can grasp on a purely non-technical level. The figure here is the most likely candidate for (3).

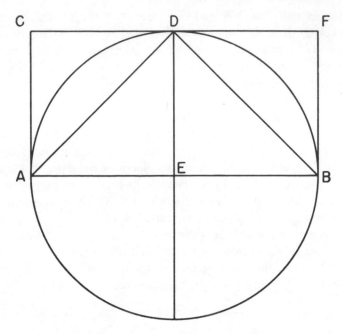

Can an area be inscribed in a circle as a triangle? Suppose it is given as a square; then, in the present simplest case, *if* its side equals the radius of the circle, it can be (as in the figure where ADE = ½ ACDE, and so ADB = ACDE); if not, other consequences follow. Note that this diagram is the same as that used with the slave in most details; this makes it an appropriate example to show Meno, and connects our new "method" with the "reminiscence" interpretation of the former experiment.

If virtue were a kind of factual knowledge, it could be taught by precept at the hands of experts; *if* it were a right opinion, the result of social conditioning, it could be taught by the example of statesmen and gentlemen. The Sophists, however, do not, if they are honest, even claim to make their pupils better men; not only can Meno assure us that he has

Gorgias' word for that, but his student, Meno, offers a living proof. What about the example of good citizens and statesmen? Here Anytus, the democratic leader who was shortly to arrange the indictment of Socrates, is brought into the discussion. Can great men teach virtue by example? For instance, there is Pericles, who was a great man; Anytus would take him as a good case in point. Socrates asks why the Athenians after years of Pericles' leadership became hostile to him. Doesn't this show that he had made them *worse* instead of *better*? Or what about the sons of Athens' eminent men; would Pericles or Aristides or Thucydides have had them taught fencing, riding, wrestling, and music, but been too unconcerned or envious to teach them virtue? Surely not; yet in all of these cases the sons and wards turned out to be either wholly undistinguished or wicked. Anytus is enraged by this criticism of national heroes; yet case after case refutes the notion that virtue is taught by example.

The dialogue ends inconclusively once more. And yet, looking at the argument again, it is clear that virtue *can* be taught in *some* sense of teaching, for the dialogue itself shows Meno improving in virtue through his talk with Socrates.

The Theory of Forms

In addition to Socrates' new notion of the soul, Plato took from Socrates an insight that he developed into what is called the "theory of forms" (or "theory of ideas"). This is a theory explaining what kind of a world we live in, and how discussion, knowledge, and moral action are possible. In its full development, the theory is a technical one; a sign of this is that every major thinker in the Platonic tradition has accepted it in principle, but failed to satisfy himself that he had clarified it in detail. In this present section, we will present some of the considerations that gave the notion its plausibility, but this can be only a preliminary consideration, rather like Socrates' own questions and suggestive insights that gave Plato's thought the direction it took in his mature philosophy.

Even a Sophist like Protagoras, who thinks that each individual has his own private world, and that all individuals are in constant change, admits that language, at least, somehow escapes this radical individuality and flow. For we can use a word repeatedly with the same "meaning" each time; and "meanings" are permanent and public in a way that physical processes are not. Although each time I pronounce the word "two," the sounds I make are made in a new context and on a new occasion, the number two, which is "what I mean," is the same. There must be such meanings that stay put if communication is to be possible at all, and if we like we can call these referents of words "forms."

But, as common sense and science recognize, counter to Protagoras, the physical things I encounter show some stubborn permanence, too; for example, they do not suddenly vanish, then pop back into existence somewhere else in some later instant. My study desk is the same desk today that it was yesterday. In trying to describe how things stay the same, the Greek scientists had already explored the possibility that we should measure ᵃnd classify their sizes, shapes, numbers of parts, and so on; or that we should study how they act and are acted on in terms of physical causality. A Pythagorean mathematician will point out, quite plausibly, that the properties that give my desk its identity as a desk both yesterday and today are like numbers or meanings rather than like physical objects. And there are rules of art and laws of nature which are permanent expressions of the way in which the desk acts and is acted on; the way, for example, in which I can "transform" it into kindling, or move it to another room. Suppose I say that my desk is a desk because it has an essential set of properties in common with other desks (so that, if I took these away, I would have a very poor approximation of a desk, or something that was no longer a desk at all), and suppose I call these characteristics a "form." Then the "form of desk" is "real" enough, but it is not a "thing," in the easy sense in which bricks and tadpoles are "things." For physical objects are always each in just one place at a given time, and there can never be two of them in the same place at once. But "forms," in the present sense, such as "two," or "desk," are not in space and time at all. There is, for example, no way in which I can make the number two larger by setting something next to it or chopping its elements with an axe, in the way I can make pairs of physical things change in number. The forms are, however, related to objects in space and time because they can be *in* or *illustrated* by many physical objects in distinct places at any moment. There are many desks in the world, and even more pairs and couples; and each shares in its form. These "structural" characteristics which we use to identify and classify things, can be called forms, and seem to be exactly the "meanings" our words refer to, which we spoke of as forms before.

Looking at the arts and crafts, we can say that they are concerned with "transformations"—ways of realizing a new or more complete form in a medium through a series of operations. I want to turn the wood I have bought in a make-it-yourself, pre-sawed bookcase kit into a bookcase; but right now, that wood is a pile of individual boards; its form is that of "board," repeated in a dozen pieces. Some ways of assembling these will make a bookcase and some won't; I turn to the "Easy Directions" to see what I must do to give my boards an added form. Some forms, then, such as the form of bookcase, can be built up from others in stages; though, of course, not all forms are related in this way; I can't build a very good bookcase out of cotton-wool.

These examples introduce still a third part that the forms play; my carpentering operations "aim at" the bookcase as finished product, and this idea of the product directs my action. In the same way, Socrates would say, the ideal or goal of "justice" directs Socrates' actions in creating a human personality and life. There is a "form of man," he might say, which attracts us all and by this attraction creates the desire we have for self-realization. The forms in this role can, therefore be goals or ideals.

The "theory of forms," as Plato puts together previous intuitions and suggestions, combines thoughts of the Sophists, the scientists, and Socrates. The Sophists, stressing the way in which language shapes "reality," still needed stable "meanings." The work of the scientists, concerned with laws and durable patterns in nature, suggested that "meanings" result from our recognition of stable features of the things we talk about; and also suggested that mathematics would be the best tool for describing such stabilities. Socrates, concerned with values as well as with facts or statements, added another dimension by showing his hearers that forms can also be goals and have value; they appear as ideals in this role.

It is by recognizing their "sharing in" these "forms" that philosophy can explain the value and reality that we and our world have. And this theme, of an unchanging realm of form shared in and attracting space-time individuals caught in flux, remains the central motif of Plato's later work and of much subsequent Western philosophy. We will, as we go on to Plato's later treatments of truth, love, and logic, see the range of problems and consequences of the theory.

The Intrinsic Value of "Justice" and the Danger of Being Practical

One of the new ideas for Western thought that originated with Socrates and was written about by Plato is the double thesis that "justice has intrinsic value" and that "a just man harms no one, just or unjust." From the treatment of this theme in the *Republic,* which we will discuss below, it is clear that most of Socrates' contemporaries held the exact opposite opinion on both points; just as, one suspects, most Americans today would be likely to. In the first place, young Greeks were told that they should be just because otherwise either (a) the law would catch up with them, or (b) even if this failed, the gods would punish them after death. In either case, it seems that justice is being presented as a constraint: it is unpleasant in itself, but one respects it through fear of external punishment. Some Greeks also argued, as some businessmen do today, that "honesty is the best policy because it pays." But this seems true only of "conspicuous honesty"—it seems not to apply to what one does if not observed—and, on the whole, it seems to be *untrue,* when we notice the relative attention paid the honest man as opposed to the more wealthy and influential, albeit less scrupulous, one. As for harming, most

Greeks, like most American admirers of western television programs or movies, were convinced that the right thing to do was to shoot or hurt bad people; their world is divided into cowboys on white horses and cowboys on black horses; the bad ones, on black horses, should be harmed by all means; this is in fact a sign of courage and certainly the right thing to do. Nor is there much doubt, on this view, that to shoot or imprison someone constitutes a genuine harm to him.

The idea of "justice" includes more in its Greek original than the word has come to mean today. It combines the notions of "observing the law," "doing the right thing," "honesty," "respect for the other person's property and rights," and "fair play" (equity), as well as taking one's share of civic responsibility. The just man is reasonable, respects the law, and does the right thing. The unjust man is his contrary.

To see Socrates' position, let us look at his three novel propositions in reverse order. First, the new discovery of the complexity of the "self" and its extension beyond the merely physical body or external fortune of a person required a new definition of harm. On this view, to "harm" someone would be to make him a worse human being, that is, to make his "self" less capable of functioning effectively and rightly. Now, if we agree with Socrates this far, we find we are committed to three consequences that must have seemed exactly opposed to good Athenian common sense. For it follows that neither physical injury nor hindrance in pursuit of profit or prestige is a genuine "harm" to anyone; it is only if he decides of his own volition that he will retaliate in kind, or will choose to be an avaricious or animalistic creature that the result is any "harm." The opposite view arises from the confusion of a self with one's body (in which case pain *is* a deterioration), or one's status and wealth (in which case, again, opposition or hindrance would amount to making one a "worse person"). But if the self is a Socratic *psyche*, it can only be by its own decision that it gives up its ideals and thinks that its identity is property or body. Further, punishment justly administered is neither retributive nor deterrent in effect and intention, but corrective. Men are punished justly with the aim of making them better, and cannot be said to be harmed or made worse by fines or imprisonments that correct their disposition to be bad. (In the limiting case, Socrates would even defend this thesis for capital punishment; this is corrective in that it destroys an incorrigible criminal who is such a nuisance to himself and others that he is better off dead.) Therefore, a just man, treating other men reasonably and equitably, may punish or restrain them, but cannot "harm" them. (These same ideas are central in later discussions of criminal law.)

Given this much, we can argue in two ways for the intrinsic value of justice. The negative argument asks what sort of psychological state leads men to act unjustly, and whether such a state, either in absolute terms or in its own, is desirable. One component of injustice is always ignorance; this combines with anger, envy, greed, or fear to motivate unjust actions. Each of these is a painful state of soul, which we would prefer to do without; each involves an erroneous notion that one may be "harmed" by physical pain or fiscal loss; none is compatible with balanced psychological functioning. Socrates is not arguing, as a later Roman might, for a suppression of all emotion; on the contrary, he quite shares the Greek feeling that life at its best is lived passionately and authentically. But he *is* asserting that in a good life, ambition and appetite have a proper degree and place; and that when either takes over from reason, and runs to excess, it defeats its own ends and sets up a psychologically pathological state.

The positive argument for the intrinsic value of justice is itself dual. All of us are aware, some more clearly and others less so, that there is some objective "form of justice" which serves us as an ideal and which attracts us. When we consider our own actions and their results as expressions of a self who acts—wondering whether it is or is not the kind we want to be—(and such consideration is unavoidable if we have been galvanized by Socrates' questions into taking "Know thyself" seriously), we find that when we measure up to our ideal, we have a sense of dignity; and we have a feeling of respect for other men who match this ideal of nobility. Both the sense of dignity and that of respect are valuable in themselves; and when one has experienced either, the attractiveness of "justice" becomes clear. A sign of this is the reaction of readers who disagree entirely with Plato's theories to his concrete portrait of Socrates: we feel respect for him, and recognize that his consistency in pursuit of justice argues strongly for the truth of his theses. Here was a man whose life was noble and worth while; who believed his own teaching, that it is only through ignorance of what nobility and justice are that anyone would choose to live with a self less than human, and lacking in dignity.

One of the things that Socrates saw clearly, and that the West has recognized, though with varying degrees of clarity and enthusiasm, ever since, is that to be "practical" in the sense of never questioning or looking beyond one's immediate culture and ambitions is really the most *impractical* thing that one can do.

The reason is that a "practical" man in this sense usually does not know what he really wants, and chooses goals that will not have intrinsic value nor even offer any durable pleasure or satisfaction. One reason that Socrates was so vigorous in his attempt to make people say exactly what they meant was his desire to unmask the confusion of intrinsic value and relative quantity.[10] An ambitious young man decides that he needs more money. If he met Socrates, the latter would ask him, "More money for what?" "How much more would that be?" "What relation is there between the ways open to you of getting this money and the sort of person you will become?" But, unfortunately, in the absence of Socrates, the human mind is able to think of "more" as a positive goal; and one can form the habit of measuring every choice against this phantom ideal of "having more"—not necessarily "more than . . ." or "enough to . . ." but just "more."

And this psychological quirk will work for pleasure or power or prestige as well as for wealth. From the outset, it must be clear that such an ideal is unattainable; however much I have, I obviously don't have more than that, and the habit of thinking I always need more to be satisfied will keep driving me on. (Today we would say that fundamental insecurity often underlies such an insatiable drive, and that the treatment must get at the causes, not the symptomatic behavior.)

Perhaps the most frequent, and futile, mistaking of the "having more . . ." formula for a positive plan or insight is the belief that the pursuit of happiness is identical with a constant increase of pleasure. Children cannot for some years distinguish between physical pleasure and comfort and the self-satisfaction that goes with happiness; so there is a native predisposition to equate them, inevitable if one doesn't mature emotionally beyond a childish state. But in the case of *pleasure*—limiting the term, here to sensations—we find that the goal we are seeking is peculiarly elusive, since each repetition of an experience tends to decrease its pleasantness while at the same time each such repetition leads to a habit that makes discontinuation more painful. Consequently, there will be no limit to the number nor to the intensity of the needs we build up if "more pleasure" is our only goal. Nor are we much better off if we take as our goal "less pain"; for that road leads into anesthetized torpor as quickly as "more pleasure" does to frustrated mania.

The "practical man" falls easily into the fallacy of thinking himself unhappy because he "hasn't more"—cash, or friends, or tangerines, or honorary degrees. (Notice that a list of "things to have more of" will coincide exactly with the rewards of "success" which the Sophists and their pupils uncritically admired.) But beyond this lies the further danger that the practical man may never realize that he has a human self, and can lead a human life, at all. Suffering from no metaphysical perplexities, he may identify his self with his body; regard other persons simply as things to be manipulated; look at the world as an outer array of indifferent facts. If Plato is right, this practical fellow has a soul that shares in something "divine"; he feels the attraction of ideals, the need for immortality; but he mistakes his inner sensibilities for the effects of the world of facts about him—or perhaps of indigestion—and mistakenly thinks of himself as really a simple center of voracity. He surprises himself, sometimes, by his inconsistency in admiring Plato's Socrates, who, after all, passed up any number of

chances to be "successful," and in the end acted on the maxim
he believed that "it is better to live nobly than for a greater
length of time." "But," as the unprincipled politician Callicles
remarked in Plato's *Gorgias*, "if you were right, Socrates,
all the values of our life today would be turned upside down!"

Language and Reality

One of the important cultural developments in Greece between 450 and 380 B.C., was a fascination with language and
speaking. The Sophists recognized clearly that when they talked
or wrote, they were using symbols as tools for communication,
and were not transferring ideas by magic or natural instinct
directly from one mind to another; and they knew that other
tools were used in other cultures. Now, this is by no means as obvious a realization as most readers will think; in our own country
and century, one of the principal reasons educators have offered
for including foreign language study in our schools is that learning an alternative language makes students aware that English
is a language, too, with its own peculiar conventions, rules, and
limitations. People who grow up in a single-speech community
with no encounters with other languages at all hold on to a
childlike belief that their language is just human talking—the
only, inevitable, and natural way of naming and communi-
cating: not an instrument for designating reality, but reality
itself.

The Sophistic study included many aspects. Gorgias, the
"inventor of rhetoric," worked on making public speeches more
effective through use of prose meters and rhetorical figures.
Prodicus, another famous Sophist, classified the parts of speech
(into "names, verbs, participles, and particles"), and began
work on a sort of etymological and dialectal dictionary. Protagoras, Gorgias, and the rest tried to find ways of transferring the clarity of logic and mathematics to statements and
inferences in legal and political discussion. The "nature-convention" dispute, mentioned above, was extended to language
and the question debated whether language (or some particular language) was "natural" or "conventional."

Inevitably, Plato was interested in this debate. For one

thing, Socrates' dialectical method usually began with ordinary language, and tried to clarify usage and meaning; for another, Sophistic rhetoric offered a competing method that challenged dialectic. Two dialogues in particular, the *Cratylus* and the *Euthydemus,* give us some of Plato's reflections as to the levels and kinds of "language" and their relation to the structure of human experience.

In the *Cratylus,* Plato has Socrates mediate between the two extreme views that all language is conventional and that all language is natural. It is a performance that at first strikes the modern reader as far-fetched and strange, since Socrates makes many of his points indirectedly through "etymologies"—the "meanings" of names—many of which have, as he admits, the look of giddy free association. (In English, these are hard to reproduce, though perhaps a fair sample is that the goddess "Hera" was given a name really meaning "Air.") But if we are patient with its punning, we find that the development of Socrates' "inspired etymolygizing" directs attention to distinctions that remain central in the most sophisticated analytic and literary discussions of language today.

Language is a tool which serves several functions, because people have, at different times and in different situations, different aims in communication.[11] For example, we may (particularly in poetry) aim at a direct, concrete presentation, where the language itself is like the meaning. Or we may have the practical aim of giving directions in a situation where adaptation or co-operation are called for. We may also aim at precise, if abstract, objective description, as we do in the languages of mathematics, or science, or contract law.

Our ordinary language is a mixture of words and devices serving all three of these distinct purposes, and unless we are selective, it serves none of them very well. It is rather like a broken wrench I once kept in my basement in Maine, which could be used as hammer, screwdriver, gimlet, or compass, but wasn't very good as any of them. The language of poetry is the most "natural" in the sense that it is specially suited to give us direct feelings and images. Coleridge's description of the site of the Emperor's pleasure dome in Kubla Khan is an example:

"And there were gardens bright with sinuous rills,
Where blossomed many an incense-bearing tree. . . ."

The description makes us see the garden; its sound is like the streams winding through the bright sunshine. But it is not the kind of description useful to a geologist or botanist; we would use another specialized language, locating plants and formations in abstract schemes of classification, if we were interested in the scientific aspect of the garden. The language of a formal kind which is specialized to purposes of logic, science, and law, is "natural" in its attempt to show the relations in abstract patterns that hold between the things it describes; often, such "language" replaces words with more abstract symbols, as when we write "A=B." In this equation, we have forgotten all about any of the interesting or useful characteristics A and B may have, and concentrated on stating their abstract relation. (Thus, what a logician might see as the formal information of Coleridge's lines is that they assert: In G [T & R].) The "language of every day," lying in between the concreteness of poetry and the abstractness of logic, classifies things by emphasizing what we can do with or about them. "Take the right hand turn," "Bring over the end table," "Catch the dog," are statements that show how, over a period of time, language develops ways of directing our attention that are economical and practically most useful. "Take the right hand turn," for instance, is not the "scientist's" way—he would give us a road map; nor the poet's way—he would tell us, perhaps, that there were roses and a schoolhouse at the corner. But neither the roses, nor the pattern of transcontinental highways, is immediately relevant to getting to the next town, and ordinary speech is so designed that it can ignore them.

In no dimension, Plato concludes, after examining the giving of names by scientists, politicians, and poets, does language exactly duplicate reality; it "imitates" it; but in no dimension is language purely arbitrary, either; for each of its purposes, there can be better and worse "imitations." The record of past human experience built into our language does shape our view of things; but there is no single consistent philosophy or world view which ordinary use reflects, and Plato concludes that the linguist must consult a philosopher when he is concerned with the relation of language to experience or to reality.[12]

The *Euthydemus* is, as was mentioned above, a devastating and hilarious commentary on the attempt to introduce the sharp either-or, all-or-none logic that works well in mathematics into the language or complex legal and ethical situations. The insistence of two belligerent visitors that he answer each question "yes or no, with no nonsense, and no qualifications!" spoils all of Socrates' attempts to discuss education and virtue, or to explain various of Plato's philosophic theories. Plato concludes the dialogue with an epilogue on "the nature of intermediates"; but even without that conclusion, we could clearly see that the kind of sharp formal logic which the brothers admire, and which the Sophists tried to adapt to legal practice, does not match the real nature of things; it gives an appearance of clarity at the price of falsifying reality. Note 4 to this chapter indicates some cases in which the modern American will do well to read Plato's *Euthydemus* and consider its epilogue.

It is usually argued that "ordinary use of language" is not "Platonic"—that is, that our common-sense observations do not support or recognize the theory of forms. This has even led some modern speculative philosophers to the thesis that philosophy "must involve *extraordinary* use of language." But I think the truth is that some ordinary types of English in use are Platonic. For example, when we say "he's a real shortstop," or "he has very good form." Or even our frequent question-comment, "Really?"

Martin Heidegger's readings of latent ontology in his "Greek etymologies" are in the same spirit as the *Cratylus* and in general, "existential" philosophy stresses the aesthetic aspect of language, its function as a tool for direct immediate communication.

.

PART TWO

Speculation and System

CHAPTER IV

Travel and the Academy

Syracuse and Tarentum

SHORTLY BEFORE HIS fortieth birthday, Plato travelled in Italy and Sicily. Although he did not keep a journal or write a detailed travelogue, we do know that his itinerary included the cities of Syracuse and Taras (the modern Tarento). One reason for the trip was to meet and talk with Archytas, the Tarentine scientist and statesman who was carrying on the Pythagorean tradition. In Syracuse, Plato visited the dictator, Dionysius I, a statesman of a very different type, who had consolidated his hold on political power, appointed himself king, and built up a brilliant local "Court."

There are many reflections scattered through Plato's writings of the study in contrasts these two cities and their leaders offered. For example, in the *Republic,* Plato's Socrates depicts the "unpleasant life of a dictator" in a detailed portrait that seems to be taken from Dionysius I. And, in the *Republic,* Archytas has been suggested as the model for the "philosophic king" who should rule in an ideal state.[1]

The meeting with Archytas was particularly significant, because it seems to have directly inspired Plato's idea of founding a new kind of educational center when he returned home. Archytas himself was carrying on the tradition of political and intellectual leadership of "The Pythagorean Order." This Order was established by Pythagoras when he came to Crotona, on the east coast of Italy, in 530 B.C. Communities of Pythagoreans shared their property, had religious and ethical observances in common, and carried on enthusiastic research

77

in mathematics. These communities also took an active part in political decisions, and until about 504 B.C., most of the Greek cities in Italy had communities of this Order. But for reasons that we do not now know, there was a bloody destruction of the Order in about 504 B.C.; most of the communities were attacked, their leaders executed or forced to escape, and the political influence of these early Utopian settlements was at an end, with two exceptions. The cities of Taras and Rhegion, in south Italy, remained "Pythagorean"; the synthesis of mathematical research and political leadership which Archytas personified shows that the tradition was still strong a half century later.

Archytas was a remarkable man. He had been repeatedly elected "mayor" of the city, by special motions making an exception in each case to the town's constitutional provision that no one should hold the office for more than one term. He is noted for achievements of two very different kinds: in pure mathematics and in the invention of children's toys. Sir Thomas Heath, in his *History of Greek Mathematics,* gives a proof devised by Archytas; it involves a geometrical imagination able to visualize the intersection of three solids in three dimensions, and Heath calls it "ingenious," "remarkable," and "brilliant." But there was presumably also a practical and human side to Archytas; for we read in one source that "he invented a new kind of baby-rattle," and in another that "he invented a toy bird that actually flew." There is a passage supposed to be quoted from him, which scholars are now inclined to accept as genuine, in which Archytas attributes all human success to skill in arithmetic and mathematics. He says that the mathematician can correctly calculate the consequences of his actions; can apply geometry to law and so secure justice and equity; can predict the economic results of public policies; devise military strategies; and, through understanding natural phenomena, he can avoid superstition. Plato, of course, would not have believed this; the influence of Socrates was too strong and convincing. And yet the prospect of applying mathematics to ethics and social planning was an exciting one.

Syracuse was very different from Taras. A series of dictators had led Syracuse and the adjacent cities to victories over the Carthaginians who held the western end of the island. Their military successes had been accompanied by increasing prosperity, and a rising standard of living. Further, these leaders had brought prestige to the city by their Olympic victories in chariot racing, and had attracted poets, sculptors, and scholars. Dionysius I was a "tyrant" in this tradition; he ruled with absolute power, and took no chances of revolution or assassination. The luxury and easy living of the court were notorious throughout Greece. But Syracuse did not delight the young Athenian admirer of Socrates; the pursuit of pleasure and comfort seemed to him a parody of true human life, and the apparatus of mercenaries and secret policy attested to the unhealthy political condition of the state. The story is told— and this time with more than usual claim to authenticity—that Dionysius I asked Plato whether the latter did not think him a happy man. Plato gave him an honest answer, that he thought no one who was not mad would ever become a tyrant. The dictator is then supposed to have handed Plato over to officers of a power then at war with Athens, to be sold into slavery. The lucky arrival of a friend who ransomed him made it possible for Plato to return to Athens as a free man. Even if this story is not true, the portrait of a tyrant in the *Republic*, with its analysis of his psychological state, and details of the picture of Atlantis (a mythical country with wealth and power but no temperance) in the *Critias*, give us a picture of Plato's reaction to his Syracusan visit. One of the pleasant parts of the Syracusan sojourn was a friendship Plato formed with the dictator's brother, Dion; this friendship was destined to bring Plato to Syracuse again, twenty years later.

The First University

Travel indeed proved stimulating for Plato; if Syracuse led him into melodrama, Taras was equally effective in starting him off on a major intellectual adventure. For on his return to Athens, we find Plato founding "the Academy:" a school and research center embodying the idea of a university, an idea of Plato's original invention.

The Academy was conceived as a community of older and younger scholars, representing experts in all fields of knowledge (for example, mathematics, medicine, and law). It was to try to realize at the same time Archytas' idea of a unity of science through mathematical method, Socrates' ideal of discovering reliable truths about human nature and conduct, and Plato's own idea of basing political action on responsible knowledge, so that no blood-bath under "The Thirty" or execution of a Socrates would occur again.

The Pythagorean contribution to this plan, directly and indirectly, was a double one. In the first place, the new (and still nebulous) notion of "social science" should probably be counted their contribution. In the city planning of Hippodamas, the praise of geometry as an aid to justice by Archytas, the definition of health as "balance" (*isonomia*) by the medical men, we find an underlying intuition that human cities, laws, and policies should be capable of the same deductive scientific study as circling planets or vibrating lyre strings. Socrates, we recall, had urged that it was absurd to spend all one's energy in planning, for example, how to get money or power, meanwhile leaving the most important concerns of life unthought of and unplanned. Mathematics seemed to Plato to offer a model of method which might apply to intelligent ethical or civil planning.

As the second Pythagorean contribution, we must go back to the interesting discovery which inspired or confirmed the general position of that school that "things are numbers." In measuring string lengths that give concordant notes, the concords represent exact small integral ratios, and the appeal of music rests to some extent on the simplicity of this "mathematics overheard." The relations of planetary periods, to a first approximation, also fit this same set of ratios; as though nature had an innate preference for simplicity in her quantitative laws. This idea suggests, by a reasonable generalization, that in every subject matter measurement will disclose relations and laws of this same simple type. Extension of measurement confirmed the confidence of the Pythagoreans that mathematics was the most valuable method of inquiry that science could have. Most important, it led to the expectation that general laws discovered in any one subject matter would have applications or counterparts in any other. For example, the periods of celestial motion, in just that form, *might* also be the ratios of the circulating impulses that make up the physical operation of the brain; if not, then some similar system of ratios certainly would be expected in these impulses.

Plato's new institutional plan accepted and prepared to take advantage of the Pythagorean ideas, (1) that nature forms a single connected system, with no drastic breaks, (2) that the laws of that system are discovered by mathematics and measurements, (3) that one of the important functions of research was to try comparing and transferring laws from one subject matter to another.

But the memory of Socrates was vivid in Plato's mind, and his influence can also be clearly seen in the institution Plato planned. Something more than pure mathematics was needed to answer the fundamental ethical questions Socrates had asked. And so neither Plato nor his plan identified (as Archytas had) the mathematician with the philosopher. Plato was convinced, also by Socrates' example, that live discussion was the way to invent and test ideas; and that "research" at its best would be "dialectical"—a round-table exchange and collaboration. The "community of scholars" aspect of the Academy is not simply a memory of the Pythagorean Order, but rather a direct and essential consequence of loyalty to Socrates' ideals of education and inquiry.

The provision for communication across specialized lines, insuring that all aspects of a topic are represented, seems to have appealed to Plato strongly. In practice, this meant that the Academy would welcome experts in medicine, politics, mathematics, law, and other "professions." A garden, a library, and a few pieces of special "laboratory equipment" completed the institution, with Plato himself its resident director.

Although there were competing professional schools, including the orator Isocrates' institute for rhetoric and politics in Athens itself, the Academy was from the outset a deserved success. Its reputation led in time to invitations for help in drafting new constitutions and codes of law; within two decades it was chosen by a Macedonian doctor for the education of his talented son, Aristotle; and it could attract Eudoxus of Cnidos, the most brilliant astronomer and geometer of his time, as guest lecturer. About Eudoxus and Aristotle more will be said later.

A discussion of the so-called "middle dialogues" in which Plato presents the speculative insights and vision that he developed during the planning and early operation of his university belongs more to a treatment of new ideas than to the present section of biography. However, it is worth mentioning the thesis of the German scholar von Sybel, that the *Symposium,* a "dialogue" on themes of love and beauty, was designed and written as a sort of program or prospectus for the Academy.[2] In the *Symposium,* instead of the dialogue form we have seen so far, a series of speeches are given, moving from Phaedrus who talks about love in poetry, through Socrates who talks about love in philosophy, to Alcibiades who ends the evening by a speech in praise of Socrates. The result is like an ordered set of "early" dialogues rather than like a single one; we can see in each speech what Socrates, given the chance, would have asked the other speakers, and why each of them would have had too specialized a view of the theme to develop any "conclusive" reply. The selected group who speak are interesting. We have mentioned Phaedrus, the "humanistic scholar"; he is followed by Pausanias, who treats of love in terms of law; then Dr. Eryximachus, who puts his ideas forward with a rather pompous "speaking as a scientist" air, yet is not very scientific; then come Aristophanes, the comic poet; Agathon, tragic poet and host for the occasion; Socrates, claiming to be repeating things he has heard from an inspired priestess; finally, Alcibiades. Each speech adds something to our understanding of the theme, and whatever Plato's immediate intention may have been, the literary form and the selection of "experts" who speak certainly seem to justify the notion that it was this kind of discussion which Plato had in mind as an ideal for the students and faculty of his "university."

CHAPTER V

The Speculative Vision: Order, Fact, and Value

Love and Beauty (*Symposium*)

As THE SUCCESSIVE speeches follow in the *Symposium*, it becomes more and more clear that love is a directed desire, that it changes behavior from normal, and that it often involves some feeling of suspension of time, a sense of or desire for eternity. We learn from poetry, medicine, and law what kinds of human behavior "love" causes; Agathon begins his speech by a reminder that this still has not explained what love is, hence *why* it causes this behavior. Agathon's own idea, put in an elegantly artificial speech that gets general applause, is that "Love is a god, and a perfect being." A few questions from Socrates, however, remind the company and the reader that in truth—as opposed to Agathon's fancy—love is a relation between the lover and some desired object or goal. If we want to personify Eros, then, the portrait must include the sense of lack and need in the lover as well as the beauty he sees in the object of his affection.

Socrates, claiming to repeat what he has heard from Diotima, an inspired prophetess, now offers his own speech. It is a speech which reminds one, both by likeness and by contrast, of Gautama Buddha's meditation on the cause of suffering of created beings, which traces to "desire." For Socrates defends the thesis that all love has its source in the desire for immortality—for "possession, and ever-continuing possession, of the good"—on the part of each finite creature.

Beauty attracts us because it presents what we lack, and offers some nearer approach to the immortality which we desire. It is therefore not accidental that love is felt to carry with it a sense of time standing still.

Even on the animal level, an instinct for the survival of the species is apparent; this often operates at the expense of the comfort, or even the survival, of the individual. This is a result, too, of a felt desire for immortality, through the "law of succession" by which it can be shared. On the human level, we feel this same force operating; but the vision of beauty may also inspire other forms of creativity.

Diotima goes on to discuss the way in which we can come to see the nature of the beautiful. At the beginning, one falls in love with a single beautiful body. Then he or she comes to see that the beauty of all bodies is similar; and from this point may sublimate or supplement the passion for procreation by other types of creation. Fine arts, virtuous souls, laws and societies, science and mathematics, each have a beauty proper to them, which is progressively more abstract; and the creative worker in any of these fields feels that he is projecting himself beyond his fenced-in finite career, creating things that transcend their creator's limitations. (It is interesting to see Plato group the creative impulse of the politician, parent, and physicist together with that of the artist; our own century may be overlooking something in restricting "creativity" and "beauty" —as we often do—to the fine arts.)

The final goal of education in beauty is the vision of "beauty itself"—the form which has given attractive power to the other beauties of persons and things. This final vision satisfies our incompleteness, when in contemplation we can identify ourselves with the form. The lover who has progressed thus far will never be deceived by appearance, and his creations will be "not likenesses, but realities."

Love results, then, from our awareness of the attractive power of something we lack. This feeling is more clearly described as the wish that one may have continuing possession of the good. Beauty attracts us because we are sensitive to the value of the forms as ideals; we are sensitive to this value because we, and all animals with us, are instinctively aware of the gap between time and eternity; between life with its constant reminders of the running-down of the body, and creative sensitivity which can reach beyond our transient histories.

Where Buddha taught the elimination of desire as the best way of life, Socrates advocates its clarification and direction. There are objective forms which attract us, and when we see them clearly, we know our real natures and in some sense actually achieve, through this knowledge, a transcendence of time.

After Socrates' speech the banquet ends with Alcibiades, who speaks in praise of Socrates. Now, in criticizing Agathon's speech, Socrates had introduced the theme that love must mediate between fullness and lack, divine perfection and human limitation, and thus must be a *daimon*—a "spirit" mediating between gods and men. Socrates, as Alcibiades describes him, exactly fits this notion of a being that is strange and inspiring, that exists in a human world yet is somehow immune to ordinary human limitations. After this speech, a troop of drunken revellers breaks up the banquet, and toward dawn Socrates is left sitting between a sleepy Aristophanes and Agathon, proving to them "that the art of writing comedy and tragedy is the same. . . ."

Philosophically considered, the *Symposium* is Plato's sustained attempt to share his vision of the forms and of the tension between ideal and actual that we feel as "love" and "desire." Probably no philosophy can be credible which does not recognize and explain the possibility of love and creativity as important and real phenomena.

Virtue and Society (The *Republic*)

The relation between the community and the individual was one problem which Plato knew from experience; to find a solution was presumably one of his goals for the new Academy. On the one hand, it was only in a social context that a full human life could be led, and such a context seemed to impose an obligation to have respect for law; on the other hand, the group wielding power in a state, whether it was a dictator, an

oligarchy of Thirty, or a democracy, could and often did use
this power unjustly; thus we could have the dilemma of Socrates, a good man in a bad state, unjustly sentenced but unwilling to set an example of disrespect for law by running away.
The possible solutions of declaring either that the state or the
individual alone was *real* and hence took priority, may have
occurred to Plato, but since he held that *both* were real, this
simple kind of solution was not open to him. Instead, he proposed to design a state such that no just man in it could ever
be treated unjustly. But before this could be well done, it was
evidently necessary to have a clear idea of the nature of justice;
as we have seen, this was a point on which Socrates, professional legal opinion, and the common sense of the time, differed sharply. "Justice" in the individual, the state, and the
universe is the theme of Plato's *Republic,* the most widely
read, admired, and criticized single work in Western philosophy. The *Republic* is a brilliant discussion, showing Plato's
ability to bring together many fields of knowledge and relate
them to a single central speculative theme. In the course of
the discussion, a state is described which is ideal in respect to
social justice; and an educational system outlined which presupposes the theory of forms, and Socrates' equation of virtue
with knowledge.

At the outset, Socrates encounters the various notions of
justice held by Cephalus ("business" ethics—pay your debts),
Polemarchus ("cowboy" ethics—shoot the bad guys and help
the good), and the lawyer Thrasymachus ("power" ethics—
justice is the advantage of the stronger). The first two of these
ideas are easily shown to be mere hearsay or guesswork; more
than accounting is meant in our concern with doing what is
right (it would be wrong to pay back a sword you owe a
friend, if he asked for it in a fit of insanity); the horses men
in real life ride have colors other than black and white (it is
not easy and obvious to tell who real, as opposed to seeming,
friends and enemies are). Thrasymachus, however, a Sophist
and practicing lawyer, has a wide experience to draw on. If
he were allowed to make a separate speech, he could doubtless
cite case after case in which the courts had acted to protect

and enforce the privileges of the group with power. He has not yet thought these facts through to find a general theory explaining why the courts behave in this way; his statement, "justice is the interest of the ruler and stronger," is rather a technician's sour observation on how things work than a theorist's explanation of why. And, in a wonderfully ironic scene, Socrates refutes Thrasymachus on a legal technicality. (My students are usually annoyed by this; they feel that Socrates quibbles, instead of really facing a serious question.) Two young men in the audience in the *Republic*, Adeimantus and Glaucon (Plato's older brothers, whom he puts into the dialogue), are dissatisfied; and, at their hands, Thrasymachus' position is brought against Socrates in a much stronger form than the lawyer could have given it.

What follows is a quick formulation and comparison of two sorts of political theory. What will Socrates, who admits justice to be intrinsically good, say to the "social contract" theorist who explains that it is a necessary evil? The "social contract" theories referred to here are those, such as Hobbes', in which men who are by nature aggressive and hostile nevertheless accept a sovereign because he offers them protection, each from all the others.

Socrates begins his answer by questioning the assumptions of this theory: as a matter of fact, men are better described as greedy than aggressive, and they will and do co-operate peacefully when their comfort and commodities are increased by co-operation. Justice becomes each performing his special work, and all sharing the production. This sounds like an "economic determinist" theory, but even for a society set up as a happy rustic co-operative in this way economic adequacy is not enough because it would provide no means of protection. The community would have to hire an army, says Socrates; and thus the "aggressive" man of the contract theory enters our "economic" state.

To have a single state which will operate without class friction, and without infinite need for expansion, we need careful selection of the soldiers and proper education for everyone. Through music and gymnastic we can teach "temperance and

grace," and so temper the ferocity of the soldier and the greed
of the producer. Supervisors of education must be added as a
third functional class in our theory; we can also entrust this
group with making public policy, if they are properly chosen
and trained.

Here is a first definition of justice. Our society is wise if
its rulers make policy well; brave if its soldiers execute policy
effectively; temperate if all its classes are harmonized by an
agreement as to which should rule and which be ruled; and
just when each citizen has and does his own proper work, not
meddling in other classes' business. These conditions of value
can be generalized to apply to other sorts of organizations, as
well as to the political one. For example, we can test the tentative result by seeing whether it will work for justice and injustice in the individual soul, as well as in the state. Examination of their conflict shows three independent "parts" in the
soul (today we would call them "faculties" or "classes of
drives"). These are the appetitive, aggressive ("spirited"—
the part that loves contests and prestige), and rational. (The
rational faculty must be separate since reason can come into
conflict both with ambition and appetite.) An excellent individual will be exactly like an excellent society: wise if the
rational part is strong; brave if the ambitious part co-operates
with reason and is not deterred by pain and pleasure; temperate if the parts are in their proper (reason-spirit-appetite)
order of subordination; and just if each part of the soul does
its own proper work. In the individual, then, justice is a psychological balance, with appetite and ambition guided by reason to their proper exercise and satisfaction. Since this balance, it is agreed, is necessary for a truly human life, justice
turns out, as Socrates had thought, to have intrinsic value for
the individual; it is the psychological state necessary to lead
human life fully and well.

The discussion returns to consider in more detail the nature
and nurture of the rulers, in terms of property, warfare, and
intellectual training. Since the rulers have absolute power, the
state seems totalitarian to some readers. On the other hand,
justice and social welfare both require equality of opportunity,

so that each person functions in the class for which he is fitted; the aristocracy is one of ability. And the principle of consent of the governed is carefully written into the definition of temperance in Book IV. Finally, the rulers are trained as public-spirited administrators, who will be objective in their judgments of policy.

Following the discussion of social classes and psychological excellence, Socrates spends some time illustrating what he means his ideal rulers to be, by describing their training in temperance, courage, and wisdom, in that order. Although he keeps saying that his illustrations are "not impossible," the account is not a practical program but a fascinating description of family life and education in an imaginary community of these guardians. It is primarily intended to show in more detail what sort of rulers his abstract aristocrats are. They must never put personal interest ahead of the welfare of the community as a whole. While the motives of gaining profit and prestige are natural and proper for the craftsman or farmer, they are not so for the legislator. The way to insure that there will be no conflicts of interest is to give the rulers no personal ties that could interfere. This means no private property; it also means no private families. Women and children will be held in common, so that the rulers form a single family. To judge from later reactions of its readers, one might think the main intention of the whole *Republic* was to advocate such communism, rather than to define justice. The proposal is shocking to the modern reader, and was meant to be so. Temperance, in this limiting case, will require a radical alteration of what Greek and American alike have always thought of as "human nature"; the natural pursuit of our own profit, and the natural tendency, even more marked then than now, to give one's own relatives preferential treatment whenever possible. This community, like the earlier discussion of society, is helping to define an idea; it is not a program that is recommended for actual operation.

The discussion of the ruler's courage and wisdom confirms this notion that Plato is making his point vivid by presenting extreme cases. To insure their bravery, Socrates goes on, the rulers should be taught to be fearless from an early age; we will take them into battle, so that they will not be frightened of pain and combat, and can make decisions of policy without timidity. To the reader of his time, who could easily visualize this "children's cavalry," this plan surely seemed startling; and no less startling was the scheme of education that follows later. The great danger in giving a group total power is that they use this in ignorance of what they are really doing; the great temptation of politicians is to rely on experience and guess-work, but in the state Socrates now describes, that temptation is to be corrected by ten years of study in pure mathematics before they are allowed to discuss public policy!

We can argue indefinitely about how literally Plato took these proposals. But we must keep in mind that, in the total discussion, they define virtue only negatively: by freedom from greed, fear, and ignorance. They do not give a constructive picture of the engaged, balanced life of the just man in the good state; Plato puts off that consideration until the end of the *Republic*.

The *Republic* now proceeds to the discussion of the divided line and the form of the good. These two concepts are so important and so technical that I have chosen to treat them separately and at greater length than would be appropriate in this overview of the *Republic*. Therefore, we will skip, for the present, Socrates' presentation of the detailed program designed to give the rulers an ideal education for the wisdom they must achieve, and go on to the point, in Book VIII, at which Socrates proceeds to classify all other "types of state and personality" as deviations from the "aristocratic" ideal.

When a group of rulers confuse national welfare with national power and honor, the result is a "timocratic" ("honor-loving") state, rather like Sparta; in the individual, it produces a man in whom ambition exceeds the limits set by reason. The appetitive motive prevails in a money-loving individual, and in a state ruled by an economic oligarchy who make policy in terms of national wealth. But at least such persons and states have a consistent policy; perhaps because of some past insecurity, Socrates suggests, they are afraid of being in want of necessities. But when appetites alternate in their claim for satisfaction and there is no fixed policy, we have the town-meeting democracy and the "democratic" personality—for whom all desires are equal. Finally (a reminder of Plato's early Syracusan travel), a mind or state gone mad, monomaniacally dominated by a single insatiable desire for individual power and pleasure, is the domain of the tyrant. A vivid picture of the tyrant's terrors and limitations is given as case study—a life of terror, surrounded by illiterate mercenaries, devoid of friends, since anyone his superior or equal seems to him a rival for his power. (Dionysius I never trusted the court barber with a razor, but had his beard singed; presently we will meet his son, Dionysius II, who was brought up in the atmosphere of fear, suspicion, and self-indulgence that Plato's portrait shows.)

Having now put before his hearers case studies and classifications of types of society and personality, Socrates finally sums up the case for justice. The good man, we can now see, is best and happiest; and it even turns out that his life, of all the lives examined, is the most pleasant. The pleasure we find in life depends on a right choice of goals, a skillful selection of means that will lead us to those goals, and an opportunity in the environment we live in to choose and utilize those means. The just man is best in all three respects. Socrates sums up, "the just man is then immeasurably better, and lives 729 times more pleasantly than the tyrant." We will not stop to show that there is perhaps some serious sense behind this joking selection of "729," for Socrates has made his point in any case. And here, perhaps, we find what the earlier discussion of temperance, courage, and wisdom lacked: a picture of justice and the just man operating in a real universe like our own, not simply being constructed like two-dimensional figures in abstract argument.

Glaucon and Adeimantus had challenged Socrates to show that justice is a good to its possessor, whether or not it is recognized by other men, or by the gods. The case has been made out without introducing gods or religious sanction; but since in fact the universe, too, is just, we should take account of our religious hope that justice is rewarded by the gods as well as men. After an aside on the dangers of poetry which only catches the superficial glitter of things, the *Republic* ends, in the Myth of Er, with a great poem. In the myth, souls are brought before the goddess Necessity and allowed to choose their next lives, from a showcase filled with patterns. The goddess shows them a model of the universe, intended to prove that the world is just and justly run, and then they draw lots and, in order, have free choice. Once they have chosen, however, there can be no exchange. Plato's description of the scene is vivid and powerful; his Socrates ends the dialogue by telling Glaucon that if this myth and the preceding argument are true, we must above all things pursue justice; for, if we keep our minds on this throughout life, "then, both here and hereafter, we will fare well."

In the *Republic,* the reader will find constant ideas that are provocative and interesting: how much have popular ideas of "justice" changed? If science in Plato's time had recognized that hereditary ability is much more equal than was then thought, would each citizen have had a turn at being a ruler? Does justice have intrinsic value? Is this state totalitarian?

One such question anticipates the following section, and is one that we can not only ask, but partly answer. What is "dialectic," which is described as the final study for the rulers in their higher education. A partial answer to this, I believe, is that an example of "dialectic" is given by the *Republic* itself; here again as in the early dialogues there is the skillful interplay of the dialogue itself as a concrete example of its subject.

Knowledge and Opinion (*Republic VI* and *VII*)

In contrast to his critic's role in the early dialogues, Plato's Socrates, in the *Phaedo, Phaedrus, Symposium,* and *Republic* develops a great system of speculative philosophy.

In the *Republic,* the Platonic "theory of forms" which is central to this system is applied to the discovery of criteria for good societies and good character. Plato offers as his ideal of social excellence a state without class friction, with rulers, protectors and producers as its three functional classes, and with assignment of status by merit.

Later readers have found a number of objectionable features in this ideal—beginning with readers no later than Plato's student, Aristotle. There has been wide disagreement as to what this discussion of justice in society really is. The theme of the dialogue as a whole is justice—in the state, the individual, and the universe—and the model of a just society could therefore legitimately overlook properties essential to realistic political theory in order to emphasize the similarities of justice in these three contexts. Let us concentrate, however, on a thesis in the argument which holds, no matter how the dialogue is read: that effective social life depends on adequate education.

To this end, the *Republic* provides three levels of public education, a common elementary school (see note 1, below, for a defense of this interpretation), a secondary school with selective admission, and a "state university" with admission still more selective.[1] The first of these institutions will teach *mousike*—literature, music, and civics; the second will prepare future auxiliaries for military and civil service posts by a curriculum of mathematics, arithmetic, plane geometry, solid geometry, astronomy, and "harmonics," in that order. (This Platonic suggestion is the ancestor of the Medieval quadrivium —the four mathematical studies of the standard "Liberal Arts" course.) Finally, in higher education, there will be five years of "dialectic," followed by fifteen more years of practical experience for the students chosen to be future legislators.

The rationale of this plan for the education of rulers is that they must be disinterested and have clear knowledge of the true general welfare of the state. The kind of knowledge adequate to the authority and responsibility they are given cannot be simply that of our ordinary politicians: there are three inferior sorts of "knowing" from which we must distinguish it. Plato is illustrating this distinction by his diagram of the "divided line," where four degrees of clarity of knowledge are represented by a line divided into four segments, as in Fig. IV.

Figure IV: THE DIVIDED LINE

The directions are to take a line divided into four parts, and let the segments represent kinds of knowledge with different degrees of clarity. A figure with equal segments is adequate to show the central distinctions Plato intends.

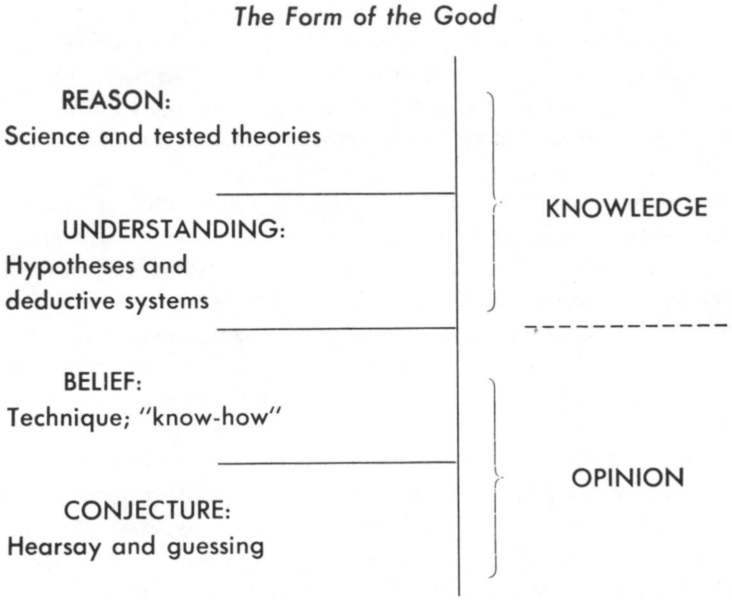

The Form of the Good

REASON:
Science and tested theories

UNDERSTANDING:
Hypotheses and
deductive systems

KNOWLEDGE

BELIEF:
Technique; "know-how"

CONJECTURE:
Hearsay and guessing

OPINION

The lowest level of Plato's line represents a kind of knowledge which he call *eikasia,* often translated as "conjecture." This is the kind of knowledge we have when we "know" something because we have been told it, or have read it in the paper. While "hearsay" may on occasion be quite true, the fact that it is notoriously unreliable is so well known that our modern law of evidence will not allow it in court.

The next level of the line is called *pistis,* a word often rendered as "belief." As Plato uses his terms, we must think of

this "belief" as differing from "hearsay" because it is based
on first-hand experience. This is the sort of knowledge a craftsman has; he knows *how* to make something, and often *what*
to expect, though he need not know *why* his predictions are
right. Plato considered the politicians of his day men who
were at best "political technicians." They knew the tricks that
got popular support, they were often right in their beliefs about
the results of policy decisions; but they were working by rule
of thumb, inexactly and unscientifically.

The third level of the line is called *dianoia,* a term often
translated as "understanding" (partly because of the influence
on our English philosophical vocabulary of the Kantian distinction between *Vernunft* and *Verstand*). To "understand"
something is to be able to explain a particular case or problem
by deductions from general laws or axioms. Such understanding, by relating the particular to a universal rule, tells
one *why* as well as *how* things behave as they do. Mathematical reasoning seemed to Plato the clearest example of the
kind of knowledge on this level of "understanding." In geometry, for example, we understand theorems when we prove
them deductively from the more universal postulates and
axioms of the system. Other passages show that Plato also intends to include as knowledge of this sort such devices as the
multiplication table or the chemist's periodic table of elements,
from which we can "compute" solutions. There is one obvious
limitation to this kind of "understanding." It only gives the true
explanation when the "postulates" from which we start are
right. We can put more than one table into the memory of a
computing machine; and, as the earlier discussion of social
theories in the *Republic* has itself shown, more than one set
of axioms and postulates is possible as basis for deductive
explanation. Perhaps, in Plato's day, it was a sound intuition
that he could not prove which led him to expect this same
kind of limitation to apply to geometry and logic. But today
we can supply abundant proof that here, too, more than one
set of axioms and postulates is possible, so that we need some
way of choosing among the alternatives they offer if we want
a complete science or clear explanation.

Plato's fourth level of his .ne, called *episteme* ("science") and knowledge by *nous* ("reason"), does not use hypotheses except as "steps to mount on." The advance of science "does away with" hypotheses. The point here is that the "scientist" in this sense has examined and compared the possible generalizations that suggest themselves as rival explanatory laws, and has determined which of them is the best, or, more usually, how all can be synthesized into a more general theory that is complete and better. The true scientist is both aware and critical of his assumptions, unlike the computing machine which cannot go beyond the facts in its memory of the rules of its program.

This Platonic account is clear, and so far not out of date. It comes as something of a surprise to many readers to find that "the form of the good" still remains, at the very top point of the line. It is this form that gives the scientist his criterion for picking the best theory. Plato, as we will see, does his pedagogical best to explain this form in another way, by clarifying our vision of it through a series of accounts moving up through the four levels of his divided line.

We should be clear as to what Plato's exact meaning is. He is not saying that any given theory in physics or social science *can* be finally shown to be absolutely true; he is saying that if his ideal legislators had an ideal science, this ought to have such certainty. What *is* absolutely certain is that we can accept what is most reasonable as most true. Plato, following his own rule that the scientist must examine his assumptions, recognized this, and found it surprising. His final argument is that this correspondence of our laws of thought and the world of fact holds because our minds are themselves part of a common reality in which both thoughts and facts are organized by a common principle of value. (It is natural for us, for example, to prefer simplicity in our theories, because nature, too, prefers simplicity, and this natural preference is reflected in the operations of our minds.) This Platonic conception leads into philosophic issues and controversies that we will not pursue here; but in studying Plato's ideal curriculum, we must remember that its aim is to clarify the student's knowledge of fact, of logic, and ultimately of value.

Certainly, the objective nature of the good, if there is such a thing which can be known, is what our ideal legislators need to know to do their work well. But what is this "form of the good," and what is the "method of dialectic" that leads to it, "using hypotheses only as steps to be transcended"? Remembering the *Meno,* we might well expect that (1) all of us are confusedly yet definitely aware of the nature of the good, since we all desire it; and (2) that to make this awareness clear, we will need to be challenged to use our own insight, since here, as in the ethical problem Meno faced, a textbook formula would be either useless or misleading.

The Form of the Good—Four Perspectives

It is certainly true that the most important condition for *wisdom* in a state is that its policy be based on real and correct evaluation. For this, the rulers need to see clearly and be able to apply their vision of "the good" which orders the world of forms. This vision is the final stage of their higher education. The appearance of "the good" at the top of the figure of the "divided line" culminates Plato's development of the Socratic thesis that "vice is ignorance." At first, in the early dialogues, "the good" appears as the cause which makes other things "dear to us." Then, in the *Phaedo,* Socrates tells of his discovery that reference to the good supplies a type of explanation which natural science needed but had overlooked; and in his Myth of the True Earth, Socrates tells a story in which this method shows that there is a connectedness and order in nature, within which we can relate our particular observations and scientific and religious hypotheses. (See pp. 38 and 109.) We do, in fact, find that all of our knowledge presupposes some criteria of evaluation: we must be able to discriminate between good and bad, better and worse, methods and explanations. Not only is this so, but those theories which are best in the sense of being clearest to a human mind prove also to be those that best match the objective order of nature, as though the same laws and limitations that guide our reasoning also operate in this objective order.

But how can we explain or define this Platonic highest form? The usual method of explaining something by showing that it is a part or special case of something more general, more inclusive, or more powerful won't work here at all. We can't conceive or postulate such a more general, or powerful, or inclusive super-form. We can't do this, not only because there *is* none (for we can postulate things that are not), but because if we did postulate such a form, it would either (a) presuppose the good as higher, because we would have to argue that the postulate was a good one; or (b) the postulated "highest form, including all the others," would simply be the good, which, on Plato's view, must include all other forms and also itself. (This requirement poses problems in analysis and logic that are still fascinating; but we will defer them until later. See p. 172.)

But, since the "method of hypothesis" does not apply, how can the good be known? Plato explains this in four ways, giving an account of the good on each level of knowledge of his divided line. There is the famous Myth of the Cave, a story about intellectual discovery. Socrates begins this attractive allegory by asking Glaucon to imagine men imprisoned in a cave, chained so that they can only look forward at the wall before them. Behind them is a lower wall and a bright fire; people pass by behind the wall, carrying "puppets" which rise above the low parapet and cast their shadows on the opposite side of the cave, which the prisoners can see. The watching prisoners take these flickering shadows for realities; they try to understand their sequences, and gain some skill in predicting which shadow will come next after a given shadow. Suppose, now, that one of these prisoners is released; he turns about and sees the puppets passing before the fire (but does not, as I interpret the story, see the people who carry them; these are still hidden from him by the low wall). Our prisoner now has an entire new dimension added to his "knowledge," as he sees what has been casting the shadows; and, viewing the puppet parade, he sees *why* the shadow of a donkey's ears

had led him to expect the shadow of its tail. ("Why," he remarks, "the shadow of the ears didn't *cause* the tail to follow
after all; it followed *because* they are joined in this order in
the whole puppet.") Now, let our released prisoner leave the
cave (by an egress, I assume, which still hides the puppeteers
from him). At first, the daylight outside is so dazzling to his
unaccustomed eyes that he can only make out shadows and
dim reflections; but presently he begins to see the things in
the natural world around him. Among the other things, he sees
a donkey; and now he knows *why* the ears and tail followed as
they did on the puppet. It was because the puppet was an
imitation of the real donkey. And the real donkey has his ears
in front and tail behind because this is the best arrangement
for a living organism. Finally, our traveller would become able
to look at the sun, and recognize it as the source of light and
warmth which made nature and life possible, and also made
it possible for him to see other things. But what a madman
he would be thought if he returned to the cave, and tried to
tell the others of his new knowledge!

Glaucon remarks that "it is a strange story, and strange prisoners"; "like ourselves," says Socrates. The stages of the journey
correspond (approximately at least, and I believe exactly) to the
change on the part of the wise man from sheer guesswork to a
vision of the forms. And, above these, the cause of their being
and being known, the form of the good, can finally be seen
directly, like the sun in nature in its brilliance and power.

It is a vivid story, but as with all allegories we need some
key to show us what its parts and stages represent. Perhaps
a map or diagram can make the position of the good in its
relation to our knowledge clear; at any rate, it is evident that
Plato has offered such a "mathematical" illustration in his figure of the divided line.

When the good first enters their discussion, Socrates describes the direct intellectual vision of it to Glaucon. It is like
seeing the sun in the natural world; the good is the summit
of the world of forms, "cause of their being known . . . and
being, . . . but beyond both in power." "Oh, Apollo!" says

Glaucon, "hyperbole can hardly be more demonic. But tell me about it." This "telling" goes on in the myth and diagram.

There remains one approach to explore: what *techniques* can men use to gain this vision of the good? The answer Socrates gives is a proposed course of studies, through ten years of mathematics in secondary school to a final (five-year) course of dialectic in the Academy. Dialectic, in the university course, will begin by reviewing the preceding mathematical studies, "with a view to seeing how they are alike." What is alike about them, as we learn from the divided line and its context, is that all pure mathematical sciences have the same *method:* they prove theorems by deduction from their initial "hypotheses" (axioms, postulates, and definitions). This first study, then, should generalize the mathematical method so that we can see it apart from any specific subject matter; when this is done, the result is precisely modern symbolic logic. Plato obviously did not have our contemporary logic at hand, nor could he have anticipated its detail; but he did see that if mathematics was to do its job of teaching his students how to think, some abstract formal logic needed to be invented. After this preliminary stage, dialectic, unlike mathematics, criticizes "hypotheses"; it uses them as steps, mounting on them higher and higher until it reaches the form of the good; this form is "non-hypothetical," in a sense we will discuss below. The details of dialectic as an abstract method are omitted, but the omission is less serious than many readers have thought; for the *Republic* is itself an example of moving dialectically beyond partial and unclear insights to a final clear vision of the form of justice.

That the first two books of the *Republic* are a clear example of the progress toward clear knowledge by the stages of the divided line, and hence an example of dialectic in action, can be shown as below. (This scheme is an adaptation of two earlier figures illustrating the point, one by Dr. Paul Desjardins, the other my own.)

Final synthesis: Comparing the "social contract" and "economic determinist" hypotheses, Socrates combines them under a more general theory.

Theoretical explanation by hypothesis: Adeimantus and Glaucon put forward their "social contract" theory to explain why justice is as it is; Socrates offers an alternative theory, just as good.

Technique and experiment: Thrasymachus draws on his legal experience to describe how justice in fact works in the courts.

Conjecture or hearsay: Cephalus and Polemarchus define justice simply by repeating what businessmen and poets say about it.

This is a fascinating philosophic vision, but in spite of Plato's four efforts, via "demonic hyperbole," schematism, myth, and method, a difficult one to share. It may be particularly hard for us today because science and mathematics have so emphasized the importance of "hypotheses" that they, and we, may tend to overlook some obvious assumptions that the very use of hypotheses in science depends on. (1) We take it for granted that logic can determine what consequences do and what do not follow from given premises: this requires a kind of stable order among our concepts and their referents. (Compare Parmenides' insight that "it is the same thing that can be known and can be.") (2) We select the simple explanation in preference to the complex and this preference certainly involves some assumption that needs justification. (3) We think that the most elegant, coherent, and comprehensive theories are going to be the most "true," that is, that they will best correspond to the observed order of nature, and it turns out that in fact they are. To a Platonist, these considerations seem to show that what we want are not just any postulates, but the best ones; and that symmetry, beauty (i.e., simplicity), and truth are properties theories will have if, and only if, they are good. There are, of course, other interpretations of our ways of knowing which do not *seem,* at any rate, to introduce Plato's assumptions and conclusions; for the present, we will not digress to look at these, because we are engaged in trying to understand Plato's theory, and must be sure we understand it before we attack, defend, or appraise it.

In what sense, we now ask, is the Platonic form of the good "non-hypothetical"? It is so in two important ways. In the first place, it must actually (not merely hypothetically) exist as the cause of the attraction we feel toward "the good." The notion that the actual and evident attraction which the good and its allied forms exert on us (which we experience as "desire") could be the effect of something which was not itself "actual" is rejected by Plato. There does seem a legitimate analogy here between "attraction" in a physical and in a psychological field; if we find very strong lines of force, we assume that there is something *actually* (not just possibly or ideally) causing them; and analogously, the attraction of the good testifies to its actuality. However, Platonism in the twentieth century reopens this question for further consideration (see p. 212). In the second place, the good is non-hypothetical because *any* use of reason "presupposes" it. We may hold that every general proposition we know is merely probable, only an hypothesis; yet we still assume that the best hypothesis is the truest, that our hypothetical method is a good one, and that what is reasonable is also what is real. These two considerations may or may not seem convincing to the modern reader; in either case, however, they may be clarifying.

The unique position of the good makes Plato's description of our intellectual vision of it sound like "mysticism." Was Plato a mystic? A little Socratic analysis is clearly needed here, for "mysticism" is a word with several different connotations, and until we distinguish them, the question will not admit any yes-or-no answer.

In the sense that his system recognizes a direct intellectual vision of some highest form of being, Plato is surely a mystic. In the sense that such a vision is different from and totally unlike all other experience, so that it is disconnected from reason and experiment, Plato equally surely is not. The vision of the good is a synoptic view which completes a progressive, disciplined clarification of our understanding; and so, any man who claims to have had it must be able to defend his claim by deduction and application "without tripping and without mistakes." Knowledge of the good, this "most knowable" of all things, is charged with value and passion; but it is not trans- or anti-intellectual in any sense of being unverifiable or wholly discontinuous with science and practice.[2]

Rhetoric and Love (*Phaedrus*)

The *Phaedrus* is a brilliant full-scale bringing together of the themes of love and logic (which proves to be "true rhetoric"). It opens with Phaedrus (whom we have already met in the *Symposium*) persuading Socrates to go with him into the country to read a speech by the orator, Lysias, a copy of which Phaedrus has with him, and which he finds enchanting. Lysias argues that a non-lover's attentions should be preferred to those of a lover, since love is a kind of temporary madness, but a calculated transaction is more dependable. Socrates thinks the speech a bad one, and challenged by Phaedrus to do better, he does so, but in an ironic way: taking his cue from Lysias, he imagines what a passionate lover, pretending to be disinterested, might say to show why his suit should be accepted. The argument Socrates' speech advances is that the lover, self-centered in his desire for unique attention and pos- session, is a desperately bad influence, since any virtues or friends his beloved may acquire will decrease that person's dependence on and admiration for him. Lovers are mad, selfish, and intolerant; "about the non-lover, let the opposite be said," he concludes. Socrates points out that his speech is better than the one of Lysias in its structure: it, at least, opens with a definition, and follows a definite topical organization. Socrates is about to go when his "divine sign," an inner voice which on occasion forbids him to do things, speaks; it speaks, he tells Phaedrus, because the speech parodying Lysias was entirely untrue, and he must now make a true one as a cor- rection and recantation.

It may well be that love is a form of "madness," but so are the poet's and the prophet's "inspiration." Love is such an inspired passion; for the soul is immortal, and falls in love when it sees a beauty which reminds it of the vision of a pure, eternal form of beauty, which it had between its incarnations. In the "Myth of the Charioteer," Plato brings together the

Meno theme of recollection and the doctrine of the three-part soul. The human soul is like a chariot, with reason its charioteer, and ambition and appetite its two horses. In general, it is the dark horse of passion which causes trouble; on seeing anything beautiful, he tries to resist the driver and drag the chariot along to immediate gratification. Between lives, these soul-chariots follow the gods in a procession around the heavens, where they look at the forms. Each soul follows in the train of that Olympian god which it most resembles; most souls are not able to get a very clear vision, and remember what they have seen only vaguely. As a result, when they are embodied again, we can recognize nine different types of personality; the difference may be explained in terms of relative ignorance and vice, or we may explain it by saying that each person loves that which is most like the god he follows in the great procession. In addition to the great procession, there are punishments and rewards between incarnations. The true rhetorician must be able to recognize and appeal to these different types of soul; the true lover must try to control his soul by reason, so that he will see the truth better, and avoid a sojourn in the world below.

Phaedrus is enchanted by the speech (with its fine myth) and transfers his admiration and "love" from Lysias to Socrates. Rhetoric now having been presented in action, Socrates and Phaedrus turn to discussion, asking what gives power to true rhetoric. Rhetoric must deal with truths, if it is to be truly persuasive; and it must use the methods of collection, division, and definition to create methodical, beautiful speeches (unlike the speech of Lysias, which does not define love, nor distinguish the kinds of love there are, nor arrange its topics in any logical order). Most of "the current textbooks on rhetoric" never even approach the level of *art*, but simply explain individual *artifices* (proper types of introduction, tactics of cross-examination, methods of case summation, ways of reasoning from "probabilities," etc.). But a true *art* consist in knowing where, when, and with what audience each of these special devices can be used for persuasion. The real rhetorician must, therefore, be able to divide correctly both his subject matter and types of audience, then see how to present the one to the other; he must, in short, be a psychologist, a poet, and a dialectician. In an appended corollary, Socrates once more expresses his distrust of the fixity of the written word by adding that a good rhetorician will not trust writing (as Lysias had for his speech), but will rely instead on direct conversation.

Notice how Plato has made the two themes of love and rhetoric converge: Phaedrus loves Socrates' second speech on love, because it is true, it is well organized (so that its truth is matched by its clarity), and it is peculiarly persuasive to a soul of Phaedrus' type. (Here Socrates has correctly recognized that myth will be important in persuading this type of soul; compare Phaedrus' role in the *Symposium*, discussed above.) What love really desires is truth and beauty, and of the three kinds of object of desire, for external, bodily, or inner goods, true love is inspired by beauty of the soul. Rhetoric is not an enemy of dialectic, nor love an enemy of wisdom. The "madness" of the lover comes from his recognition, in the person loved, of a vision half-remembered, a vision of the eternally beautiful. The persuasiveness of the true rhetorician rests on the combination of his knowledge of the truth and his presentation in an organic form, which makes his hearer see that truth combined with beauty.

Socrates ends the *Phaedrus* with a prayer: "Beloved Pan, and all ye other gods who haunt this place, give me beauty in the inward soul; and may the outward and inward man be at one. May I reckon the wise to be the wealthy, and may I have such a quantity of gold as a temperate man and he only can bear and carry.—Anything more? The prayer, I think, is enough for me." "Ask the same for me, for friends should have all things in common." "Let us go." This has been true rhetoric; and for Socrates, as we have seen, the prayer was granted.[3]

Myth and Belief: What We May Hope

After his travels in Italy, Plato begins to have Socrates counter his opponents, in the dialogues with the Sophists and their pupils, by presenting myths. Evidently, Plato feels that there is more to the religious intuitions reflected in these Orphic-Pythagorean stories than the Sophists had recognized. Greek religion at this time included two distinct movements; on the one hand, the worship of the Olympians was carried on as a kind of civic ceremony, accepted and shared in as a matter of citizenship; on the other, the "Mystery religions" claiming to trace back to Orpheus (and actually rooted far deeper in Indo-European tradition) taught a doctrine of reincarnation and offered salvation to a group of the initiate. The Pythagorean Order had accepted much of this Orphic belief, and had apparently rationalized and extended its images and legends to a considerable body of allegory. The Sophists and Ionian scientists had tended toward a religious scepticism, while this Pythagorean religious revival was taking place on the western frontier in Sicily and Italy.

If Socrates opposed the literal-minded trust in ancient poems as revelation that Euthyphro held, and even agreed with the Sophists that many beliefs of the public religion were superstition, Plato shows him as recognizing that the Orphic myths are not to be discarded entirely. Socrates often uses them in Plato's dialogues to give added depth and meaning to discussion. In the hands of a philosophical poet, myth can do more than argument to show vividly and concretely the kind of god, freedom, and immortality that are consistent with an immortal human psyche, in a just world under providential direction. Where argument can prove abstractly that the world shows evidence of design, that men who can know eternal forms must in some degree share in immortality, or that science finds respect for value in the natural order, myth can do more. Abstract concepts are not as vivid and persuasive in some ways as concrete stories, in which we see concepts personified in the aesthetic detail of a time between incarnations when souls line up to choose their next lives. Personification and concrete picturing give the ideas of philosophy a personal reference which helps to show that these ideas refer to us and our world, and are not merely abstract theses for argument. The myth remains a statement of "what we may hope"; the sort of thing, in a concrete setting, that would be consistent both morally and aesthetically with our philosophic findings. The myth as record of what men have hoped, as poetic projection of their intuitive aspiration and awareness of form and order in the flow of things, has philosophic value, though one would not take it literally. We will see, in fact, that there are different ways of visualizing the soul's freedom and its career which are equally plausible, but not compatible if we treat them as literal revelation: Plato is concerned with a religious vision, not a dogmatic doctrinal system, and apparently either by chance or even by design selects his fables and allegorical pictures in such a way that one cannot take them literally and get a consistent picture, as a Euthyphro (or some of Plato's Hellenistic admirers) would try to.

The myth fits into the interplay of abstract reason and concrete imagination which is the distinctive feature of philosophy in dialogue form; in his *Statesman,* in fact, Plato presents the weaving together of myth and formal methodology as the proper function of philosophy in action.

Some of Plato's most famous myths may be summarized to show the range and function of this philosophic poetry in the dialogues.

The *Gorgias*

(1) As opposed to Callicles' doctrine that men should cultivate their appetites to the limit, Socrates recalls the Pythagorean story that the human soul is like a cask. If it has many wants, its possessor must spend all of his time trying to fill them, as one would a cask full of holes; and his satisfactions have no lasting value. (2) As opposed to Callicles' insistence that justice is merely convention, Socrates tells a myth of the last judgment: after death, all souls are judged by a court in another world; they appear without their clothing or their bodies, so that their quality is plain. The just souls are rewarded, the unjust punished for their correction; Callicles should remember that the man who acts unjustly will be properly punished by a court from which he has no appeal.

The *Meno*

We have seen Socrates introducing the myth of knowledge as recollection of truths our souls have seen before their present incarnation. Socrates' comment, that he will not assert that this story is literally true, but that he *is* certain that we can discover truths we do not know if we inquire, seems characteristic of his attitude toward mythology.

The *Phaedrus*

In addition to the "Charioteer," the *Phaedrus* also contains a much briefer myth, the "Myth of Theuth and Thamus," an "Egyptian" fable contrasting the merits of live discussion with the relative inadequacy of ideas pinned down in writing.

The *Republic*

In the *Republic* the conclusion—after a criticism of poetry as mere imitation—is the great poem of the Myth of Er. This is the report of Er, a visitor returned from the next world, on the choice of lives which souls make. At a place beyond the heavens, the Goddesses of Destiny first show the souls a model of the universe (which makes evident the existence of cosmic justice); then offer them a choice of their next careers from a showcase of roles or parts. The souls choose freely; but once the choice is made, it cannot be reversed. After the choice, the souls drink from the River of Forgetfulness (some, intemperately, drink more than is required), and then return to earth to be reborn, in a shower of shooting stars. The relation of human freedom and the "necessity" of natural law is brought out beautifully, as is the part that men's ideals play in their fortunes. It seems, from a passage in a later dialogue, that Plato means the "moment of choice" to symbolize each present moment of our lives, as we decide which goals to follow, and that the one-time character of choice in the myth is not to be taken literally. On the other hand, the irreversibility of the choice once made, and the tendency of habit to repeat, are both literal fact.

Another myth in the *Republic* is the "Myth of Metals"

which is a "tremendous fiction" that the rulers tell their subjects, and that we try to have them believe themselves. The
fiction has two parts: first, that all men in the state are
brothers; second, that they differ in ability because they have
different metals and alloys in their souls—but they do not in-
herit these from their parents, so that "iron" parents may have
a "golden" child. There is an Oracle, they are told, that social
function must be based on ability: "disaster will come to the
state if it is ruled by men who are not of gold, but iron."
Here the "myth" is, in fact, so far as the treatment of heredity
goes, a piece of "popularized science"; it is not literally true,
but the relations of heredity and aptitude that it images are so.

The *Phaedo*

This dialogue concludes, as we have seen, with the "Myth
of the True Earth," which is rather like the other myths of
judgment or myths of the structure of the world, with interesting conjectures from contemporary science fitted into an account which shows the presence of the good as an ordering
cosmic purpose.

The *Timaeus*

To be discussed below. This entire synthesis of empirical
sciences is put forward as a "myth," a "likely story." It is a
story of creation, in which God's purposes and plan give a
framework of laws of nature, and a kind of constructive hy-
pothesis-building connects the plan with the full detail of
observed fact.

The *Statesman*

A myth of "Cosmic Reversal"—in which the universe runs
forward and backward alternately, with the ideal directly causing the actual in the forward phase, but with increasing deviation in the backward—comes near the beginning of this dialogue on politics in the light of philosophic method. We will
discuss it in more detail below.

Mythology supplies concrete imagery needed to fully grasp
the meaning of abstract concepts and ideals. Argument sets

certain directions and limitations, e.g., no evil can happen to a good man, men are free and responsible, the gods are just, the cosmic order respects justice, the good is a principle of the actual world. And the story of a concrete person like ourselves facing a last judgment or a choice of lives, while not literally true, is the sort of poetry men can believe, and an expression of what we may hope.

The Order of the Forms

The possibility of science and logic, and that of sound common sense as well, rest on two facts: first, that the forms are an ordered system; second, that their order sets limits and imposes patterns on the world of space and time in which their instances appear.

Because the forms are unchanging, and are systematically related, we can think about them and discover their patterns of order. For example, some forms always "include" others. Take the case of "odd number" and "three." Each of these is a form and three is one of the forms included in odd. This means that every group of three things is also an odd-numbered group; the idea of "a triple that is not odd" doesn't make sense, nor can we find any technique that could construct "an even-numbered set of three." In "thinking," we take advantage of the fact that if form O includes form T, and a is an instance that shares in T, then a must share in O. In planning, we have rules of this sort: if a is a T, then there is no cause or operation that can change a from being an O without making it cease to be a T. This is an abstract way of putting something so familiar and sensible that it is obvious; it is so obvious, indeed, that only a philosopher would be likely to wonder about it. I can't do anything by way of cutting, adding, moving, etc., to my triple of things that will make it lose its odd number without also changing it so that it is not a triple, but it will become a new set with more or fewer than three things in it.

This is taken as showing that "the forms limit both relations in being and operations of causes in becoming," and that "if there were no system of forms, understanding would have nothing to rest on."

Exploring a bit further, we see that "inclusion" can hold between more than two forms—for example, since number includes odd, and odd includes three, number must include three. But *exclusion* will relate some forms, too. Odd, for example, excludes even; and since this is so, no particular number or set can be both odd and even at the same time.

There are many differences between the stable system of forms and the changing world of our experience. For example, if time can make a difference, there are some senses in which "the same thing" may change in form. ("The unfinished work on my desk" can change from twenty to fifty unread examination papers, and, with the passage of time, too often does so. Or, as a more precise example, if an animal participates in the form of life, death is a radical "transformation.") Further, remembering that the form is sometimes described as an unchanging ideal or perfect type, it is clear that concrete things approximate it more and less closely, hence that "a is O" (where a is some concrete instance, O a form) is a different kind of statement from "T is O" (where T and O are *both* forms).

One more property of order is important. If the forms are a coherent system, there must be a single form (for instance, the "form of system") at the top. And for any pair of forms that exclude each other, as odd and even do, there will always be some higher form (number, in the present example) that includes them both. This insures that "contradictory hypotheses," whether in philosophy, politics, or physics, are special cases of some still more general theory.

In this discussion, the word "form" has deliberately been used in a general way; we have neither specified what kinds of unchanging things will be allowed to serve as forms, nor what relations of "level" hold between different types. But if the forms are in fact a system, we can at least say with certainty that all of them are definitely related in some way. And we can add that the causal patterns in nature are limited by the logical patterns we find among the forms in our abstract thought.[4]

It remains for the Academy and its successors in philosophy to find out how the forms are articulated, how closely and by what means they limit the things that share them, and how, if at all, the same forms can be fixed patterns, meanings, and ideals. But it is an insight of central importance to Platonism that being, thinking, and doing all operate within limits of pattern which we have been referring to here as "the order of the forms."

PART THREE

Experiment and Analysis: The System Tested

CHAPTER VI

Science in the Academy

Astronomy, Chemistry, Physics, and Medicine

THE STUDY OF *astronomy* had fascinated the Greeks from the early engineers of Miletus to the late Pythagorean mathematicians. Unlike the Near East, where there was stress on arithmetical computation and prediction, the Greek astronomers thought in terms of geometric cosmic models. Their results never reached the algebraic accuracy of their Near-Eastern contemporaries, but neither did their cosmological hypotheses go into wild astrological absurdities.

The Academy's scientists could draw on some vague notions of Near-Eastern work, on the Ionian world-machine models, and on some Pythagorean variations, including their metaphor of the music of the spheres.

There were two discoveries of first magnitude which had appeared in Greek astronomy. The first was mechanical, and was the achievement of the engineers of Asia Minor. This was the two-component model of planetary revolution. If we imagine ourselves and the earth at the center of the heavens, the fixed stars present no problem; they come back in the same relative positions every twenty-four hours. But the sun, the moon, and particularly the planets are quite another matter. In fact, the name "planet" echoes the perplexity of Greeks, well before Thales' time, at the behavior of these brightest of the stars, which change their place nightly among the stable constellations, for the name means "wanderers." Suppose, however, that the sun, moon, and planets each have *two* motions. Every day, the whole heavenly sphere revolves once on

115

an axis running from the north to south pole; but at the same time, these bodies are revolving at an angle in an opposite direction, much more slowly. As the sun, for example, moving "backward" along the ecliptic, approaches its "lowest" point, the day is very short; but as its orbit brings it further above the horizon, the daily circular motion of the skies makes it trace a longer path, and the days are long. Now, suppose the planets are also moving along the ecliptic slowly in the opposite direction. Each day, their reverse proper motion will have shifted them slightly in their relation to the stars that are fixed, and they will "drift through" the skies predictably and periodically. The period of return is the rate of each one's proper, counter-stellar revolution. The Academy inherited this two-component theory from the tradition of earlier Greek astronomers; it was a major discovery of a hidden regularity in nature, and Western astronomy, through a history that runs from two motions to fifty-five, from circles to epicycles, from epicycles to ellipses, has never given it up altogether.

The second discovery was that of the "music of the spheres." Pythagoras, or early Pythagoreans, had found that if we measure the lengths of string on a stringed instrument which give concordant sounds, the ratio that produces an octave is exactly $1:2$, a fifth $3:2$, a fourth $4:3$, and a second $9:8$. Their experiment can be repeated easily, using a ruler, a movable bridge, and a single violin string. The secret of the beauty of music thus rests on a system of relations which have extreme arithmetical simplicity. In fact, if we take the first numbers, 1, 2, 3, and their squares and cubes, the relations of these give us the proportions underlying the musical scale. Now, as Fig. V. shows, if we take the periods of solar, lunar, and planetary motion, as a Greek observer would have calculated them, the same set of "simple" numbers (plus their products) are the ratios of the celestial periods to one another! It is as if nature, like art, preferred simplicity and beauty; that the same mathematical relations worked for songs and stars was a Pythagorean discovery of great importance, and it is no wonder that it was thought to prove that "things are numbers." Nor have we ever quite lost this feeling for the

Figure V: THE SIMPLE RATIOS

For the Greek astronomer, taking one year as the unit, the observed periods of the sun (and Venus and Mercury, too close to the sun to be correctly observed) would be 1; the moon's period, 1/12; Mars' year comes out 2; Jupiter's is 12 (4 times 3); and Saturn's, with more drastic rounding-off, is 27 (perhaps later, the Academy took the alternative simple approximation of 32). Now going to Pythagorean experiments in music, taking the diagram made of the series of powers of 2 and 3, the ratios of 2:1, 3:2, 4:3, and 9:8 determine the fixed intervals of the scale. If we allow products in our table of elementary integers and ratios, the planetary periods also follow from this diagram.

---

magic of "the music of the spheres"; Newton and Kepler, at least, both felt the appeal of mathematical simplicity as strongly as any Pythagorean.

Several features of this hypothesis are excellent. In the first place, it applies easily to the seasonal variations in latitude of the sun, bringing all the familiar farmers', sailors', and soldiers' awareness of solstices and equinoxes within its scope. In the second place, it preserves the geometrical simplicity of a cosmos that is a sphere, and orbits that are circles: these are a natural first choice for cosmological models, and not simply for Greek ones. Although we have had to recognize the ellipse, we would still be stunned today if we had to adopt a model in which our universe was not a sphere—or at least, in which it was not sphere-like in having space equal in every direction. In the third place, the measured periods of proper motion approximated ratios which had a special arithmetical simplicity.

In Plato's *Timaeus,* the principal speaker Timaeus, a Pythagorean "who has made a special study of the universe," describes how God must have planned and created the total system. Timaeus' God is described as a "craftsman," and we are to imagine him creating an outer circle with a daily motion and inner bands with contrary motion, in the light of the "two-motion" hypothesis. In determining the periods and dimensions of His work, Timaeus' God begins with the "Pythagorean" simple ratio diagram, so that the heavens carry out the same simplicity in their intervals as does the musical scale. There is evidence of simplicity, system, and order; there are also some left-over anomalies of planetary motion which the Academy was able later—through the ingenious work of Eudoxus—to incorporate in the framework of circle and sphere, but for which Timaeus gives us no explanation.

In *chemistry,* the theories of "elements," including the classical version of the atomic theory, offered a challenge to the scientific ability of the Academy. On the one hand, separate atoms combining purely mechanically seemed incapable of producing complex organisms, with parts functioning in the whole; and the notion of the space between these particles as "pure nothing" appeared radically unintelligible. But on the other hand, the notion of quantized elements did explain many phenomena; it was particularly effective in explaining compression and rarefaction.

Platonic *physics* starts with a direct inspection of the field of "space." If we empty our minds of specific content, what remains is a direct confrontation with a continuous, dynamic spread of extension, without parts or form. Such a space can be given structure if it is differentiated into "places," which are determinate, separate, and able to be differently shaped or qualified. An interesting line of thought is used here: if we can subdivide a region indefinitely into smaller regions (e.g., triangles) similar to the original, there is no reason to think that space suddenly becomes a void with atomic lumps; it would rather seem that the properties of larger regions still apply even to places of almost vanishing smallness.

The least elements from which Plato and the Academy built their own molecular theory are minimal plane triangles; a solid results when these adjoin in such a way that they stably enclose a three-dimensional volume of space. These solids will be the "molecules" of the theory. Platonic molecules have four distinctive properties:

1. They occur in differing sizes
2. They have a finite number of shapes; for two reasons: (a) because common sense recognizes just four primary qualities in experience (hot, cold, moist, and dry); (b) because even on this level we expect nature to show some respect for simplicity and beauty
3. The bounding planes must be in a kind of equilibrium which will resist constant pressure from the field around them
4. To account for such phenomena as condensation, rarefaction, and some chemical reactions, a transformation of molecular matter into pure space seems necessary.

Now as it happens, the discoveries of a brilliant young mathematician, Theaetetus, who had developed the "solid geometry" not yet invented when Plato wrote the *Republic*, included a proof that there are five "regular solids"—solids which, inscribed in a sphere, and having equal faces, divide the sphere exactly equally between their vertices. These have at the same time the unique aesthetic symmetry required by condition 2(b), and the needed mechanical stability under pressure for condition 3. And, by equating four of these solids with particles of earth, air, fire, and water, the correlation of qualities in ordinary experience and postulated molecular structure could be made. Conditions 1 and 4 could be satisfied by having the elements of the theory be small triangular planes, which come in similar shapes but different size; and which can "fold" to bound volumes, but can also be thought of as separating and recombining to explain transformation.

The qualitative properties we observe are traced back to quantitative characteristics of their particles, and the models correlate rather well.

Figure VI: PLATONIC PHYSICS: THE TRIANGULAR ELEMENTS

The molecules of Platonic chemistry are the "regular solids" illustrated in any standard geometry, except that the twelve-sided dodecahedron is not included. These are built from bounding planes, the cube from squares, the rest from equilateral triangles. The real elements of the theory, however, are all triangular, either isosceles or right triangles with sides in ratio $1:2:\sqrt{3}$. These are capable of building the larger square and triangular planes, as shown below; and, in addition, they are "the fairest," so that some aesthetic principle is at work even on this level.

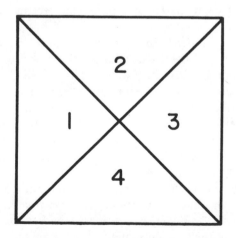

Construction of square bounding planes

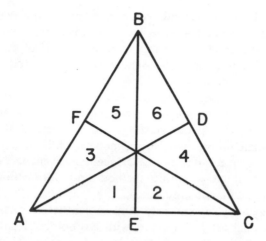

Construction of triangular bounding planes

On this microscopic level of size and behavior, the Academy apparently felt able to accept the quantitative, mechanistic explanations of phenomena that were the strong point of the atomic theory; but without accepting that theory's theoretical concepts or constructs (indivisible particles, pure empty space, etc.) which seemed to them philosophically objectionable.

Balanced between the organized whole of the cosmos and the miniature molecules, with their mechanical interaction, it still was necessary for the scientific synthesis to account for events of a different kind, in order to include biology, medicine, and psychology.

Throughout the history of Greek culture, the medical men and their tradition offer a strand of careful observation, common sense, naturalistic explanation, and one could almost say reluctance to theorize which provides a valuable balance to the mythologies of the religious tradition and the speculative dash of mathematicians and engineers. The Academy could draw on the work of two schools of medicine: that of Hippocrates, in the eastern Mediterranean, and the Sicilian school (of which Empedocles had been a member) in the West. With its Pythagorean context, the latter of these schools had apparently developed considerably more theoretical framework for their practice, and the Academy generally followed the Sicilian rather than the more empirical Hippocratic theory.

We are beginning to recognize again in our own century that what is "the philosophy of science" depends on *which* science we choose as our starting point. If instead of physics, with its small, stupid particles, a modern philosopher were to begin by taking zoology as the science par excellence, our generalizations about scientific method and verification might have a very different look.

The Academy, at any rate, had to synthesize certain facts which medical art presupposes with cosmological and microscopic molecular theories. One such fact is that individual organisms are in many ways isolated systems; they adjust to compensate for changes in environment in a way that preserves their own structure and function. This high degree of organization is more like the system of astronomy than the utterly unorganized mechanism of physical molecules. A second fact is that there is close physical-mental interaction wherever we can observe or infer a "mental" pole. Predictable psychological phenomena are the regular result of certain human physical illness and injuries, for example. Thus, a theory of mind or of the self cannot posit a sharp separation of mental and physical, though in extreme cases the two may operate in considerable independence. There also seems to be a law of conservation of species at work in nature (here Greek biology, with its very short knowledge of time, was related to our modern theories as a special case; it is all right, if the time covered is short enough). Such a law demands explanation: often the actions that conserve the species are detrimental to the individual. One might rather have expected, particularly after listening to the Sophists' opposition of "nature" to "custom," that every individual would always and instinctively seek its own immediate greatest comfort, pleasure, or power.

On the one hand, our scientists turning to biology found that there were types of organic adjustment which seemed to involve other kinds of "cause" than the mechanical collisions of molecular theory; such concepts as organism, function, and abnormality were needed. But on the other hand, the systematic mathematical model of the universe didn't fit the needs of biology entirely, either; it did catch the mutual adaptation of parts, but an organism, unlike a solitary universe ("able to be its own companion, hence in no need of a friend") is constantly running down and colliding with other entities—material, personal, or ideal.

Consequently some balance seemed needed to introduce the needed new types of explanation and causality.

Experimental Apparatus

Admirers of Plato have often felt that apparatus and model-building were entirely alien to the spirit of the Academy, where scientists preferred to depend on pure mathematics and reason. There is certainly some ground in Plato's writing for thinking that he held this view. For example, there is the story that when two of his colleagues solved a standing geometrical problem by building a machine that generated the curve required, Plato told them indignantly that the purpose of geometry was to develop human reason, not to inspire mechanics to gadgetry. In the *Republic* we find Plato's Socrates dismissing all arts and mechanical crafts as illiberal and unsuited for secondary or higher education, and telling the astronomer that his science is concerned with the theory of motion, not with the variegated appearances of any physical model, however beautiful—not even if the physical model should be the stars and planets themselves.

But on the other side of the ledger there is the story that Plato set the Academy the task, in its astronomical researches, of "saving the phenomena" by setting up a simple mathematical model that would exactly generate the observed anomalies of planetary motion. There is the further fact, not always noticed by Plato's admirers, that arts and crafts evidently fascinated him; for there are repeated examples throughout the dialogues of contemporary technology used as illustration or clarification of an idea or discussion. Eel-traps, looms, potters' wheels, bronze-smith's work, trireme construction, spindles, sculptor's lead rulers, carpentry, lathes, and a host of other items from Athenian technology appear in the dialogues. There is even a story, though not authenticated very well, that Plato built himself a primitive alarm clock.

What goes particularly badly with the thesis that Plato had on principle no place for experimental models or gadgetry is the presence in four passages of what seem descriptions of models, including occasional mechanical language that would be appropriate to a model but not to its archetype.[1]

These four passages are all concerned with astronomy. The first is the Myth of Er that ends the *Republic:* the souls about to choose their next lives are shown by Destiny a set of nested hemispheres of varied colors, moving at different speeds. From a detailed description of the sizes and colors of these "bowls," it is clear that this is a model of the cosmos; from their vision in cross section, it seems clear, too, that the souls are being shown a model which the goddess holds. The second passage is a myth in the *Statesman.* From time to time, according to this myth, the cosmos reverses its motion, and turning on a fine pivot, runs backward. The result is a widening gap between ideal and actual while the world "runs down"; the two directions which the myth treats as successive sound very like the two simultaneous motions that result in cosmic change in the more scientific *Timaeus* astronomy. But the language once more suggests that Plato has in mind some definite model, imitating the periods of seasons, night and day, and capable of reversing its direction. The third case is the description of God's creation of the framework of the world in the *Timaeus.* The process is one of mixing, spreading into strips, cutting and marking, bending and fastening—terms that are exactly those that would describe a metal-worker building a metal-band "armillary sphere" to order. Last, later in the *Timaeus,* we read that the conjunctions and oppositions the planets go through as positions "in their dance" cah, apparently, only be understood and calculated with the aid of models. I say "apparently" because the text is not absolutely certain here, and because there is no record of any technology in the literature of Plato's time that could even approximate a moving "orrery" model, with speeds that are analogues of actual planetary motion.

Thanks to the work of my colleague, Professor Derek Price, on the history of science, particularly that of the clock, and to his suggestions, I think we can be pretty sure that Plato's passages do refer to four distinct models; and as their detail becomes clearer, a reason appears as to why they should be different, and why there should be just four. Within about half a century of Plato's time, metal band descendants of the sun-dial and water-operated celestial globes rotating once in a day were common features of the Greek market-place; Athens had several. The water-clocks told time, whereas the band models were used rather to keep track of the seasons. If we assume that this evolution took some time to reach its relatively finished third century state, the metal-band model and revolving globe town water-clock exactly satisfy the descriptions of the mechanism Plato had in mind in the first *Timaeus* passage and in the *Statesman*. Further, a later archeological find from Roman times has proven that an age may have advanced technology which leaves no record in its literature, so that we can no longer assume that the second *Timaeus* passage refers to something that would have been technologically impossible when it was written. The statue holding the band model is also suggestive: if this was also traditional, the picture in the Myth of Er of a goddess holding a cosmic model for souls to see is more natural and understandable. It seems fair to say that the Academy probably had, or was familiar with, actual mechanisms matching the four passages, and referred to them on occasion for explanation or illustration of phenomena and calculations.

This rather changes the traditional picture of science by stylus and waxed tablet alone, without apparatus, that had been held up to 1961. Four models were needed, I suggest, because four aspects of cosmic process had to be singled out for close separate attention. The mythological machine in the *Republic* directs attention to the phenomena themselves; the "town clock" in the *Statesman* catches the more familiar cycles

of public time and seasonal progress; the moving model cal-
culates relative planetary positions; the "band" model demon-
strates that the basic measurements of the universe follow a
pattern of arithmetical simplicity. The models themselves thus
seem to lead from sheer appearance to scientific theory in
stages corresponding to the "divided line," which was discussed previously.

Were there other models and devices as well? Certainly,
some were used in the study of solid geometry, and others
must have been in forming hypotheses about "molecular structure." Further insight must await future archeology and history of science, but it would not surprise some of us if it
turned out that indeed there was, in the Academy, no notion
at all of an antagonism between the latest gadgetry and the
purest reason.

Some Ideas of Permanent Scientific Value

The *Timaeus,* we have seen, represents a compendium and
synthesis of the science of its time. The very organization of
the work, if we study it carefully, illustrates an idea of considerable importance for science and philosophy: for it seems
that the section on mental and physical diseases at the end of
the study can be understood only if one already knows something about cosmology, God, space, and inorganic chemistry.
All nature is interrelated on Plato's view, and the living organism, particularly man, lies at a point of very complex intersection of the over-all cosmic plan and the mechanical acci-
dents of history which deviate from the ideal order. It is still
suggestive to ask whether a modern school of medicine ought
to adopt this notion of medical education: today we are rather
closer to Hippocrates, who concentrated on specialized training, than to the Academy, and our "common sense" has been
colored by our practice sufficiently so that at first the notion
that a physician will practice his own art better if he knows
something about astronomy and something about the traditional problem of evil seems nonsensical.

Nonsense or not, we must credit Plato and the Sicilian doctors on whose work he drew for one insight that, periodically

forgotten and recovered, retains its medical validity. In dealing with an organism which is a conscious complex of "soul" and body, it is unrealistic to treat the one without the other. Psychic ideas, passions, and events may be reflected in the physical organism as medical symptoms—of the sort, Plato says, that the Hippocratic physician can't diagnose or cure. Our own century is increasingly aware of the tricks that "mind" can play on "body"; when we read Plato's brief case study of the man with great psychic ambition but a frail physique, whose soul is dissatisfied with its body, we can supply modern theories and counterparts for this classical description of megalomania. Just how ideas and organs interact is a problem, both for the Academy and for the physician today; but surely, in spite of its quaintness, Plato's account of the liver as responding physically to the ideation of the brain is on the right track.

This suggestion of psychosomatic interdependence follows, we have seen, from the more general conviction that nature forms a system, so that different specialized sciences and subject matters are related to one another, and can be understood better when we see their systematic connection than they can if we merely examine them separately. Beyond this, Plato combined the insights of Socrates and the Pythagoreans into the idea that nature is governed by general laws which can be stated mathematically, and which imitate the beautiful and the good by having maximum simplicity. The original Pythagorean "music of the spheres" motif reflected, we have seen, their discovery that aesthetics and (approximate) astronomy rest on quantitative ratios of small whole integers, and their products, to one another. Plato seems to go one step further, in his scientific synthesis, to the idea that things have the laws and numbers they do because things are beautiful, and the economy and simplicity of the underlying laws and periods of the universe give them their beauty. The degree of approximation of actual observed phenomena to these underlying, limiting laws varies with type and scale. Studying the cosmos as a whole, it appears close, though certain planetary aberrations remained unexplained by Plato's approximation, and left him wondering whether other formulae might improve the accuracy of his theory without destroying its simplicity—and in works of fine art (the musical scale, the canonic statue of an ideal human type) there is often an equally exact approximation. But smaller regions of space and time, such as individual persons or societies, are not isolated systems: they are not self-sufficient and are in constant interaction with an environment which varies; as a result, small scale phenomena present more difficulty to the scientist anxious to trace the role of the ideal in the actual.

A further Platonic idea, that there is a God who has created this world from an ideal plan, actually involves two distinct notions, one of which has been widely accepted throughout the history of Western thought, the other seriously entertained once again only in the twentieth century. Plato's creative deity is powerful and good—and so far Christianity in its orthodox form would agree—but Plato's God is already given the raw material of a "ch..os" of fluid space, and His power is limited by the fact that this plastic medium will not accept or retain form perfectly. The result is, that evil results from failures of the cosmos to imitate the perfect plan properly; there is a certain slippage, erosion, and interference which is the necessary consequence of space-time existence. God is not responsible for disease, death, war, and similar phenomena, and presumably disapproves of them; but He is not all-powerful, and our cosmos is the most beautiful, unified, yet varied world which can be created in the field of becoming. Here Plato differs from orthodox Christianity, which holds that God is all-powerful and that He created the world "out of nothing," so that matter did not exist independent of creation, and was brought into being as a result of Divine decision. Plato's God is not portrayed in the *Timaeus* as knowing the course of history in full detail; he foresees general laws and cycles, he admires the cosmos as a "beautiful shrine," he knows the laws of nature in their eternal simplicity, but there is no clear indication that he also "marks each sparrow's fall." And though Plato himself attributed omniscience to God or the gods in his latest work, the logic of the *Timaeus* does not require it, and may suggest the contrary. Thus twentieth-century theologians—still unsatisfied with the traditional view that God foreknows human choices in full detail, creates men who make those choices, but holds His creatures responsible—sometimes go back to the position of the *Timaeus* and argue that God is neither omniscient nor omnipotent in the orthodox senses, so that there is no conflict between divine goodness and the existence of evil, nor between divine wisdom and true human responsibility and freedom.

Other Platonic ideas that continue to operate in the history of science are the notion of space, the molecular theory of matter, and the complex character of natural causality. Great as the ideas are of system, structure, simplicity, and law, the notions of "cause" that occur in Plato's synthesis of sciences seem equally true and useful. We have already noted the clarification of the "field" concept of space, and the modification of the "atomic theory" to a solid geometry of molecules, and so we will turn to an examination of Platonic science and causality.

It is still of interest to see that Timaeus, as a responsible scientist, recognizes the complex character of "causal" explanation in his lecture.

First, one must distinguish "causes" from "conditions"; a creative God will have some reason for making the world as He does, and that reason will be to realize some good. This good is "the true cause"; the number and assembly of space-time components is rather an "auxiliary cause." Thus, animals have vision because this is a good; but in order to realize it, they need organs properly designed. There are two ways of analyzing such organs: we can study them as *wholes* in which retina, lens, and optic nerve work together as functional parts; or we may, if we push analysis to their smallest components, see them as complex mechanisms, small particles acting "by necessity" on one another. Timaeus calls such chains of particles "auxiliary conditions" (*symmetaitia*), and neither "conditions" proper (*metaitia*) nor "causes" (*aitia*).

The moral for the scientist, ancient or modern, is that he must at least consider the possibility that there are different kinds of "causality" at work in nature, and that different parts of science may be more interested in one level than in another. Cosmology is for Timaeus the study of an organized closed system, where the ideals of simplicity and order are clearly evident in the laws of nature. Inorganic chemistry, on the other hand, is the study of the separate, insensitive interactions of small elements. Zoology and physiology work with organisms, wholes in which the parts are adapted to some over-all function. Medicine, psychology, and philosophy are concerned with higher organisms in which consciousness introduces freedom and thought; such organisms are sensitive to purposes and ideals, unlike the atoms, but can be mistaken in their choices of roles that will give them self-realization, unlike the stars.

Causality in Timaeus' science is a two-way relation: *wholes* cause the over-all adaptive behavior of their parts, but the proper number and order of parts are necessary conditions (and in this sense also "causes") of their ordering "wholes."

CHAPTER VII

Reason and History: The Atlantis Legend

Plato's *Critias*

WITH THE COMPLETION of the *Timaeus,* Plato and his students must have been pleased to see that the latest results of the science of their time agreed with the *Republic.* The *Republic*'s doctrines of interdependence of subject matters, simplicity of the laws of nature, the value of mathematics as a model of method, even the conviction that the universe is "just" had been checked against available detailed observations and were holding up well.

But Plato's plan for a set of dialogues to relate the *Republic* to natural science and history included more than the *Timaeus;* there were to have been two further dialogues, the *Critias* and the *Hermocrates;* of these, however, the *Critias* was never finished and the final dialogue never even begun. The reasoning behind this three-step program is not hard to see. The *Timaeus* had analyzed the role of the forms in the physical world, through its account of "reason persuading necessity." But in applying the result to political theory, it would not be enough to find that the ideal was truly *relevant* to the actual, without some measure of the *distance* between the two. Given the friction, competition, and restless change of human history, could a small but virtuous city (one approximating the ideal in the *Republic,* for example) last any length of time, or would its "idealism" have too little power to resist external pressure and aggression?

As relevant to this point, Plato's main speaker in the *Critias* tells Socrates a "true history" of a war in the remote past between an ancient Athens and Atlantis. Atlantis, a rich and powerful nation, had conquered and enslaved Europe and Egypt; and the Athens of that day, a small state "organized in every way like the ideal city in the *Republic*," was left alone to meet a final Atlantean attack. Athens withstood the attack, and in the end set Europe free; Atlantis itself (a continent in the Atlantic Ocean) sank beneath the sea in a great earthquake; and only "ancient Egyptian inscriptions" preserved any record of its existence and misadventure.[1]

Almost the entire section of the *Critias* that Plato completed is a description of Atlantis. It is a remarkable piece of writing; it has such an air of concrete factuality that generations of readers have taken the story to be true history. (A look at a chart of the North Atlantic floor will show a "Plato" and an "Atlantis" group of peaks near the Azores, named by readers of the story.) The Atlantis legend is widespread through folklore, but every version of the story can be shown to originate with the dialogue by Plato. I would suppose that the abrupt destruction of the Minoan empire still had left echoes in Plato's time in the form of stories of a great seapower that "vanished overnight." And sailors' stories (some of which figure in the *Odyssey*) about the unknown ocean to the west (protected from Greek exploration by the Carthaginian trade monopoly) doubtless suggested a site "beyond the Pillars of Hercules" as the lost continent's location.

But the many details that give its verisimilitude to Plato's story seem to have been selected by him from a great many places and items on the contemporary scene; and the selection is so definitely made to bring out the contrast of Atlantis and the city described in the *Republic* that Plato's creative talent was certainly at work, and we are not dealing with a simple copy or literal repetition either of some early tradition or of "Egyptian inscriptions." The menu Plato cites which emphasizes Atlantean intemperance, for example, reminds us of the state dinners he had disapproved of in Syracuse; the "voracious elephants" he mentions as inhabiting the forests may be a dash of Carthage; the over-specialized military organization is reminiscent of the conscription laws and army of Persia.

Apparently, Atlantis had everything except wisdom; there was unlimited manpower, an economy of abundance, and an "almost superhuman" technology (used for irrigation ditches, fortifications, and the construction of colossal race-courses and temples). As long as the Atlantean kings (who had a share of divine nature thanks to their descent from Poseidon) and their subjects were content to enjoy their lives in comfort, and not to prize power, wealth, or pleasure as highly as virtue, all went well. But at last greed and ambition corrupted them, and the career of world conquest began which was announced by Plato as the main theme of his story. The fragment that Plato did complete ends just as Zeus, seeing this change, is about to address a council of the gods which he has called to decide what shall be done.

Two things stand out in the description of Atlantis: the absence of any reference to education or educational institutions, and the lack of any rationale behind the details of its social order. Every reader recognizes some likeness between Plato's imagined capital—with its hot and cold baths separately for men, women, and horses, and its approach via bridges and tunnels, plus its cult of "the bigger the better"—to Manhattan. Most readers also will admit that the selection of details is made in part to show how opposite Atlantis was to ancient Athens—where, for example, there was only one "temperate" spring used both summer and winter, only one type of military training, and rule by an aristocracy of ability, not heredity. But here readers divide as to whether Atlantis is meant as an outline of a wholly bad society or as a prevision of utopia! "It looks like us, so Plato must have thought it was great," say some readers; "it looks disorganized and never did pursue virtue intelligently, so Plato must have thought it was bad," argue others. Both groups agree that power and wealth are no substitutes for wisdom and temperance, and that this is one central moral of the Atlantis story.

The further moral, or conclusion, that there is no necessary reason why a small but just state cannot endure through time, even in a context of less virtuous neighbors, was already announced in the outline of the story; Plato seems to have put off completion of the *Critias* in the interest of other discussions and experiments in the political application of science, logic, and philosophic theory.

CHAPTER VIII

Eudoxus and Megara: Brilliant but Provoking Neighbors and Colleagues

Eudoxus

WE KNOW OF a number of remarkable achievements by Plato's contemporary, Eudoxus, but unfortunately almost nothing of the man himself and of his association with the Academy. Certainly, there was contact between Eudoxus and his students and Plato's school; but some conservative scholars hold that this may have been limited to a brief visit, while others take as true the later story that Eudoxus and his students actually moved to Athens in a merger with the Academy; and some would hold that Eudoxus was the acting director of Plato's school during his absence on his first voyage to Sicily. Recent study seems, at least to the writer, to be confirming Professor P.-M. Schuhl's conjecture that "perhaps the three persons who had the most influence on Plato were Socrates, Archytas, and Eudoxus." At any rate, the contact or communication seems, from sound internal evidence, to have been a significant and provocative one for the Academy.[1]

Eudoxus is called a student of Archytas, and certainly had mastered the latter's approach to geometry; and with or without the inspiration of Plato's program, he carried out two of the most important specific parts of the plan Plato put forward in the *Republic* for the advancement of mathematics and astronomy. In addition to mathematics, however, Eudoxus was interested in other areas; he had developed theories in ethics and philosophy (along Pythagorean lines) which differed radically from the ideas held by Plato. His evident genius in logic and science must have made the impact of these other dissenting views a profound one; and whether he was interim director or merely *in absentia* consultant, Eudoxus must certainly have been a most admired yet most exasperating contemporary of the Academy.

Eudoxus devised a new definition of "equality of ratio between quantities" which finally conquered the "irrationals" that had vexed Pythagorean theorists, and that brought arithmetic and geometry together in a single general theory of quantitative relation. If, as the Pythagoreans had, one thinks of "quantities" as either whole numbers or as ratios of whole numbers to one another (they preferred this notion of ratio to that of fraction in their arithmetic), geometry evidently contains some lengths, such as $\sqrt{2}$, which are determinate enough, but cannot be defined; and the usual techniques of calculation do not seem to apply to these left-over "irrationals." For, on this theory, the number series consists of ordered sets of monads, all ratios are relations of numbers, and thus neither numbers nor ratios form a compact continuum. Eudoxus hit upon the alternative conception of a definite quantity as a dividing cut, separating all other quantities (including ratios) into two classes: those greater and those less. And these relations hold for all equimultiples, so that if a/b is greater than c/d, every multiple of a/b is greater than the same multiple of c/d. Mathematics was thus equipped to go ahead with the study of quantitative relation in general, rather than having to look separately, and use separate approaches, for the cases of continuous vs. discrete or rational vs. irrational quantity. At last the pattern was clear in virtue of which "the mathematical sciences were akin." Further, since most Greeks intuitively accepted the notion that "beauty consists in magnitude and order," such a new theory must have seemed to hold out exciting potentialities as an aesthetic and philosophic tool. For philosophy, in fact, this seems the most important breakthrough in mathematics until the seventeenth century. Eudoxus also used a form of "the method of exhaustion" for finding values of convergent infinite series that, though less elegant, was still a modest advance toward the theory of limits that offered mathematicians a way of avoiding (not of solving) Zeno's paradoxes in the nineteenth century.

In his role of research director, Plato is reported to have set the Academy the problem, in science, and especially in astronomy, of "saving the phenomena," that is, of discovering simple mathematical laws which matched the full detail of empirical evidence, within limits of probable error. The apparent motions of the planets are the most spectacular and complex cyclic natural phenomena which the Academy's science was called on to "save." The puzzles not explainable by the two-component model were the periodic "retrogradation" (an apparent reversal of direction of motion) by Mars, Saturn, and Jupiter; and a "wobbling" in planetary latitude, departing from predicted exact circular orbits. These were not a simple challenge: it almost seemed (for example, to Plato when the *Timaeus* was being written) that nothing less than an exercise of capricious free will by the planets could account for their reversals of direction. Here Eudoxus showed the same remarkable spatial imagination Archytas had earlier employed: if we imagine a set of nested spheres, with different angles of inclination and rates of rotation, we can get a point on the innermost sphere to trace a figure-eight curve (the hippopede) which will make a planet's apparent motion alternately advance and retrograde. The simplicity of nature and the power of mathematics to explain appearance both seemed to have new confirmation; and the ingenuity of this solution still commands enthusiastic admiration. It must be from about this period that there begin to be treatises "On the Sphere," in which a new and rigorous scheme of logical proof (of the type Euclid adopted in his *Elements*) was used to show the consistency of theoretic prediction and observation, by strict deduction of what an observer would see from the centers of "universes" differing in shape, containing planets differing in

paths of motion. (For example, if there were not one fixed
cosmic axis, the stars would not seem to move in smaller circles as they approached the pole; if the universe were a cone,
fewer stars would rise and set than we observe; and so on.)
We can see that it was exciting to discover the precision with
which the ephemeral world of appearance could be "saved";
and inevitably this achievement must have suggested trying
further extensions of the technique to problems of philosophy.
Could a Platonist, for example, prove that some version of the
theory of forms is necessary to "save the appearances" of motion and time? It is not certain that Eudoxus himself originated
the rigorous scheme applied to the sphere, though many scholars believe that he did. But I think I have shown, in another
book, that Plato, in his *Parmenides* (to be discussed below,
p. 146), did relate various interpretations of the theory of forms
to the appearance of time in precisely the proof-pattern used in
the later astronomical "phenomena-saving" demonstrations.[2]

Turning now from Eudoxus' work in science to the field of
ethics, we must begin with the idea that appears both in the
fragments attributed to Archytas and in Plato's dialogue the
Protagoras, that mathematics is useful for living well, because
it enables us to measure and calculate the consequences of our
actions—in terms of pleasure and pain, on the most evident
level. Eudoxus followed this line of thought and developed a
"rational hedonism" as his ethical theory. "Hedonism," the
thesis that the good life consists in maximum pleasure, was by
no means a new philosophical idea. But it had been fairly simple for Plato to show the theoretic and practical weaknesses
of the "pursuit of pleasure" theory of Callicles in the *Gorgias*
or the "maximum intensity of physical pleasure" principle
which he seems to have attributed to his contemporary Aristippus; Eudoxus' formulation was more difficult to attack. Eudoxus
begins with the postulate that all things by nature seek pleasure
and avoid pain; as though by an intuition that pleasure is either
the good or at least *their* good; and this instinct turns out
badly only when mistakes or inexperience result in our mis-
calculating either the degrees or consequences of the pleasures
that we choose. Plato had in fact used a somewhat similar

argument in Books IX and X of the *Republic,* where he tried
to show that the noble and the good are also pleasant; but he
was entirely unwilling to identify "pleasure"—a motley col-
location of human causes and conditions—with the good.
Things that are good are pleasant to a good man; but they are
not good *because* they are pleasant, rather they are so because
they represent some realization of man's ideal perfection.
Eudoxus, however, now defended the thesis that *because* and
insofar as things are pleasant (to the prudent man), they are
good; and that "the good" is *really identical* with pleasure.
Plato's discussion of hedonism in his last Socratic dialogue,
the *Philebus,* seems directed against this position.

Eudoxus also held the philosophic view that the forms were
not separate from the field of space and time, but rather were
boundaries marking off states and events *within* that field. He
revived Anaxagoras' notion that reality is a "field" with continuity, in which everything but mind is mixed, and took this
as part of his own position. This way of construing "forms"
would limit philosophy to the description of recurrent or similar space-time boundary patterns; it is hard to see any use for
"transcendent" forms, or how any value form such as the good
could serve in a Eudoxian philosophy as an organizing prin
ciple for reality.

These ideas and discoveries presented a wealth of issues and
problems to the Academy. Plato seems to have decided that
he would first try to defend his theory of forms, in detail and
with logical rigor, then return to the ethical issues. Once the
theory of forms was established, it would offer a stable frame
of reference for discussion of the question, is pleasure really
"natural" in any sense that makes it unqualifiedly good, or the
good for human life? Plato evidently planned to introduce
various visiting experts as leading speakers who raised technical questions in the first set of dialogues; Socrates would
return to consider the ethical question; and the program may
also have envisaged his return as central speaker in a final
summing-up of the "analytic" set. In spite of distractions of a
practical political experiment, Plato's late dialogues very nearly
carried out this program.

Megara

Some of Socrates' friends and admirers were from the near-by city of Megara. Plato mentions one of them as present at the death of Socrates in his *Phaedo,* and presents the *Theaetetus* as being read to this same Megarian, Euclides, and his friend Terpsion. There is a tradition that after Socrates' execution young Plato left Athens and visited for a time in Megara.

The philosophers of Megara claimed to be carrying on the work of Socrates, but with special attention to the tools of formal logic, which the Eleatics, Parmenides and Zeno, had invented. Over a period of several generations, our sparse historical information is uniform in representing the Megarian school as centering its attention on formal logic. We hear, for example, of a controversy in the school as to the conditions under which an "if . . . then" hypothetical proposition should be considered true; of exploration of problems connected with the meaning and logical function of the copula "is"; and a bit later of a pamphlet (surely constituting one of the first attacks on Aristotelian logic) by a Megarian contemporary of Aristotle named Eubulides.

This is only one part of the story, for the Megarians also had a "theory of forms," as Plato's Academy had. It is reported, for example, that Euclides equated the Socratic "form of the good" with Parmenides' "single absolute reality." The main difficulty with Megarian theory was that it reduced *everything* to forms, with no "field" left over, and it made the "forms" mutually exclusive and sharply separated from one another. Probably this sharp insulation was a consequence of their admiration for the new logic.

Eleatic logic depends for its effectiveness on there being a "sharp disjunction" between different terms or classes. Zeno's own critical work, for example, confronted the Pythagoreans with a dilemma: their position had to be either A *or* B *or* C *or* D; and Zeno then showed that A, B, C, and D, taken severally, each led to inconsistency. This form of argument uses what we now call the "exclusive" *or:* this kind of "or" relation assumes that the alternatives it connects are mutually exclu-

sive, hence that no new synthesis can be developed by con-
joining them. If a logic with this formal structure applies to
reality, it seems reasonable to think that it works because the
world to which we apply it also contains things separated by
"exclusive or" relations. If we should agree with Socrates, that
there are objective and permanent "essences," and at the same
time are convinced by the argument of Parmenides that changing things have no share whatever in reality, the world of sensible things will seem to us to consist simply of "clusters" of
unchangeable abstract "ideas."

But this result, although it is clear and useful for analysis,
is not so good philosophically. For example, the attempt to
think of concrete things as built from unchanging abstractions
—shapes, shades of color, hardness, etc.—runs into Zeno's
own paradox of the "arrow" at the outset. ("If a flying arrow
rests at every *instant* of its flight, when does it move?" Or,
more generally, how can growth, change, and time—real *or*
merely apparent—be constructed from static, timeless abstractions?) And to insist so strongly on the purity and separateness
of "forms" leaves no way to explain how such completely
separate forms can be related to things.

Further, the logic is misleading if one tries to apply it to
ethics or aesthetics: sometimes events and properties are so
complex and tightly interconnected (as the "parts" of a work
of fine art usually are) that an "either-or, yes-or-no" approach
is bound to falsify the situation it is used to describe.

Plato was certainly aware of the philosophic work going
on in Megara; he seems to have admired its precision at the
same time that he was sensitive to its dangers and limitations.
Consequently, we will keep Euclides as well as Eudoxus in
mind when we try to understand the creative work and the
intellectual atmosphere of the Academy from about 369 to
347 B.C.

CHAPTER IX

Knowledge and Opinion Once More

The *Theaetetus*

IN THE LIGHT of the *Republic*'s sharp distinction between the scientist (who has had the ideal education outlined), the prescientific theorist (Socrates counts himself and Glaucon in this class), the mere man of experience, without a real theory (this, we have contended, describes Thrasymachus), and men who take their ethical (or other) ideas on the basis of hearsay (Polemarchus and Cephalus are in this category), Plato evidently believes the difference between knowledge and opinion to be a real and crucial one. Not only practical men, however, but some philosophers would deny this; and the *Republic* does not offer a very adequate analysis or defense of its central thesis, that the four kinds of knowledge schematized by the divided line are different and not reducible.

It is oversimplified, but not entirely inaccurate, to see the "logical" group of Plato's later dialogues as centering on this question of kinds and reducibility of "knowledge." The *Parmenides,* which will be treated in the next section, can be read as showing the limits of *dianoia* (descriptive, hypothetical, deductive, thinking) as opposed to *nous* (a "synoptic" vision of various hypotheses as parts of a whole, which is based on an insight into the good that is non-hypothetical). The *Theaetetus,* with which the present section is concerned, centers its attention on the "incommensurability" of knowledge and opinion, the central distinction of the divided line, and a crucial distinction in the scientific synthesis of the *Timaeus* as well. The

Sophist, to be treated below, proves that even the most perverse of reasoners must admit a difference between fact and semblance; the *Statesman* finally shows that all art requires objective forms, in their old role of criteria of value.

The question of whether there is a difference in kind or only in degree between collected items of information, working techniques, and "knowledge" in a strict sense has continued to challenge philosophers from Plato's time to our own. Positivism, logical empiricism, pragmatism, and formalism, all are attempts to show that we do not need *four* kinds of knowing, but only one, two, or three. Knowledge consists, ideally, of laws and propositions which are universal and admit of no exceptions; also, it answers the question *why?* as well as *how?;* and in many cases the knower feels that these are, in fact, distinct questions. Sense experience, on the other hand, is always particular: I perceive just this individual thing or quality, just here and just now. Can we find a way of interpreting our general statements as shorthand for many concrete experiences or experiments? If we can, philosophy and science can be considerably simplified from Plato's "four-story" view. But it seems we cannot effect this simplification in most cases. The very obvious thing to try is the philosophic hypothesis that we associate experiences which are similar, and expect sequences that have always come together in the past (remember the shadow of the ears and that of the tail on the wall of the cave) to do so always in the future. In defense of such a radical empiricist view, we can point to the fact that whenever we can, we look to sensible models and operations as aids in making our ideas clear; whenever we can, we draw on past funded experience as a guide to planning the future. But there are several difficulties here. In the first place, we need an idea of similarity, one of unity, and one of dissimilarity to use in sorting out our experiences. But these three ideas are abstractions which do not occur in our sense experience; the theory therefore presupposes something other than its atomic concrete data.[1] In the second place, it seems not only arbitrary, but perverse, simply to say that we believe the future will resemble the past, and that we can give no reason for that belief. It is perverse because the assumption of an experience which comes in the form of separate present items provides no real connection between present and future, so that we are entirely cut off from observation or knowledge of it. Even though the future *has* always resembled the past up to now, the empirical theory can never show that such a conformity will hold in the new future. There are other related issues, and the controversy continues to be vigorous in our own time.

In Plato's dialogue, Theaetetus, a talented young mathematician, knows the answer to a difficult problem in irrationals, but does not know "what knowledge is."[2] Questioned and encouraged by Socrates, he tries out the positions that knowledge is identical with sensation, that it is identical with technique, that it is identical with technique plus explanation.

The dialogue opens with a brief memorial to Theaetetus, recounting his death and the great promise he had shown, a promise which Socrates had noted. Theaetetus looks like Socrates, we learn from the older mathematician, Theodorus, who introduces them. Socrates opens their conversation with the question, "What is knowledge?" Theaetetus gives instances of things we know, then realizes that what is needed is a general definition. He knows the kind of answer required, he says, because he and his friend, Young Socrates (who will figure in this set of dialogues later on), solved a mathematical problem of this kind. Theodorus had been proving, case by case, the incommensurability of a unit side and lines equal in length to square roots of two, three, etc., to seventeen. Theaetetus and Young Socrates were able to generalize this into a classification of all lines into lengths and surds; their result is probably an extension of Euclid X. 9. But the young man cannot do this for "knowledge"; his courage fails him. Socrates tells Theaetetus that he, Socrates, is "an intellectual midwife," who helps others to give birth to their ideas, and then tests them; he encourages the young man to answer, and Theaetetus suggests that knowledge is perception. This, says Socrates, is also the thesis of Protagoras who had said that "man is the measure of all things," so that whatever appears to each man is true for him. But there are several reasons why Socrates would criticize the theory. For one thing, it would reduce knowledge to auto-biography; for another, it would seem to preclude the possibility of arts which actually exist. For the artist, with his technical skill, knows in a way which the amateur does not what results to expect, and how to produce them. Consequently, not all things that seem are true; for example, Protagoras himself claimed to know better (that is, more truly with respect to prediction) than anyone else what a jury would do in a legal case. Theaetetus now believes that knowledge is technique: the man who can enumerate the parts of a wagon and put them together knows what a wagon is. But Socrates is also dubious of this: it seems to him, and Theaetetus agrees, that there is a difference between "all of the parts" and "the whole," and that the function of the whole is essential to the knowledge of, for example, what a wagon is. In the course of this, it turns out to be equally impossible to explain "thought" as a process or technique for combining individual perceptions "in the mind." For all of the standard metaphors for such models of thought that Theaetetus suggests—the wax tablet on which experience writes, the tablet on which sensation makes impressions as a seal does on wax, finally the mind as a mad aviary in which a small bird-keeper rushes about with a hook—make no provision for universal truth or for error in handling general concepts; yet we do know some universal truths (this is something of which a young mathematician is, of course, aware) and we do make errors in abstract thought (as when someone believes that $7 + 5 = 11$). And even if there were not these objections, doesn't each of these models smuggle in a small hidden observer who needs explanation? If experience writes, someone must read the writing; if impressions are sorted, someone who knows the nature of similarity and difference—which are not impressions—must do the sorting; if ideas fly by in associated flocks, someone must catch and identify them, and so on. Theaetetus at last hits on the idea that knowledge is "knowing the parts and operations of a thing, and having in addition a general explanatory formula which characterizes it." This would be excellent if it were not circular; but this is the same as saying "knowledge is know-how *plus* knowledge." And the dialogue ends inconclusively.

Many traits of the early Socratic dialogues are present here: Theaetetus becomes both wiser and more courageous as the conversation goes on; he has certain knowledge of the relation of incommensurable quantities, yet cannot say what knowledge is, nor what the common measure is of knowledge and opinion; Socrates is not teaching, but asking questions in a joint inquiry; and the outcome is to establish the need for distinguishing knowledge from either conjecture or opinion, as it was distinguished in the divided line of the *Republic* and by postulate in the scientific inquiry of the *Timaeus*.

Knowledge in some way involves an insight which goes beyond and cannot be finally confirmed by sensation or experience. The mind, not the senses, must be involved; it must bring with it certain ideas which are needed even to make comparison of our sensations possible; it must be able to recognize or be reminded of some universal characteristic in the particular in virtue of which we can see functions, concepts, and laws, that go beyond mere memory and experience, with their particularity. This is an excellent dialogue for the contemporary reader interested in philosophy to read and think about; the translation and notes of F. M. Cornford and the introduction to the Liberal Arts edition by Irving Copi, as well as a comparison of the fate of "7 + 5" at the hands of Immanuel Kant and Rudolph Carnap or A. J. Ayer, will add depth and interest to this study.

The One and the Many: The Theory of Forms Defended (*Parmenides*)

Probably just before leaving for his experiment in Sicily, to be described presently, Plato completed a dialogue, the *Parmenides*, in which he gives an indirect defense of his own version of the theory of forms, as against either Eudoxus' interpretation (which seems to make the "forms" too material) or the Megarian version (which seems to make the "forms" too sharply separate both from the physical world and from one another).

It is a brilliant and baffling dialogue, reflecting the equally brilliant and baffling issues and ideas that were in the air when it was written. Plato represents Socrates at a very youthful age, engaging in conversation with Zeno and Parmenides, the great philosopher from Elea. In the first part, the young man (provoked by Zeno's paradoxes) tries to explain his notion that there are "forms" in which sensible things "share"; the forms do not change, and they give the things sharing them their identity. But Socrates at this age is not a very good logician, and not very clear: he tries explaining his "forms" by making them spatial things, he tries defining them as completely separate from anything in space and time, he tries identifying them simply with "notions in our own minds"; but he is shown each time by Parmenides that the interpretation is logically inconsistent and will not do.

Parmenides, however, also believes in a theory of forms; and in a second part of the dialogue, he offers young Socrates a model of the logical method one should use in such discussion. The model takes the form of examining the consequences of various hypotheses concerning the relation of *unity* and *being*. Although he does not say so, Parmenides' program is highly relevant to young Socrates' own philosophic problem, as well as to his need for a lesson in method. It is so because, on young Socrates' view, (1) each form is a unity, though many instances "share" it; and (2) each space-time thing is a single thing because the flow of time and space is arrested and given structure by a single simple or complex form. Parmenides continues through a dry, compressed, formal examination of eight consequences of each of eight "hypotheses as to the relation of the One and Being."

Plato has Parmenides explore the possibilities (1) that *being* forms a single, continuous field; (2) that there are "many *beings*," units of *being* separate from one another. For each of these cases, in turn, he considers the alternative possibilities (a) that the several *beings* or the single field is spatial and temporal, and (b) that the several *beings* or the single field of *being* are formal and thus not changing and not in space or time.

The results can be summarized by saying that four different world-views result if the typical unit of being is viewed as Form, Substance, Process, or Atom.

Figure VII: THE ONE AND THE MANY (THE PARMENIDES HYPOTHESES)

THE ARCHITECTONIC OF THE HYPOTHESES

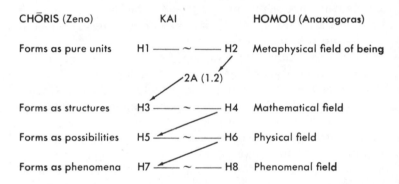

TO HEN (Parmenides)

CHŌRIS (Zeno)	KAI	HOMOU (Anaxagoras)
Forms as pure units	H1 ——— ~ ——— H2	Metaphysical field of being
	2A (1.2)	
Forms as structures	H3 ——— ~ ——— H4	Mathematical field
Forms as possibilities	H5 ——— ~ ——— H6	Physical field
Forms as phenomena	H7 ——— ~ ——— H8	Phenomenal field

Parmenides moves through eight positions in order; the four on the left give trouble because the "form" is in each case too separate, and it is hard to see how it combines with any field (of the things it informs); but the alternatives on the right, if we think of unity as being "right in" the field, are too formless to satisfy him. (The figure is from my *Plato on the One*, New Haven, 1961, reprinted with permission of the Yale University Press.)

Parmenides first shows that if unity belongs solely to a "form" which (as isolated, unique essence or ideal) has *no* plurality or diversity, there is no way to explain how any other property or thing, including existence, can relate to or share in such a form. But, second, if unity is simply identified with the total field of being, so that it ceases to have any distinctive identity of its own, as it melts down and diffuses through time and space, such a unity is not a "form" at all; not even an indeterminate "something."

The postulates that units of reality are *indivisible particles, abstract possibilities,* or separate *type-specimens,* all prove equally unsatisfactory. In each case, the result is valuable for the insight it gives, but also in each case the account proves neither consistent nor complete. Our experience is too varied to be exhausted by any of these alternative notions as to what its component units are, and for different purposes each type of unit provides a useful approach. For example, for the "technical" objectives of invention and control, the "atomic theory" has proven itself a most useful mind-set; yet for contexts in which aesthetic values of creativity and novelty are central, the notion of a single "creative process" proves the unit closest to the reality.

Certainly, by the end of his long demonstration, Plato's Parmenides has shown two things. If there are no "forms" at all, things will have no stable similarities by which we can recognize them or describe them. But if there are forms *entirely* isolated from space and time, there will be no way in which these can be relevant to us and our world at all. Young Socrates, therefore, was mistaken both in his first attempt to treat his "forms" as though they were physical things (although this is the way that Eudoxus later tried to interpret them), and in his subsequent attempt to define the "forms" as completely isolated, "pure," essences (although that was apparently the way Plato's contemporaries of the Megarian school defined them).

This is not the argument's only important consequence. It also seems that unless we human beings can see some systematic relation between the different kinds of "unity" and plurality" which our minds and sense encounter, we cannot devise a philosophy that will be consistent or complete. The way in which the dialogue establishes this constructive point is a negative one. Early in their conversation, Parmenides and young Socrates agree that there are forms of "beauty, justice, and the good"; and young Socrates prefers thinking about these to working out detailed puzzles about forms of "less attractive" things. However, neither these forms of value nor the faculty of reason (*nous*) which knows them appear in Parmenides' logical demonstration. And without the vision of a system of being ordered by the Good Parmenides' logical skill leads only to contradiction. On the one hand, each of his many hypotheses has *some plausibility;* but he treats them as mutually exclusive, so that every consideration that makes one of them true will falsify the others. When we study the history of Western philosophy, we find defenders of each of Parmenides' alternative accounts of what the units of reality truly are; we find philosophers assuming that these alternatives are mutually exclusive; and we find a debate continuing for two millennia without resolution.

The conclusion of this dialogue is certainly a defense of the Platonic theory of forms as against the Eudoxian or Megarian interpretation. At the same time, it seems to offer an indirect proof that we need the beautiful, just, and good as criteria by which reason can harmonize our many abstractions and assumptions into a single pattern with harmony and value.

Plato's indirect argument in the *Parmenides,* if it is what we have just presented, has neither been fully reconstructed, nor appreciated, nor tested against the details of the history of philosophy. These are all difficult enterprises, but they seem worth while.

CHAPTER X

The Political Experiment
In Sicily

Dion and Dionysius II

ON THE OCCASION of Plato's first visit to Syracuse, he met, as we mentioned, Dion, brother of Dionysius I. Dion's friendship with Plato continued over the years; his name appears on an index compiled later of "Members of the Academy" (which may have stretched a point in listing "corresponding members," as it were, as well as scholars in residence), and all evidence attests to his interest in the University. Prince Dion was a complete contrast to his brother; at first one wonders how he had survived the atmosphere of suspicion and intrigue in the "Court," which young Plato had found so offensive. But Dion seems to have been the sort of person even his brother would not suspect of secret intrigue or concealed desire for power: candid and outspoken, with a tendency to see things in black and white, and a tendency to judge other men's characters by his own, he seems to have been critical, somewhat aloof, trusted, and tolerated. What later proved perhaps his tragic flaw was a tendency to see situations as simple questions of principle, where they were in fact very complex. When Dionysius I died, and his son, Dionysius II, succeeded to the dictatorship, it seemed quite sensible to Dion to invite Plato as teacher for his nephew, to train him in the part of the "philosopher-king" which Plato had described in the *Republic*. The young dictator approved of the plan, and apparently the invitation was sent to Plato with no notion on Dion's part that his philosophic friend would not feel a favor had been done him; and with no notion, either, that his nephew might have second thoughts about the role of disinterested austerity of a true "philosopher-king."[1]

The invitation would have been very difficult for Plato to refuse, for several reasons. In the first place, there was his friendship with Dion, who had devised the plan. Second, the Academy and its "philosophy" were under attack for their impracticality. From the near-by school of practical political training run by the orator Isocrates, and from various comic poets, we find the Academicians made fun of for their researches in method and their "idle talking." It annoyed Plato that so many critics failed to see the practical value of the sort of philosophy he was after; it reminded him of Socrates' annoyance at people who insisted on "being practical" in ways that were short-sighted and not truly practical at all. We don't need to guess about this, for in his writing between 369 and 367 B.C., Plato is bitter about the practical men ("lawyers and speakers" in one passage, "the general public" in another) who call philosophy "useless" and "idle babbling." Loyalty both to friendship and to philosophy itself demanded acceptance of the invitation. Still, Plato had misgivings; and here it is only a guess that a third factor in his decision to accept was a feeling of optimism and luck on his side: he had, in fact, scored a tremendous practical success with the Academy; a tremendous literary success with the early Socratic dialogues; and an intellectual triumph for himself in the philosophic vision of the middle dialogues, and the scientific synthesis of the *Timaeus*. It would be surprising if these had not led him to hope that the Sicilian experiment had a chance to succeed, even though any dispassionate appraisal of the odds should have shown its success to be impossible.

And so, in 367 B.C., Plato and some of his students from the Academy (including Speusippus, his heir and favorite nephew) set sail for Sicily. Dion had been right in representing young Dionysius as intelligent and intellectually curious; wrong in representing him as patient and idealistic enough to carry through any extensive course of intellectual discipline. Dion had been right in assuring Plato that his visit would be welcomed by all of the court; for Plato was by now one of the men of intellectual eminence in the Greek world, and his visit had great prestige value. But Dion did not mention, and did not realize, how unwelcome Plato's longer stay and its purpose would be to officials who were dependent on the current order of things, and who could no doubt recognize that under a Platonic ruler, they would lose their high standard of living, their jobs, and quite possibly their lives as well. (For, unless they were stupid, it must have been evident that they were not qualified junior guardians, and that a Platonic ideal ruler would summarily replace them by promising young theorists from the Academy.) Nor could Dion see that along with intelligence his nephew's character combined hostility and insecurity—a mixture of brilliance, ambition, and paranoia, almost impossible to avoid for a sensitive young man whose misfortune it was to have had Dionysius I as his father. Had Dion noticed this, he might have understood better why his nephew was susceptible to suggestions from people who gave him reassurance by flattery; something we can be certain his uncle had not done.

These factors, which Dion had not seen or had not felt important, meant that the Academicians had been invited to walk into a deadly trap. Young Dionysius wanted to be a great speculative philosophic writer right away, not a patient beginning student of elementary logic or astronomy; and it was surely pointed out to him repeatedly by interested parties that if Syracuse were to have an ideal ruler, any number of people—Dion, or Plato's nephew, would at once come to mind among them—were better qualified for the post than Dionysius himself.

Although at first the young ruler set about mastering elementary mathematics, and "geometry, for a time, was a fashion in the Court," distrust, impatience, and slander from hostile courtiers had their effect. Convinced that they were plotting to depose him in Dion's favor, Dionysius placed Plato under house arrest; Dion fled to the mainland, his property confiscated, his family imprisoned. Plato and his party, partly through the diplomatic influence of Archytas, still a leading figure in near-by Tarentum, were released and allowed to return to Athens. Though the plan, from the outset, had no chance to succeed, still it was disappointing to have it end in such a violent failure. But this was not as yet the end of Plato's involvement in Sicily.

Dion, indignant and outraged, began to contemplate an armed invasion; and, in 361 B.C., Dionysius agreed to negotiate toward the restitution of his property and release of his family, provided Plato would serve as arbitrator. So once more Plato set sail for Syracuse, knowing this time that the adventure was not without attendant danger. The negotiations did not succeed; again Plato found himself *non grata* with a Syracusan dictator, but again managed an escape. In spite of his advice, Dion determined to invade; their final conference seems to have been held at the Olympic Games in 360 B.C. Dion enlisted an army, including many volunteers from the Academy, among them Plato's nephew as member of the intelligence staff, wintered in the harbor of Zankle, and then attacked and conquered. Dionysius held out for a time in an island fortress, Ortygia, in the harbor; but at last withdrew to Corinth, where later tradition says that he passed the rest of his life as a teacher of philosophy! Dion set up a limited democracy, retaining to himself rights of appointment and veto. He was neither flexible enough nor unscrupulous enough to succeed in this role of benevolent semi-dictator, however, and a year later his assassination plunged Sicily into chaos and factional war.

Later, Plato wrote an account of the affair, in two long "open" letters, designed as much for Athenian as for Sicilian readers; at least, most scholars agree that *Letters VII* and *VIII* in the collections of Plato's papers were his own, and had this intention. That was the end of the affair in Sicily.

CHAPTER XI

New Philosophical Analysis

Shifts in the Dialogue Form

THE CONCERN WITH analysis—logical testing, clarifying, applying—which was a third step in Socrates' method, was Plato's central interest during the third main period of his career. The "late dialogues"—*Parmenides, Sophist, Statesman*—are only now acquiring a circle of appreciative admirers; the nineteenth-century lovers of Plato could hardly believe him their author. They are rather more technical in content, and less likely to appeal to a general reader who does not see the point. And the point is not easy to see, because Plato in this set of writings has combined features of his early and middle dialogues with new technical methodology and lecture style to produce a new and unfamiliar literary form. Perhaps, by indicating the way in which these "dialogues" resemble and differ from the much more easily appreciated earlier group, we can help to prevent the reader from being alienated and outraged at Plato's change in style and apparent shifts in thought. For the following three sections, however, patience and close reading, even of the present summary presentation, will be required. This demands a faith that if Plato did these things, they must be important and worth while; and the reader unconvinced on this point may want to skip the present sections, to the treatment of Plato's very last works in ethics and law.

In the first place, Socrates is no longer the central speaker, but is replaced instead by "experts" who take over his role. We have already seen, in the *Timaeus,* that a Pythagorean

scientist presents the new scientific synthesis in what is practically a continuous lecture; now, the philosopher Parmenides,
in the dialogue bearing his name, conducts his demonstration
of the difficulties of the theory of forms and its necessity
mostly with a young respondent who gives only monosyllabic
answers. (Socrates as a young man appears only in the opening scene.) In the *Sophist* and *Statesman,* a Stranger from
Elea, who is both "a student of Parmenides and Zeno and a
true philosopher," carries forward inquiries of a logical kind,
while Socrates listens.

The audience, too, is changed; the Stranger has as his partners successively Theaetetus and Young Socrates (the former
of whom is an image of Socrates in looks, the latter of whom
shares his name), young men of excellent ability and enough
training to follow what seems a tedious exercise in near-lecture
form. He proposes to define first the Sophist, then the Statesman; as though he were carrying the discussion forward from
the *Theaetetus,* and answering the question, "What is knowledge?" both by a display of methods and a definition of "knowing" that involves various senses and kinds. There is a dry,
lecture-like formality that to some extent remains when Socrates returns as leader in the *Philebus* to discuss value and
pleasure.

All of this suggests that Plato had settled down to write
philosophy in a literal, lecture form, and that the literary
critic will find these technical dialogues unpromising material.
At the same time, the continued presence of Socrates—
whether in his youth, by namesake, by semblance, or as mod-
erator—suggests that the early dialogue form is not wholly
irrelevant. At major transitions, literary devices are used to
mark the shifts in method or topic; responses stress the intellectual improvement of the young respondents; unexpected
poetic words intrude; and the whole enterprise is held together
by continuing metaphors of the hunt and the net. There is a
sense, too, in which these dialogues on method are, like the
earlier ones, self-referential: the lecturer uses the patterns he
is discussing; the exploration moves through inconclusive essays, ending in jokes or critical asides, after which "new

weapons" are taken up for the hunt. Thus, the first definitions
of the Sophist are Sophistical—only semblances of correct
definitions—and the definition of the Statesman as measurer of
value requires us to measure the relative value of successive
methods of classification.

These features suggest that perhaps in the later dialogues
Plato has invented a new literary form; the excitement of the
chase, and the high ability of the audience, create a tension
between the successively rejected ideas of method, which in
part replaces the dramatic tension between characters in the
earlier form. This suggestion has never been followed up in
detail; but perhaps it ought to be. Just possibly there is more
in common between the early dialogues and the later lectures
than scholars have discovered.

The Logic of Unreality (*Sophist*)

One of Plato's achievements most admired by modern logicians and analysts is his solution to the problem of meaningful
statements about "non-being." As Whitehead wrote repeatedly,
and as Socrates knew, "consciousness and intelligence require
negative judgments." To "think" about something, we must
recognize what this something *is not*, and how it differs from
other things like or opposed to it. But just here the Eleatics
left to Greek philosophy a very tricky problem. What do negative judgments refer to; what are they "about"? Now, truth is
taken to mean that "a proposition says what is the case"—in
one familiar type, for instance, it indicates a subject and pred-
icates an attribute of it. (And this notion that truth is "to say
the thing that is" is deep-rooted in Indo-European ordinary
language and common-sense semantics.) How shall we analyze
the proposition, "No elephants are in this room"? It seems true
to me, but what subject does it indicate, and what is it about?
I try turning it around, and get "Nothing in this room is an
elephant"—which is even more curious. For I seem to be "indicating" or "referring to" a kind of non-being as though it
were a positive, existent class or entity. But Parmenides had
already insisted that "nothing" can't possibly *be* something;
"nothing in my room" is not an existent thing, of the sort a

proposition can refer to; and how can it "be true," that is, "say what is," when it refers to something that *is not?* It can't very well be called false, either, in the absence of any reference; it seems just nonsense.

This corollary to Parmenides, that "falsehood is impossible because no one can think or say a thing that is not," appears to have delighted some young Sophists and logicians; in Plato's *Euthydemus,* mentioned earlier, Euthydemus uses this Eleatic argument (that no one can say what is not) to defend the thesis—which Socrates "had heard of as the thesis of Protagoras"—that all falsehood is impossible. "A pretty clatter!" comments one of the hearers; but what is the answer?

In Plato's *Sophist,* the Stranger, having corrected two earlier flaws in his own method of division, is on the point of "catching his quarry in a net of definition" by saying that the Sophist is "a maker of semblances". The Sophist raises a philosophical question which is the old non-being theme. "You accuse me," he says, "of making poor imitations, that is, things somewhat like but less real than their originals. But how can you call my works 'less real'? That would require them to have a kind of non-being, and, of course, non-being can't *be* any thing or property or 'in' anything." It's like the elephants that aren't here.

The Stranger has to review the history of philosophy to show Theaetetus that earlier thinkers have been telling us myths in their accounts of *being* and *non-being.* We must distinguish kinds of *non-being* or *nothing.* The first is sheer, pure non-existence, like the non-being in Parmenides' philosophy, about which nothing definite can be thought or said. But a second type of non-being is the logical relation of *otherness* between forms or things. This is a perfectly definite relation, and any field of discussion that we divide separates into parts, each of which is the same as itself, and other than the others. *Non-X* is of this second type; it is a name referring to everything that is other than *X.* So, when I say "no elephants are in this room," I am talking about all elephants, all things in the room, and the relation of otherness between them; there is no mysterious "presence of non-elephants" involved at all. Perhaps, the special case of otherness that holds between original and likeness—otherness in degrees of resemblance and reality—should not be counted as a third co-ordinate case; the Stranger convinces the Sophist fairly easily that this is a significant relation, once the major objection is disposed of. And statements about things may be more or less *other* than the things they refer to.

In order to explain how a statement can be meaningful, but false, we need to look at the forms which are "meanings." From our earlier consideration of language, it is clear that a word can be "meaningful" in several ways, and that there are several levels of "meaning." In discussion and conversation, we are able to think of individual forms in relative isolation from their total systematic context, and we can construct new separations and combinations. This is like the paying of selective attention by which we can think of "non-X" as though it were a single form. It does not mean that the forms themselves are really capable of being sorted, separated, and recombined; nor that the forms are simply identical with meanings of terms. In fact, in the very next dialogue, the *Statesman*, the forms return once more in their role of ideals and criteria of value. But it does mean that levels of knowledge below reason on the Divided Line give a kind of forms which we can think about and recombine in many ways. And it also means that the way in which we refer to the forms in statement and thought is very complex. We are prepared for this in part by the distinctions in the middle dialogues of degrees of clarity of knowledge, which involve degrees of clarity of vision. This complexity of reference, and the complexity of "role" that the forms must play if they are to give meanings to words, intentions to concepts, and value to entities, bring Plato's late dialogues close to the contemporary interests of analytic philosophers working in philosophy of mind and philosophy of language. But Plato does not seem to feel that such detailed analysis changes his vision of the theory of forms, however much it poses problems for clarification, such as that of the being of non-being.

The Method of Division (*Sophist, Statesman*)

From its very beginning, a central concern of Plato's philosophy is with methods for achieving clarity. We need a clear vision of ourselves and of the forms in their complex articulation; the techniques of education in the middle dialogues are sometimes "ladders" on which we mount from an unclear awareness of some presence to a clear view of the form that gives that presence its attractiveness. And, of course, sound method also requires that we be able to divide; the method of "collection" must be supplemented by a method of "division" or "discrimination."

A great rule of division, which Plato appreciated, even though it gave rise to some of the puzzles about "unreality" which his *Sophist* explored, is that every class, A, can be divided into two sub-classes, B and non-B, which will exhaust it. And such division by subclassification can be carried forward indefinitely. For all sharply defined classes, there are no borderline cases; so "nothing can be both A and non-A" is a second rule of the logical scheme. These simple rules have remarkable power; it becomes possible to "reason" almost automatically with no mistakes in inference. These, plus three more rules of the same type, govern the operation of our modern card-controlled information handling machines. It might not be too surprising, then, in the infancy of formal logic to find the Academy as fascinated by "A equals AB plus Anon-B" as the Pythagoreans were with the equally simple and powerful "Theorem of Pythagoras"; and one can imagine Plato devoting a dialogue to a visiting lecturer who explains classification by this rule.

But there is evidently more involved in the Stranger's lectures than a simple demonstration of the great $A = AB + A\bar{B}$ rule of classification. We can see this by noticing what new qualifications and restrictions he adds to his division technique as successive examples are shown in the *Sophist* and *Statesman.*

Figure VIII: CLASSIFICATION: SOME GENERAL RULES[1]

It is sometimes instructive to look at the generality and power of something as obvious as the classification rules.

$$1. \quad A = AB + A\bar{B}$$

A and B represent any classes; $\bar{A}$ and $\bar{B}$ their complements (non-A and non-B). AB is the class "*both* A and B," '+' is the logical sum of the two classes (A +B equals all of A plus all of B, that is, everything that is *either* A or B).

Some classes are "empty," that is, they have no members. For instance, the class "both A and non-A" surely has none. Let '= 0' describe such an empty class, so that, for example,

$$2. \quad A\bar{A} = 0$$

We can then discover a second general rule, namely, that if a class is empty, all of its subclasses are empty:

if $A = 0$, then, since $AB + A\bar{B} = A$, $AB + A\bar{B} = 0$, so that
$$AB = 0 \text{ and } A\bar{B} + 0.$$

Conversely, if a class is not empty ($\neq 0$), then at least one of its subclasses is not empty, either (as in ordinary addition, $0 + 0 = 0$)

if $A \neq 0$, then $AB + A\bar{B} \neq 0$; but if AB and $A\bar{B}$ were both $= 0$, their "sum" would not be A; so either $AB \neq 0$ or $A\bar{B} \neq 0$.

The Academy was working along the lines of these "laws of thought," but for the most part using geometrical figures rather than equations with letters, as in the illustration here.

The abstract patterns of Fig. VIII need the following qualifications:

1. The mere collection of the names we call a thing may not constitute a definition or accurate classification of it; ordi-

nary language frequently fails to offer the exact names we need to mark the classes of divisions.

2. It makes a difference what we start with; an initial mistake—such as the false assumption that the Sophist is essen-- tially a hunter rather than a maker of semblances—can vitiate the reasoning that follows from it.

3. It may be important to keep track of "empty" and "full" classes in the division, since we could not usually draw any conclusion about existence from the properties of a class with no existent members. For example, if all Athenians who commit injustice voluntarily are better than those Athenians who commit it involuntarily, we are still not entitled to conclude, "Therefore, there exist some Athenians who commit injustice voluntarily"—if we believe Socrates, there aren't any.

4. Often an *ideal* case or formula is not an adequate definition of *actual* instances, unless we also have some clue as to the way in which the ideal is attained in the actual. To know that "weaving is the art of making cloth" tells us the ideal function of the art, but we may need to weave together a more informative definition by specifying, in addition to this function, the medium used and the successive operations that the art employs. The model we are given will be shown in Fig. IX. This "definition" shows the stages and operations by which the medium is changed into the product.

Different methods of division are not all equally valid or useful for philosophic purposes. The classes into which we divide should all be of the same "type." This requirement amounts to a demand that we not mix up stages or levels of subclassification, as we would, for instance, if we divided "animals" into "Greeks, fish, birds, and non-Greek land animals." Even more important, however obvious, is the necessity that the intended use of our divisions must be kept in sight throughout. In the case study at hand, the Stranger's problem is one of defining an *art;* to do this, he wants to locate it by its product, material, and operation. His "divisions," then, must be divisions of arts, products, operations, and materials. More generally, to guarantee that a classification is relevant to our purpose in classifying, we need a common property connecting all the wholes and parts of our division; thus art should divide into arts, science into sciences, value into values, and so on. Finally, we are told that there should be some technique for finding the right size and shape for ideal classes. This normative condition, like the others, is familiar enough (there are certain proper proportions for works of art). The Stranger puts off as too long an account of the art of measure which would give a method for such evaluations. The only obvious general condition I can see is that if a given proper operation makes completion of a product impossible, there has been an error in quantitative measure. For example, in weaving, if the twisting operation twists the warp too loose, there can be no cloth: the twisting was the right operation at that stage, but quantitatively wrong. We will discuss this further in the following section.

The Measurement of Value

The techniques of classification in the abstract are essential, but not yet enough. In the *Statesman*, the Eleatic Stranger moves on to the question of the measurement of value; as a case study, he classifies and evaluates the types of rule in human states. In our previous discussion of division, we noted that a definition of an art which specified product, medium, and operational stages gave one criterion for saying something was "too much" or "too little." This was the case when an operation was of the proper type, but nevertheless made impossible the completion of the product because of improper measurement.

Unlike the *Parmenides*, the *Statesman* has been relatively neglected. With the ideal state of the *Republic* and the detailed legislative code of the *Laws* available, this "halfway stage" in political classification has not seemed important, except perhaps as marking a transition phase in its author's thought. Yet of all of Plato's dialogues, this is the most interesting in its interrelation of an abstract logical problem and a concrete situation, and it is the most baffling in its superficially jagged over-all organization. It is also the most annoying, to the reader and to Young Socrates, because the Stranger insists that a true statesman is "above all law."

The discussion begins with a straightforward definition by subclassification of the statesman as the custodian of a human herd—the classical image of "shepherd of the people" taken literally. (Thrasymachus had used this analogy in his argument with Socrates in the *Republic;* "the stronger" had an *art* of shepherding the people, which meant, for him, getting them fattened for a mutton roast. In the "strict sense" [which legal definitions would have] such a strong man could never make a mistake as to his interest. Socrates' counter was that, in this strict sense, the shepherd is an expert in tending, not in eating his sheep; and, by analogy, the "ruler" would have an art which benefited his subjects—his own wealth or pleasure would not enter into his qualification as "expert" shepherd of the people.)

The shepherd definition runs into immediate difficulties: there seems to be no one who exercises an undisputed and total authority over the state, attending to feeding, protecting, entertaining and doctoring his flock. The Stranger tells a long myth to show why the definition failed: the universe, it seems, sometimes runs forward—this is a golden age, in which divine shepherds attend to our human needs. But in another cycle, the cosmos reverses its motion; in these reversal phases, the law and order of the golden age erode; the demigods leave their human charges; and men must struggle for survival. We have mentioned some of the details of this myth in earlier sections. In particular, the interesting notion is developed that when the cosmic cycle reverses, so do all the subordinate planetary and life cycles. The first error in the definition, concludes the Stranger, is that it defines a ruler of the golden age, not of our present "iron age" world. In other words, he and Young Socrates have delineated an ideal case which is too remote from actual conditions to be a useful definition.

There is nothing in the science of the time that corresponds to this "periodic reversal of cosmic motion," except perhaps for some Egyptian fancies mentioned in passing in the *Timaeus* but given no scientific foundation. However, throughout the cycles in the *Timaeus*—from planets to circling impulses in individual human minds—the phenomena that we observe are a resultant of two simultaneous opposite motions, called those of "the same" and "the other." The "motion of the other" introduces deviations from the predictable simplicity of "the revolutions of the same," so that, for example, a single daily circling does not describe planetary motion, but a contrary deviation is needed. If the *Statesman* myth is read in this context, it seems that it is treating as separate periods two phases of cosmic process that actually occur together: one a regular, predictable imitation of an ideal; the other a contrary, perhaps aberrant, departure from this by the actual. A divine shepherd defines the ideal statesman for an ideal universe in which there is no backward component, but it will not apply to the actual mixed world we ourselves inhabit. Our definition must catch the statesman in the present world order; and the myth points out the kind of world to which it must apply.

The Stranger now proceeds to try to describe the ruler by a further set of formal logical classifications, of the type the *Sophist* had illustrated; but in each case the classification would include many citizens besides the ruler.

Saying that the main point of their discussion should be to explore method, the Stranger moves on to a use of "example" as a step toward the definition they seek. It is imperative to distinguish two kinds of measure; descriptive and normative. The nature of normative measure, the method by which we judge something as "too large" or "too small" (as opposed to descriptive, where a six-foot table is just six feet long), would require a long digression; but since there are arts, such measurement must be possible. Let us take "weaving" as an example to be defined: we must discriminate its proper product and function from the co-operative arts (spinning, loom-making by the carpenter, sheep-shearing, and so on); and must then specify the operations and medium which lead to the proper product.

By this time, returning to the statesman's art again, the Stranger has demonstrated and discarded three techniques of definition: the unspecified ideal was not satisfactory—it took in at once too little and too much. The myth showed us the medium in which the stateman's art must operate, but did not have the generality needed to define anything. The net of descriptive classifications turned out to be too inclusive.[2]

The statesman's art, like the weaver's must be defined by stating (a) its product, (b) the stages of production, (c) the material at each stage, and (d) the successive operations which the craftsman must perform. Like the warp in weaving, descriptive classification provides a background into which the concrete facts must be woven. Neither logic nor myth alone is adequate. In the state, analogously, we are weaving a pattern; our citizens and subordinates are the medium; the stable background is given by custom and law; and executive actions provide the operations. The true statesman will be guided by his vision of the product of his art. He cannot, it is clear, be defined *operationally:* a man is not a "statesman" simply because he exercises power in administering policy; we could not, therefore, accept a Sophistic notion that the man who can tax, kill, or exile whom he will is the statesman in a community. But neither can we define our statesman, as Greek conservatives would, as the uncritical protector and preserver of custom and law; because the statutes of a society are general, with an eye to the public good; but the medium of the statesman is always a particular situation. His art is above all laws; a conclusion which shocks Young Socrates and the modern reader. It is more an apparent than a real paradox, however; for the art itself provides norms and operations that limit the statesman; as far as traditional custom goes, he *is* immune, perhaps; but the temporary characterization of the statesman as "bound by no law" is quickly modified in the sequel.

The statesman directs policy of the state; he is therefore superior to the general, judge, and educator, each of whom has a "co-operative art" with subordinate function. Apart from the state of a golden age ideal with its divine ruler, policy may be made in a state by one man, a few, or all; and may be made with or without the stabilizing limits of respect for law. For every form of state except the pure ideal, respect for law produces a better social order; it avoids the "melting into chaos" of a world running backward, and gradually losing all "memory of the God's laws"; and, resting on funded experience, custom and law in fact usually involve approximate recognition of some objective norms. Social direction, Plato holds, is more effective and consistent if one person does it than if many do. He thus gets a classification of seven types of "state:" (1) the Golden Age ideal; (2) rule by one man with law—monarchy; (3) rule by a few with law—aristocracy; (4) rule by all with law—democracy; (5) rule by all without law —no special name exists; this is democracy of a second sort; (6) rule by a few without law—plutocracy (since in these cases the "few" are a wealthy elite); (7) rule by one man without law—tyranny. And these are ordered from best to worst; the concentration of power without respect for law is less good than its dispersion.

Part of the good ruler's "weaving" aims at combining "gentle" and "irascible" personalities to produce a well-ordered society. This is done by proper allocation of subordinate functions; by marriage counselling which tends to prevent breeding of imbeciles or maniacs; and by education, which "harmonizes opinions as to the good and the right" throughout the society.

Young Socrates, who has been making progressively more intelligent responses as he follows, gives a truly statesman-like summary at the end of the dialogue: "Now, Stranger, I believe that you have given us a most beautiful and complete ruler and statesman." Some editors think that this is a remark by the older Socrates, from whom it would in fact be appropriate. But although the jump in Young Socrates' intelligence is greater than Plato usually permits young respondents, he has been trying to have the responses show that the young men in the audience are actually learning from the lecture, and he would have indicated it if this final comment were by another respondent than Young Socrates.

I have summarized this dialogue at length because it is *an example* of the "art of normative measure," for which Plato never seems to have written out a set of formal rules of method.

The Stranger "weaves together" myth and pure logic, neither of which is satisfactory, into an artistic definition; the statesman weaves together the components of his society; the abstract discussion of method is illustrated by the concrete example of defining statesmanship in the lecture, as it is too ideal, too empirical, too formal, and finally just right. In the *Laws* we will see Plato attempting a specific task of statesmanship; in his Lecture on the Good, we will see a final attempt to explain the technique of normative measure; but there should be further study and appreciation of the *Statesman* both by Platonic scholars and by general readers of Plato.

Figure IX: THE OPERATIONAL-LOGICAL DEFINITION PATTERN OF THE STATESMAN

The definition of the art of weaving which the Stranger gives as an example of the way we should define the statesman's art can be schematized as in the figure blow. The end product lies at the upper right, the initial raw material at the lower left; the successive operations on the left transform the material (in successive times, the *t* on the bottom); and the stages of production, which give the desired definition of the art and its product, lie along the diagonal.

WEAVING

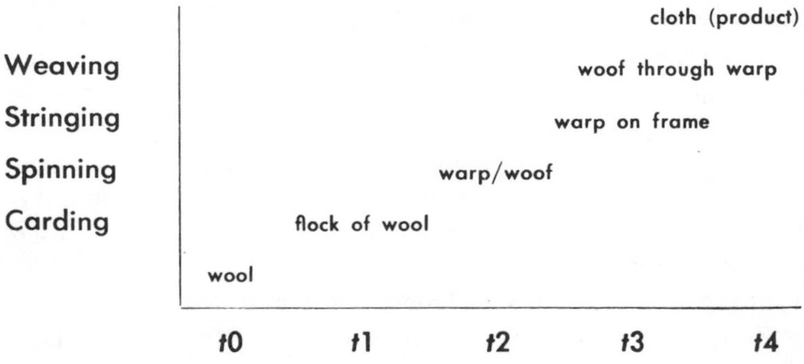

					cloth (product)
Weaving					woof through warp
Stringing					warp on frame
Spinning				warp/woof	
Carding			flock of wool		
	wool				
	*t*0	*t*1	*t*2	*t*3	*t*4

PART FOUR

Plato's Latest Work

CHAPTER XII

The Late Discussions in the Academy

WE HAVE SEEN that in the later dialogues there is a change in the dialogue form: a leader now presents and criticizes alternatives at length, and his audience is sufficiently talented and trained to follow out the interconnections of the lectures. The element of shared inquiry still is there, but the lively drama of ideas of the early dialogues gives way to a more patient and abstract procedure. One reason for this is, no doubt, the change of emphasis in the Academy from concern with discovering synthesizing principles to attempts at their application. Eudoxus' detailed work in astronomy, Plato's in legislation, and the general study of methods of classification, for which the Academy in this period was notorious enough to be satirized by comic poets, all involve a shift in this direction.

Aristotle refers on occasion to "Plato's unwritten doctrine" as though he were recalling lectures; and that Plato did lecture on occasion we know from the fact that he gave a large public lecture on The Good. We have suggested that Plato's program for his later dialogues left room, at least, for a final dialogue defining "the philosopher"; such a summing-up should have developed in detail the "art of normative measure" which is deferred in the *Statesman* to "some other occasion"; and we would hope that there would be a positive proof that what is real is good, which the *Parmenides* showed only indirectly. This enterprise might involve carrying forward the dialectic of the *Republic,* and using the "kinship of the formal sciences" as a "step" toward some general theory of value. The final summarizing dialogue was never written, and the lecture which attempted to communicate the final answer was not successful; the very fact that Plato was willing to give such a lecture at all may have meant that in his own mind some implications and transitions of his ideas were too unclear or uncontrolled for him to write in any variation on the dialogue form.

Four ideas from this lecture, and from other reports of Plato's teaching in this period, will be briefly treated: (1) that "there is one good"; (2) that "the forms are (in some sense) numbers"; (3) that forms work causally on space and time through mathematical structures; and (4) that the meanings of the term "form" need distinction and clarification.

1. The Lecture on the Good which proved that there is one good was "highly mathematical" according to Aristotle, and it "disappointed most of the audience," who hoped for something more practical. Plato was evidently returning to the philosophic issues: (a) whether there is some final convergence of truth, goodness, and beauty; and (b) whether there is some common referent for all our uses of the term "good," or whether, instead, there are disparate categories or types of goodness, with lines we cannot cross. Plato—at the expense of most of the audience—evidently addressed himself to a formal proof of this convergence and unity; this shows no change, except perhaps in tactics and technicality, from the ideas he maintained throughout the dialogues.[1]

2. The proposition that "the forms are numbers" may not have figured in this particular lecture, but it is reported by Aristotle several times as Plato's doctrine. Connected with this is the further report that Plato held that each level of reality is a "field" (an "indeterminate dyad") which is given determinacy by a form (a "one"). What, exactly, Plato said or meant is hard to specify; though the one and dyad are similar to ideas put forward in the *Philebus* and *Parmenides*. But to equate the forms with numbers seems neither philosophically sensible nor consistent with the other doctrines of Plato's philosophy. It is just possible that, since Aristotle himself held that measure is always a *number* of some kind, and also that "forms" should be limited to *specific* forms; and since Plato

called his specific forms "measures" on occasion; it is this reference to the form as measure that Aristotle meant. Otherwise, something very hard to understand took place in Plato's lectures and discussions.

3. In this context the notion appears that form operates by "projection," as the ideal of a table is projected into space and time by way of the blueprint that guides the carpenter's construction. The doctrine seems latent in, and consistent with, the role of forms and structures in the dialogues themselves, and raises no special problems.

4. Reports of statements and lectures agree with the late dialogues to some extent in recognizing that the term "form" is being used in a number of different senses. Different "methods of division" (and, presumably, "methods of generalization" as well) will trace out different patterns and lines of demarcation among the "forms." There are twelve central roles the forms play; and to explore these was a concern of the Academy. Aristotle's various lists of the things which "we Platonists say do" or "do not have forms. . ." no doubt are echoes of lectures and discussions aimed at the clarification of stricter and broader senses of "form."

It may be helpful to indicate here the twelve most important senses of "form." The "forms" are at once meanings of words, referents of concepts, and entities in their own right; and, since they are causes of unity without which nothing could exist, they must be present and effective on every level of reality. The following matrix is meant to be suggestive, if not definitive:

	WORDS	THOUGHTS	THINGS
1	philosophic meaning	theories	ideals
2	formal syntax	hypothesis	abstractions
3	ordinary use	technique	types
4	poetry	expectation	elements

Value versus Pleasure (*Philebus*)

The *Philebus* is a dialogue directed against hedonistic ethics in general, and probably the position of Eudoxus in particular.

Plato makes Socrates the main speaker once more; he has him examine the respective claims of knowledge and pleasure to be the good for human life. While a general line of argument disproving the claims of pleasure can be seen clearly enough, Plato seems anxious to put into this final dialogue in which Socrates appears *all* of his insights and ideas that are directly or indirectly relevant to the method and content of ethics. Among these are medical ideas from the *Timaeus,* metaphysical ones from the *Parmenides,* and notions of method from the *Statesman.* The result is that the detail of the *Philebus* seems jagged and is compressed almost beyond belief.[2]

Philebus, for whom the dialogue is named, has been explaining and defending the thesis that "pleasure is the good"; Socrates, who has been listening, is inclined to think that knowledge is better. Protarchus, the main respondent in the dialogue, and the other young men with him, are impressed and almost persuaded by Philebus' case; but either they are not such consistent hedonists that they avoid discussions because they find them unpleasant, or else they enjoy inquiry. Plato's Socrates, at any rate, engages them in a conversation in which he seems to know and take advantage of the inquiries in science and logic that the late dialogues had carried on (inquiries which Plato presents as led by visiting experts, but with Socrates present), and he is able to redefine the problem at hand in a way which keeps the ethical issue on the level of "the good for human life." A human life would be less good (signs of this are that it would be "less desired" and "less sufficient") if it consisted of pure reason with no pleasure, or pure pleasure with no reason, than it is if it has both. Socrates is not, therefore, going to concentrate on proving a total opposition between knowledge and pleasure; the question will be which parts and proportions of these are the essential conditions and causes of a life's value.

1. First a question of methodology arises. Socrates would like to classify "pleasures" into kinds; he suspects that some pleasures may be good, others bad. Protarchus, however, insists that all pleasures, *as* pleasures, are the same, so that Socrates would be wrong if he were to subdivide the class into

contrary subclasses. This insistence is contrary to all rules and precedents of sound method: knowing involves more than recognizing a common similarity in a class, or an infinite diversity among its possible instances. What art and science do is to distinguish a finite number of relevant subclasses between the one large class and the infinite possible differences among its members. Vocal sound, for example, is a single class; but the different sounds a voice can make lie in a continuum, which would have an infinite number of potentially distinct sounds. The art of grammar begins by recognizing a finite and determinate set of consonants and vowels, which are the relevant elements of meaningful speech; it then studies the combinations of these subclasses and the new properties of their compounds (how it does this is illustrated in the *Cratylus*, discussed previously. See p. 71). It seems, by analogy to all other sciences and arts, that one must begin the study of ethics by examining and defining relevant kinds of pleasure. Even if Protarchus still wants to insist that all pleasure is good, he will at least admit that some pleasures are true and others false (such as the pleasure of anticipations resting on false opinions).

2. But granting (a) the general rule of method, that we must divide into finite relevant subclasses, and (b) that pleasure is capable at least of *some* type of subclassification; we still need to know (c) how pleasure and knowledge relate to nature and to human nature: in a sense we are asking what, in the nature of subject matters, makes the method of finite subclassifying a possibility and a source of knowledge. Here Socrates, asking to be allowed to use "weapons of another kind" in the fight between wisdom and pleasure, offers a general characterization of the dimensions of "mixed" things such as human life. In nature, we can distinguish four classes: an animal, a life, an event or an experience belongs in the "mixed" class because it lies at an intersection of an "infinite" indeterminate field, and a "finite" specific structural determination. Hot and cold, for example, are an indefinite continuum (from hotter to colder) of opposite qualities; it is when number and measure determine a given region to have *just so much* heat

that we deal with definite and measurable "temperature." We must recognize the fluid medium that underlies a concrete thing, the determinate structure that imposes limitations of shape and number on the flow, the "mixture" of these which is the concrete thing itself, and as a fourth class a "cause of mixture" which is responsible for the selective combinations of "finite" and "infinite" (classes which would never combine without such a cause). Protarchus asks whether Socrates would also like a fifth class for his scheme, a "cause of separation." Socrates "does not need it for the present."

Socrates now divides knowledge and pleasure against the background of his four-class scheme, as in Fig. X.

Since physical pain and pleasure result from the loss and restoration of harmony of the body, physical pleasure is always mixed with pain. We distinguish these "pleasures of deviation and restoration" from the "pure pleasures" of simply sensed beauty, and from a "neutral state" that constitutes proper function with no departures from the norm (this latter state could be called "well-being" or "happiness"; it does not include the type of pleasure which is simply a removal of pain). Turning to knowledge, we must note, says Socrates, that human life requires applied as well as pure knowledge; "otherwise, for example, a man could never find his way home"—however much he knew about abstract geometry.

Now, what properties of the "mixed life" make it good? We can agree that symmetry, truth, and beauty are three "touchstones" by which we recognize any good thing. What causes these in a mixed life is *measure;* after this come the measured, reason, and pure science, which are "most akin" to symmetry, truth, and beauty; third place is awarded to mind; fourth to applied knowledge as a needed component; as fifth we add the "pure" pleasures which are entirely compatible with the rest. But the physical pleasures cannot claim sixth place; for they destroy the measure and balance of the good life we have been sketching in; and a wise man will not admit them as ethical criteria.

The dialogue ends with Protarchus agreeing, yet still not wholly satisfied: there remains "one small point" that he thinks

Figure X: THE FOUR MAIN CLASSES OF THINGS
(PHILEBUS)

Socrates and Protarchus first agree on a general scheme,
dividing things into four classes:

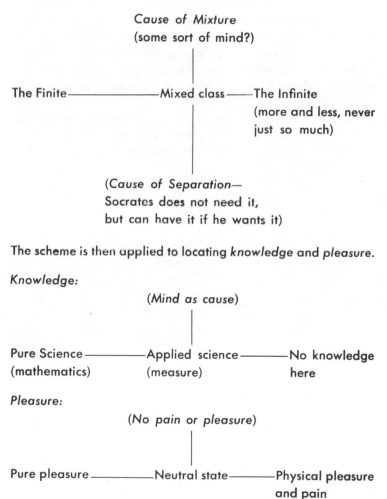

Cause of Mixture
(some sort of mind?)

The Finite————————Mixed class————The Infinite
(more and less, never
just so much)

(Cause of Separation—
Socrates does not need it,
but can have it if he wants it)

The scheme is then applied to locating *knowledge* and *pleasure*.

Knowledge:

(*Mind as cause*)

Pure Science————————Applied science————No knowledge
(mathematics) (measure) here

Pleasure:

(*No pain or pleasure*)

Pure pleasure——————Neutral state————Physical pleasure
and pain

Socrates has not considered, but he does not say what it is. Throughout the discussion, however, he is learning and moving toward a wiser ethical theory.

In this final summing-up, Plato's Socrates combines the ethical interest of the early dialogues with the refined logic and advanced science of the later ones. His final appearance here answers Eudoxus effectively: for in the case of every physical pleasure, which owes its existence to removal of pain, the total excess of pleasure over pain is simply zero. Our "natural" or "instinctive" pursuit of physical pleasure is rather a natural "pain avoidance" which restores us to a normal state; the pure pleasures, on the other hand, do offer a gain in positive value to human life.

Plato now turned his attention to describing the specific operations and medium that could combine in right measure to constitute a good society where a good life could be led by every citizen.

CHAPTER XIII

Plato's Last Project: The Model Legal Code

AMONG THE MOST controversial of Plato's major works is the *Laws,* his model in twelve books for a municipal code; the controversy does not center about the meaning of what Plato said, but rather about what he did not say. As we have mentioned, the Academy had been invited to send experts in philosophy and legislation to help draw up constitutions and codes for new colonies. This is an exacting job of detailed work, but at the same time a challenge to philosophy to prove its worth in practice. Unlike the *Republic,* or even the *Statesman,* a code of statutes for an actual contemporary Greek town was limited by actual conditions; it had to work. In the *Laws* Plato paid meticulous attention to the sort of detailed regulation that he casually "left for the younger guardians to decide" in the *Republic.* This last of Plato's works was never edited and polished, and was "published" in an unfinished form; yet there is no indication that any major changes would have been made in a final editing; Plato's project is substantially complete.

The speakers in the *Laws* are three old men, able to draw on long political experience, representing the states of Crete, Sparta, and Athens. The leader of the discussion is an elderly "Athenian Stranger," often thought to be Plato himself. In the legislation they propose, these men agree that an optimum arrangement is one which compromises between a straight aristocracy (the "order of Zeus" which proportions rewards and responsibilities to merits), an oligarchy (which takes account

179

of differences in wealth as making a difference in political status), and a democracy (an "order of arithmetical equality").
They construct an interesting, carefully balanced fusion of
aristocracy and democracy, including a shrewd use of the
desire for profit and property, as well as of the desire for
honor, to motivate the citizens. Education is to be public and
compulsory and to include gymnastics, music, mathematics
(emphasizing theories of measure, rather than formal method),
and civics (in which course, the laws are to be studied). A
Nocturnal Council of older men and young associate fellows,
meeting by night, will carry on research and study, and will
recommend changes in the laws.

The laws themselves (in spite of the criticism of inflexible
statutes offered by Plato in the *Statesman*) are fixed and stabil-
ized in such a way that they look almost impossible to change:
for a change in law, everybody must concur from the public
assembly to the Oracle of Apollo at Delphi! In addition to
education, a belief in natural theology—the existence, goodness, and providence of the gods—is required by law, and
heresy will be punished. We find some striking omissions: the
system of education contains no critical "dialectic" at its summit; no one in the state will have the sort of virtue which is
grounded in certain knowledge as opposed to conditioned opinion; and it is doubtful what the fate of Socrates himself would
have been under Plato's late legal system.

A selected list of provisions of the code may show the
planned weaving together of equality, merit, profit, and prestige; and the sensible application of mathematics to institutional social planning. Each citizen, for example, will own an
estate which he cannot sell or mortgage; his additional income
and property (up to a statutory maximum) locates him in one
of four economic "classes" which the laws recognize. Elections
for the Assembly, a representative body, are regulated in such
a way that representatives of the two lower economic classes
are in effect elected by voters of the two upper classes, and
vice versa. (This is done by having voting on nominees from
each class on successive days of the election period. A fine for
non-attendance is imposed on the lower class on the first two

days, when representatives of the two upper classes are elected; and no penalty at all for the lower class but a heavy one for the upper class is imposed for not voting on the days set aside for electing representatives of the lower two economic classes.) Certain specific offices—such as those of the Superintendent of Education, and the Magistrates—can be filled only by citizens meeting high requirements of experience and merit. Others are by appointment, others by popular election; for example, membership in the state Academy of the Nocturnal Council is strictly appointive. Slaves constitute a fifth group; they are protected by law from arbitrary mistreatment, but are severely punished by the laws for any failure to keep their place. And a difference is recognized by the laws in the behavior expected from members of each economic class. For example, cowardice on the part of an upper-class citizen, who is expected to set a responsible example, is fined much more heavily, in proportion to his respective property, than it is for one of the lower class; but insolence (e.g., an unjustified challenge of a state official's conduct in office) brings on the lower-class offender a proportionately heavier penalty. With at least a partial prevision of the prestige value of "conspicuous waste," sumptuary laws allow the upper class *proportionately* more as maximum expenditure for funerals and for wedding feasts than the other classes.

Other provisions of the law show that Plato has not forgotten the Pythagorean notion that mathematics can be applied to the design of a well-run community. There is to be a standardization of weights and measures (including the calendar) on a duodecimal system. The number of citizens will be held fixed at 5040, a "wonderful number" with sixty divisors. The town and highways will be planned in advance and laid out on a radial plan. There will be fixed prices, and state inspection of weights and measures. This will include state supervision of hotels, so that guests can be fairly sure they will neither be robbed nor assassinated—an assurance apparently lacking in the typical hostelry of Plato's time. Detailed regulations are also put forward of such miscellaneous items as guardianship of orphans, riparian rights, responsibility for irrigation ditch maintenance, and so on.

After reading through this extensive work, we can agree that Plato is following the notion of the *Statesman* in weaving the state together with a rigid warp of law and a more pliable woof of citizens and resources; but he is certainly limiting himself to applied, "low-flying" philosophy. Many of Plato's admirers—particularly, I would say, those whose admiration is relatively greatest for the late dialogues—do not see this limitation as introducing any *inconsistency:* the laws are, they maintain, simply a detailed application of the more abstract and ideal principles of, say, the *Republic.* Plato's student, Aristotle, saw the relation in this way; he used the *Laws* to supplement the *Republic,* and indeed he absent-mindedly refers to the "Athenian Stranger's" ideas as "what Socrates says in the *Laws.*"[1] But Platonists who appreciate the early and middle dialogues more than they do the later group, see a veritable betrayal of philosophy in this dull colonial city; no dialectic; no one whose virtue rests on knowledge rather than pure conditioning; no one allowed to ask questions about the state religion; very few old men allowed even to recommend any social change, and even then, almost certain to fail in getting adoption of such recommendations; a slave population; a didactic education more like that of Gorgias than of Socrates; all these elements figure in their critique. Nor is the situation remedied or clarified by the *Epinomis,* an appendix on knowledge and the Nocturnal Council related to the *Laws* as the Myth of Er is to the *Republic.* The highest science here is astronomy, studied in conjunction with natural theology and the state religion. The authenticity of the *Epinomis* will be treated below; but if it is not Plato's own appendix, it is probably the work of his close associate, Philip of Opus, who might be expected to know Plato's intention.[2]

I do not see how this debate can be resolved. Certainly, Plato may have *intended* his citizens to advance some day to the point of reading his *Republic* and Socratic dialogues; but he certainly nowhere *says* that they could or will. Certainly, many of the principles of Plato's philosophy carry forward, and we can sometimes see how they offer a latent rationale for his meticulous detail. But it is just as certain that the attempt to limit the discussion to the level of what Plato thought might work next week in a small Greek colonial town lead to the omission of institutions and ideas, of plans for progress, that seem to vitiate many of his earlier philosophic insights and principles. The speakers are old men, substituting funded experience for abstract reasoning; perhaps, given these characters, it would be dramatically inconsistent to have them suddenly offer or follow arguments that went far beyond Cretan, Spartan, and Athenian politics or natural piety. But, if that is so, this very selection of speakers may concede too great a distance between ideal and actual where the actual is an imaginary contemporary town.

Repeatedly, in the history of philosophy, great men have tried to treat some immediate practical situation: Plato and Kant, both at the age of eighty, write on law; Descartes takes up medicine; and so on. And they are determined not to be "unrealistic" or over-theoretical; they are so aware of the distance between their advanced theory and the limitations of immediate practice, that they exclude the theory rigorously in concentration on what is practical. Medicine, education, and law have all found major philosophers producing works of some interest but no great overt philosophical content, and works that limit the treatment in a way inconsistent both with their own philosophies and with the true importance of ideas and ideals in the special fields treated. This is true of Aristotle's, Kant's and Whitehead's practical writings on education; of Berkeley's and Descartes' ventures in medicine; and of Kant's and Plato's "practical" legislation. Yet in each case, in spite of this conscious over-limitation, the philosophic ideas are still operating in the background, and a later reader is able—preposterous as it seems—to improve on these masters by making explicit the suppressed (or even sometimes unrecognized) connection between their total philosophies and their practical suggestions. One can improve on these works by correcting their pessimistic exclusion of "difficult" or "over-theoretic" ideas from craftsmanlike treatises on a more popular level.

It is in this spirit that defenders of the *Laws*, from Aristotle on, have recognized its essential consistency with the *Apology* and the *Republic*, and have minimized or overlooked its contradictions of these. But it is in this same spirit that critics of the *Laws* stress the need to reject some of its assumptions and accommodations to practice because the *Republic* and *Apology* have (correctly) convinced them that such limitations are not necessary, and in fact *are not truly practical.* The *Laws* remains a masterpiece of coherence, with frequent insights that we can admire; but at the top of its intricate tapestry, we may feel we can improve on Plato's design by replacing an empty space with the *Republic*'s vision of the "city in the skies."

PART FIVE

History

CHAPTER XIV

The Fortunes of the Academy, 347 B.C. to 529 A.D.[1]

WHEN PLATO DIED in 347 B.C., his nephew, Speusippus, inherited the Academy property and became the next head. Aristotle left to visit Hermeias, a former fellow-student, who was now ruler of a city in Asia Minor. Whether this leaving was a protest against the new leadership, or an attempt to extend the Academy by developing another center in Asia Minor, it marks the beginning of a sharp divergence among Plato's students as to what Plato had taught.

Speusippus modified his uncle's views, which he evidently thought were both too optimistic and too static. The Good seemed to Speussipus to be a goal, as Plato had thought, but a goal that few things ever reached or approached, and then only for a short time. Animals, for example, desire the good; that is, they instinctively want the freedom and power of alert maturity; but most never attain this, and none retain it for very long. Plato's value forms seemed to his nephew not to be actual controlling factors, but, if anything, possibilities rarely realized; and the nephew's philosophy moved toward a Pythagorean view of "form" as abstract quantitative structure, and toward a Heraclitean reaffirmation of "reality" as restless process and flow.

Aristotle advocated a different revision. He was very impressed by such objections as those Plato himself had offered in the *Parmenides* to "forms" separate from individual concrete things. The form should be *in* each thing as those essential properties which give the thing its identity. In some cases, there are no typical things for forms to be in; "animal," for example, is a general form that is never realized in itself; for the beings we encounter are all *specific kinds* of animal, never pure "animalness" without further specification. So Aristotle distinguished forms into two kinds. Forms in his strictest sense which he called "formal causes" of things, he limited to determinate species. More general abstractions are forms only in a secondary sense; they are classifications abstracted from the species of the first kind.

Xenokrates, who succeeded Speusippus as head of the Academy in 335 B.C., apparently tried a "back to Plato" revision of Speusippus, which would once more make the forms actual and separate values. This was accompanied by a rejection or weakening of the mathematical structures that Speusippus had made important in his philosophy. Concerning the separateness of the forms Xenokrates is quoted as saying that the forms "exist *in a place* outside of the visible heaven . . ." —a dangerous figure of speech for any Platonist to use, because it will destroy his whole philosophy if he takes it too literally. (See above, p. 146.)

The Academy in general, if not Xenokrates himself, seems to have become literal in its acceptance of such an interpretation of Plato. As we shall see, this set the stage for the three major phases that mark the next seven hundred years of Platonism: scepticism, eclecticism, finally mysticism.

Before we trace these fortunes of the Academy, perhaps one comment is in order on the reinterpretations by the generation just after Plato. Although both Aristotle and Xenokrates had done some philosophic writing in dialogue form, the same temptation to be clear and eliminate variables that had led Plato to offer his Lecture on the Good made them change from dialogue to lecture as their preferred philosophic form; Speusippus seems to have gone from dialogue to diagram and equation. This change has its price: when we study Platonism presented as textbook or lecture (including, unfortunately, this presentation), it always seems to short-change the concrete, human dimension of reality which the dialogue

form, *but not the lecture,* always embodies. Plato's ideas, abstracted from his dialectical presentation, seem to leave out
process, individuality, space, and time. Speusippus' correction
makes dynamic process more important; Aristotle's puts a new
emphasis on the individual. Xenokrates seemed to try to return to Plato by simply denying Speusippus' emphasis on
process, but the result was an over-correction that left him
with separate, remote "forms" once more.

Within three Academic generations after Xenokrates, the
Academy had become a center of philosophic scepticism. This
reversal has sometimes puzzled scholars, but there is an inner
logic in this history that seems quite clear.

If we accept two propositions, (1) Certainty is possible
only through the recognition of a Platonic form acting causally in things; (2) The forms exist outside the heavens in
another place; therefore, (a) They are inaccessible to us as
knowers, and (b) There is no way to explain their operation as causes on the things around us, within the heavens;
it clearly follows that "knowledge in the strict sense" is impossible. Proposition (1) is Plato's own; (2) is Xenokrates'
explication; (2) (a) and (b) are corollaries drawn from (1)
and (2). Then, since "knowledge" is impossible, philosophy
must settle for "conjecture" and "opinion"—and these are at
best, as Plato had proven, probability, not certainty. The Roman Empire created a setting in which the individual felt
insignificant and uncomfortable, alone in a world he could not
control, and a world with sharp corners. Philosophy restricted
its central interests to ethical inspiration and consolation, and
in this frame of reference, the "probabilism" of the Academy
was defended for its ethical value. For, argue the Sceptical
Academicians Arcesilaus and Carneades, if we have no illusion of certainty, hence no intellectual commitment that makes
us feel sure of the future, we will not be disappointed; and
prudence can still be useful on the basis of probability calculation.

In the latter half of the first century B.C., however, the official Academic position changed from critical scepticism to
scholarly eclecticism. Granting all the sceptical arguments, it

finally was also conceded that these apply to the sceptical position itself: in the absence of *any* commitment or certainty, philosophic doctrines will all stand upon a foundation of equal probability. A premonition of this change can be seen in Cicero's treatment of Plato's dialogues as urbane conversations which are deliberately inconclusive because no conclusions are to be had. In effect, a position of tolerant eclecticism can be more sceptical and less philosophical than the doctrinal view of a professional sceptic. For a hundred years, during its period of eclecticism, we lose track of the Academy. "Scholarship" may have occupied their attention; if a small and dismal reference supplement of *Definitions* appended to older Plato manuscripts dates from this lost period, as I believe it does, history's neglect was certainly deserved.

With the second and third centuries A.D., the doctrine known as Neo-Platonism appeared and dominated the Academy. This is a strong reaction against scepticism, in either its dialectical or eclectic form. The Neo-Platonists, in effect, accept the following propositions:

1. Knowledge depends on the recognition by the knower of "forms" which act causally on their instances;
2. these forms exist "yonder," in a place beyond space and time;
3. nevertheless, certain knowledge is possible.

These involve the further proposition:

4. We cannot understand how certain knowledge is possible, but we must accept its possibility as a matter of *faith*.

A feeling that there is a causal power exerted by transcendent form leads Plotinus, probably the greatest metaphysician of the Hellenistic Age, to the "theory of emanation." The ultimate reality is The One, which lies beyond being and knowledge (compare, above, Plato's argument in the *Parmenides*). The

One creates by overflowing itself, emanating as a light does in darkness, in orders of emanation: highest are Mind and The Good—which contain the system of forms "yonder"; then the soul; finally, physical reality. Each level strives to "return" to the higher order of unity from which its existence emanated, and strives to escape the limitations of its own order. However, a soul may mistakenly choose to "look down," and, becoming infatuated with matter, lose its own purity. Such souls are condemned to reincarnation in future lives. The aim of philosophy, within this world-view, is to escape from the round of reincarnation and to attain the destruction of individual identity. (In this, Plotinus reflects the concern with insulation and escape typical of Hellenistic thought.)

Philosophically, the one possible improvement on Plato which Neo-Platonism, with its gaudy metaphors, offers, is in the doctrine of "semblance" in aesthetics. Sometimes, this doctrine recognizes, an imitation which is not an exact model can "remind" us of a form better than the model could: a drawn square which does not have exactly equal sides *looks* more like squareness; a column with a slight curvature looks ideally straight; and so on. This improves what seems to have been Plato's original view. But in ethics, the change from Plato to Neo-Platonism introduces a desperately one-sided escapism, pessimism, asceticism, and passivity. In science and logic the change is marked: mysticism, magic, and aesthetic intuition become the only reliable tools. There is no way to *understand* how the forms of the Neo-Platonists are at once separate and causally operative; *that* they are both is a matter of faith, and we accept it at the price of giving up clear understanding.

By the fifth century, Proclus, the head of the School, had given final development to the insights of Plotinus. We will encounter his *Commentary on the Parmenides* later in our history, in connection with the Christian tradition of "negative theology." Proclus' successor, Damascius, was the head of the Academy when the Emperor Justinian closed the pagan schools of philosophy in 529 A.D. Damascius, with a part of the Academy's library, took himself and the Neo-Platonic philosophy to the court of the Emperor of Persia.

Some Dialogues of Questioned Authenticity
(*Alcibiades I, Hippias Major, Epionomis, Cleitophon*)

Not only do we have no record of authentic Platonic writing that has been lost, but the Academy and Alexandrian library over a period of time had included with their "Plato" papers a number of items clearly from other periods or by other authors, some of which were included by the editor Thrasyllus in his "tetralogy" arrangement of the works of Plato.

In some cases (for example, the *Definitions*), the material is clearly *not* authentic; but there remain a set of writings of disputed authenticity, which, if genuine, are either very early, very late, or incomplete drafts. These are worth brief consideration because if they are authentic, they somewhat change the account we have given of the development of Plato's thought and literary style; even if they are not, they help us to see what other writers in the tradition appreciated when they read Plato.

Had the real point of the early Socratic dialogues been simply to show the importance and difficulty of getting Plato's contemporaries to generalize inductively, had a theology always been central to Plato's doctrine, then the *First Alcibiades* might claim authenticity. (The *Second Alcibiades* is a later critique of Stoicism produced during the sceptical phase of the Academy.) The choice of characters could be evidence in favor of the authenticity of this little dialogue: there is evident dramatic appeal in a conversation between Socrates and the brilliant, unstable Alcibiades.

But the argument of the dialogue is clumsy, its dialectic constantly refers us to God for philosophic answers, and its central point of method—tediously made—is simply the difficulty of getting the young respondent to make a generalization. There is almost none of the interplay of concrete situation and abstract argument that marks the indisputably authentic early dialogues of Plato. Further, the *First Alcibiades* includes an almost textbook summary of the ideas that are central in the authentic dialogues of Plato's "middle" period; so markedly,

that it was in fact used as an introductory textbook for fresh-
man Platonists by the Neo-Platonic heads of the Academy. It
seems to me that the difference in literary skill prevents us
from thinking of the *Lysis,* say, and the *First Alcibiades* as
written at or near the same time; and it seems that the *Lysis*
must have been done practically at the beginning of Plato's
literary career. The absence of any other dialogue with such
a patchwork textbook character also argues against authenticity, and it would be surprising if this thin illustration of the
tediousness of induction were ever Plato's own exclusive philosophic theme: he had too many other ideas to explore and
offer.

The same considerations apply to the *Major Hippias,* with
one difference. Hippias in the dialogue is less a character than
a caricature; he is a pompous walking encyclopaedia of facts,
devoid of ideas; and it is almost impossible for Socrates to
lead him toward generalizations. But in this particular case,
there is the possibility that the choice of central character explains the thin and unusual content and emphasis: Plato *just
might* have been annoyed enough at the vanity of the historical Hippias to portray him in this way. Yet even as an *ad
hominem,* atypical venture, the tedious conversation is hard
to accept as authentic.[2]

The *Lesser Hippias,* on the other hand, which was discussed
above, has every sign of being genuine.

The *Cleitophon* presents a slightly different problem. It is a
brief dialogue in which young Cleitophon (who figured briefly
as an associate of Thrasymachus in Book I of Plato's *Republic*) charges Socrates with "exhorting young men to be virtuous, but then offering no clue as to how virtue is to be attained." The little exchange looks authentic enough, and
Republic II-X could be read as an extended answer by Socrates to the challenge. But if we take this as complete as well
as authentic, and independent of, or even a later appraisal of,
the *Republic,* this short conversation must be recognized as an
almost perfect presentation of the idea that philosophy is engaged inquiry which can never offer answers. Man's essential
nature and virtue, if we follow the lead here given, would lie

in his ability to be provoked into asking what his virtue is. More study is needed of the *Cleitophon;* my own notion is that it is *incomplete* but *authentic.*

A collection of thirteen *Letters* attributed to Plato offers a baffling set of items. Two, the *Seventh* and *Eighth,* deal in some detail with Plato's part in Sicilian politics. They seem "open letters" of explanation, designed as much for Athenian as for Sicilian readers, and there is widespread acceptance of their authenticity. The others either are forged by various hands, or at least betray a strange multiplicity of personalities and roles if they have but one author. Would Plato actually have allowed his own character to seem, even in correspondence, a mystagogue (II), sycophant (I), plagiarist (XI in the context of stories of his stealing Pythagorean doctrine), rotarian (VI: "dependability is the only true philosophy . . ."), and niece-ridden mendicant (XIII)? If so, we can add a good many details, not all of them flattering, to our picture of Plato; but these letters are highly suspect, and, apart from VII and VIII, at least as likely to be later inventions (which could have been sold to the Alexandrian library for a handsome price) as they are to be genuine.

Finally, among the doubtful works of particular interest, the *Epinomis* has been mentioned; this is presented as an "appendix" to the *Laws,* praising astronomy and natural theology as the high points of the research of the Nocturnal Council. It is disappointing not to find the transition here from measurement and myth to the "science of the good" of the middle dialogues. On the other hand, the limitation of "wisdom" to astronomy and theology is consistent with the practical tone and applied philosophy of the *Laws* itself, and there are defenders of the dialogue's authenticity. The defense, however, claims only that this is what it purports to be—an appendix on education to a practical treatise—not that it is Plato's final revelation, nor a proof that its author had rejected all of his earlier speculative philosophy.

Some of Plato's admirers could write good Socratic dialogue; but none could equal Plato in his best early work. And the doubtful works which are at all persuasive as to their authenticity do not change our picture of Plato's development or his philosophy.

Platonism, 529-1962 A.D.[3]

In brief outline, the history of Western philosophy shows alternating displacements and revivals of Platonism; in different fields of study, these revivals sometimes coincide, but sometimes are out of phase (for example, there are periods in which mathematicians are Platonists, but theologians Aristotelian).

But in spite of gains and losses, it seems reasonable to say that until the thirteenth century, Christian thinkers worked within a frame of reference that was essentially Platonic. St. Augustine established a synthesis of Christian doctrine and Neo-Platonic philosophy which to the present day remains central to Christian theology; and this synthesis served as a philosophy as well (for those thinkers interested in philosophy —by no means all were) until the work of Aristotle, rediscovered by the Latin world in the thirteenth century and elegantly interpreted by St. Thomas Aquinas, displaced Platonism for a time.

Within this common early Mediaeval frame of reference, there was still ample room for intellectual controversy and for diversity of interpretation. For example, the work of some anonymous fifth-century writer, incorrectly attributed to St. Paul's companion, Dionysius the Areopagite, initiated and supported a tradition of "negative theology." Pseudo-Dionysius seems to have taken from Proclus the doctrine that all reality culminates in and depends on a "One" which lies beyond knowledge and being, in an inconceivable and unique highest station. If God is identified with this One, then theology can at best describe Him negatively, as unlimited by any of the properties we are familiar with, and only direct mystical experience can supplement this negative way by any positive "knowledge." This is a radical Neo-Platonism; it is a position likely to appeal to the mystic and the poet who distrust abstract, precise doctrinal speculation.

But on the other hand, a Latin translation of the first part of Plato's *Timaeus* served as a model and inspiration for work in science; Chartres in the twelfth century and Oxford in the thirteenth saw a keen interest in natural science, particularly the laws of physics and optics, quite different in implications and tone from the conservative theological and the radical mystical traditions. Roger Bacon, who wrote a treatise in defense of "Experimental Science" (and as a result got into trouble with his conservative superiors), typifies the way in which this Platonic theme continued. And probably in the same line of descent we should include the "magical" tradition of alchemy, astrology, magic, etc., deriving from a fusion of Plato and Near Eastern elements, which throughout the Middle Ages played an important role in the history of experimental science.

Mention of the Near East is a reminder that Plato's influence was also felt there; this is a field still in need of study, and we will only mention the fact that translations of Plato and of commentaries on his works were made into Georgian, Arabic, Syriac, and Armenian.

After the thirteenth century, Aristotelianism displaced Platonism to become the dominant philosophy; it tended, however, to crystallize into textbook formulae and doctrines; and was displaced in favor of a revitalized Platonism by the Renaissance, which we can think of philosophically as running from the fourteenth through the seventeenth centuries.

Plato was rediscovered, as it were, first by the Italian humanists, who at one time had their "Academy" in Florence. The Plato they admired was a great literary stylist, a thinker who by his teaching of man's power to envision the ideal proved the *unlimited* creative power and dignity of man (Plato would have been most surprised at this interpretation), and a philosopher whose awareness of the interconnectedness of nature justified magic and the occult as proper methods of science (again, Plato would have been astounded). In Italian science, on the other hand, the revival of Platonism was influential in a return to mathematics and measurement—as opposed to qualitative cross-classification—which mark the beginning of physical science as we know it today.

The seventeenth century ("The Age of Reason") reached, among the English group of "Cambridge Platonists," and even more the great "Continental Rationalists" (Descartes, Leibniz, and Spinoza), a high point in the development of modern speculative philosophy, at the hands of thinkers who, if we take their own statements, had been inspired by Plato and were carrying out his speculative program against Aristotelian opposition. Then, under combined pressure and attack from empiricism, critical philosophy, and romanticism, the temper of modern thought changed away from trust in speculative system towards more emphasis on detailed factual observation in science, sensitized romantic intuition in literature and aesthetics, and greater acceptance by both art and science of a common sense that was distrustful of the theory of forms.

In the twentieth century, particularly in the work of A. N. Whitehead, Platonism is resurgent once more. Whitehead tried to bring together the two separate lines of development of science and human creativity, which had diverged throughout the nineteenth century. He set himself the task of devising a modern Platonic cosmology which would simultaneously do justice to science's concern with fact, common sense's practical concern with adaptation and control, and religious and aesthetic concern with value.

It is a difficult synthesis to effect. The separate dimensions of Whitehead's program, identifying philosophy with analysis, with practical efficiency, and with intuitive sensitivity, are currently all pursued and defended—usually with an insistence that a Whiteheadian synthesis cannot meet the standard of clarity, or utility, or mystical insight, which these separate inquiries respectively admire. But, in the modern world, with the centrifugal forces of specialization and technology tending to tear apart society and individual personality, it seems fair to say that such a Platonic synthesis as Whitehead proposed is *necessary;* even though there may still be some question as to whether it is *possible.*

CHAPTER XV

The History of Plato's Text

EXACTLY WHAT HAPPENED to Plato's text in the period between 347 B.C. and about 50 A.D. is still not known; there is a sharp difference of scholarly opinion on the matter. We do know that the text was copied and fairly widely read, and that the copying was not always carefully done.

In the first century A.D., Thrasyllus, a scholar and editor, prepared an "edition" of Plato's complete works, arranged in groups of four—"tetralogies." This arrangement was followed in most later manuscripts and is still used by classicists in their editions of Plato. Diogenes Laertius, in his gossipy "Lives and Opinion of Eminent Philosophers" (a kind of scrap-book put together in the second century A.D.), describes this great edition and gives a table of the critical marks its editors used for their marginal annotation. He tells us that the manuscript was so magnificent that scholars had to pay a fee in order to consult it. Thrasyllus' sources, whatever they were, evidently had some direct line of descent by way of scholarly and competent copyists from the Academic originals themselves. (The tradition he followed probably included more material than just the complete works of Plato—at any rate, as we have seen, other works do appear in Thrasyllus' sets of four.)

The "popular" editions in general circulation were written on papyrus, and we have some fragments of these from dates much earlier than Thrasyllus. The reason we have these fragmentary papyri is that Egyptian embalmers frequently bought up "used books" and used them for mummy wrapping; so that on occasion a piece of papyrus with a Platonic passage has been identified and read. The oldest such papyrus fragment goes back to the third century B.C. But their texts are inexact, hasty copies with omissions, corruptions, and paraphrases; apparently conditions in the ancient world did not favor accurate, yet inexpensive "paperback" editions. The papyri are of some, but to date not great, help in textual study.

Our earliest extant manuscripts of Plato are two single volumes from two-volume "de luxe editions" prepared for scholars of the ninth century A.D. The Oxford manuscript E. C. Clarke 39, usually abbreviated as *B*, was (according to a note at the end) "copied for Bishop Arethas by John the Calligrapher in the year 895 for a fee of thirteen byzants." It is the first volume of some standard two-volume arrangement of "complete works." Cod. Parisinus Bib. Nat. MS grec 1807, usually abbreviated *A*, is of about the same date, and luckily is the *second* volume of a two-volume complete edition. *A* must be a copy of the edition of Plato edited by the Patriarch Photius, Arethas' teacher, who was responsible for a revival of classical studies in the ninth century, rescuing Greek literature and philosophy from the relative neglect that followed the closing of the Schools by Justinian in 529 A.D. At one time, all of our other (178) manuscripts of Plato's works, in whole or part, were thought to derive from *B*, *A*, and Venice *T* (a twelfth-century manuscript, almost certainly a copy of the lost first volume of *A*). In turn, *B*, *T*, and *A* have been very plausibly traced back to a single common ancestor of the fifth century A.D. Although they are apparently careful copies, errors occur: some through misreading of letters that looked alike (thus $IC\Omega C$ for $\Pi\Omega C$) or through pronunciation—either when copying from dictation, or from a scribe's repeating aloud to himself the text as he copied.

Without exaggerating the extent of such scribal errors, it would not be too satisfactory a situation to find ourselves unable to reconstruct the line of descent of our Platonic text from any date earlier than the fifth century. An unknown thousand years would offer time enough for considerable cumulative mechanical error, and the confidence of the Neo-Platonists that they understood Plato perfectly would have offered a strong temptation for editorial re-writing or retouching (of which we have records of a few cases in point).

We can be glad, therefore, that the notion of reconstruction dead-ending in the fifth century is not correct. Editors have been able to take advantage of the "indirect tradition"— cases in which Platonic passages are quoted verbatim by other writers, such as Aristotle or Plutarch, and the quotations transmitted in their original form. In about one case out of ten, where there is a difference between the manuscript and indirect traditions, the latter preserve the correct text (this, at least, was H. Alline's figure in 1898). But, what is far more important, there are no large-scale discrepancies; and this strongly suggests that there were no systematic or extensive changes in the text during the Neo-Platonic period.

In addition to new work on the indirect tradition, we have had to change our notion of the "copyist" of the Mediaeval period to that of "editor." For cases keep coming to light where we can show that a supposed direct copy, with arbitrary corrections or emendations, is in fact a composite text based on several sources which the "copyist" compared and chose from. This finding means that we must complete more detailed study of the 178 extant Plato manuscripts; over half of these have not been studied in any detail, on the assumption that, being later than B, T, A, they are mere copies of one or more of these, with no independent value. However, collating and textual history are painstaking, tiresome work, and there has been relatively little recent enthusiasm for this needed textual study.

A notable exception to my last remark is the most recent work on Plato's *Gorgias* and *Meno* by Professor E. R. Dodds and Dr. R. S. Bluck. This finally clarifies the status of a thirteenth- or fourteenth-century manuscript, Vienna F, the exact relation of which to the other sources was not determined previously. New study shows that the ancestry of F goes back along a line independent of that of our other mss to an archetype of the second- or third-century A.D., from which it derives by way of a "popular" rather than a "scholarly" or "expensive" edition. For the dialogues that F contains (among them the *Gorgias, Meno, Republic,* and *Timaeus*) there now is evidence that from the third to the ninth centuries there were no drastic interpolations in, or modifications of, the main lines of descent of our Platonic text.[1]

Some specific examples may show the sort of thing that Platonic textual study finds interesting.

A. Revision in the light of preconceptions. This is dangerous, but detected cases that come to mind are infrequent. In the Hellenistic world, astrology had become respected; and so Plato's passage that comets and conjunctions "bring terror to men not able to calculate . . ." was "corrected" in one version by omitting "not." The key had been lost to Plato's astronomical details in his myth at the end of the *Republic,* but someone with a theory of his own re-wrote the passage to make the "widths of their rims" correspond to the apparent magnitudes of the planets—this was surely not Plato's intention. Again, a modest erasure probably changed an "each" to a "hundred" in a passage on human history, where a very large number was expected but hard to extract from the text.

B. Sharpening of images and analogies. Copying error weakened the fear God expresses in the *Statesman* myth that the cosmos might run down and "fall into an ocean of non-being" to "fall into a place of non-being." A similar error would make Parmenides hesitate at the thought of "the multitude of words I must prove through . . ." rather than "the ocean of words I must swim through. . . ." There are many such minor items.

C. Other. Other aspects of this sort include emendations, classifications of sources, and new editing on the basis of such classification. The interested reader will find references in the Bibliography.

PART SIX

An Appraisal: The Academy's
Program and Ideas,
2500 Years Later

CHAPTER XVI

The Program for Formal Logic

WE HAVE BEEN dealing primarily with Plato's world and his philosophy, though without losing sight of the relevance of that philosophy to problems and ideas of our own. It may be interesting to compare Plato's programs and expectations with the actual course of history, to see what progress he would see, and what program he would offer, if he were to return to our contemporary scene.

In formal science, mathematics and logic, we find Plato's program for first-year dialectic almost completely carried out; the early twentieth century saw the final discoveries needed to complete this work. In technology, there has been so much progress that it would have seemed incredible to an ancient Athenian—though he would have seen some new dangers to virtue that would make him wonder whether this dream-like vision was not the beginning of a nightmare. In ethical sensitivity, there has been remarkable progress since Plato's time. But in the common sense and applied philosophy needed to hold together these gains in human society and life that give increased virtue and nobility, there has been little progress, if any at all. One reason may be, that our philosophy itself has either turned away from speculation altogether, giving up any responsibility for this integrating function, or has turned away from concern with ideals and forms because it is fascinated by process and flow. Philosophy and art want to discover something we call "the concrete." This, they assume, will be at the opposite pole from "abstractions"; and by abstraction they mean "empty form." It is true, in a sense, that the "forms" of

205

our science and logic are empty: they describe but do not evaluate. It is even truer that the "forms" imposed on life by our technology are "abstract"—we get from place to place efficiently, in straight lines, but without a chance to adventure and wander. But if one tries to avoid the empty forms by removing form entirely, what is left is merely an indeterminate medium, equally empty of value. "Concrete existence" was realized in Plato's time by the combination of medium and form; by the form, conceived as an ideal, giving direction and structure to the flow of space and time. In our look at contemporary philosophy, we will be particularly concerned with the relevance of new philosophies of process to the classical problem of the ideal and the actual.

Nothing in the modern world would be likely to please and interest Plato more than the tremendous advances of formal logic we have made in the nineteenth and twentieth centuries. There has finally been detailed development confirming Plato's two programmatic notions or happy conjectures, (1) that the deductive methods of mathematics make an excellent general model for science, and (2) that study should show some more general formal system in virtue of which all the mathematical sciences are "akin."

What was required for these advances was the generalization of the notions of "logical order" and "scientific proof," in an algebraic manner, away from Aristotle's deliberate restriction of scientific method to the demonstrative syllogism as its canonical form. From Plato to the present, the ideal of a "universal method" has haunted the Platonic tradition. Eudoxus, with his universal theory of ratios; Raymond Lull, the thirteenth-century Scholastic philosopher who devised a "great art of combination"; Descartes, in the seventeenth century, with his *Rules for the Direction of the Mind* and his new general four-step method; Leibniz, co-inventor of the calculus, with his "universal characteristic"; are among those who felt this notion's appeal. It remained for Whitehead and Russell, in the twentieth century, to complete the program of consolidating logic and much of arithmetic and geometry in a single deductive, systematic form.

Perhaps the most important step involved is the generalization of the ranges of variables and the rules of inference that can underlie "reasoning." To show how this operates, suppose that we begin with the traditional observation that all of our descriptive discussion takes place in the form of propositions: statements which make some assertion, and that are either true or false. Generalization enters when we note that the truths of all complex propositions (such as "he was poor but sometimes honest") depend only on two things: the truth or falsity of their simpler components, and the patterning of their connection. Thus the "truth value" (true or false) of any compound argument can be represented as a "function" of the truth values of its components, and each type of logical connective defines such a function. In other words, we abstract from the specific content of our propositions and treat them as variables or dummies in order to isolate and study the abstract form of argument. For example, if 'p' and 'q' are variables each representing any proposition, then 'p and q' (written 'p.q') represents the pattern of conjunctive connection of any two propositions; the conjunction, of course, will be true as a whole only when both of its components are so. We can tabulate this functional relation, using 1 and 0 for the "truth values" of truth and falsity, as shown below.

p	q	p.q
1	1	1
1	0	0
0	1	0
0	0	0

There are various ways of handling this notation; for example, there is the useful theorem that "the truth value of a conjunction equals the product of the truth values of its conjoined components." Other functional relations hold for complex patterns of "if . . . then," "not," "or," and so on.

Beyond such a general algebra of truth and falsity for propositions, we have already seen how to develop a formal algebra of classification. Let us think of our general terms as names of classes, and our propositions as information about cross- and sub-classification. Then a few very simple axioms and postulates give an abstract picture of classifying, an algebraic picture first discovered by George Boole in the nineteenth century in his *The Laws of Thought*. The algebra of classification gives the exact structure of operation of modern card-controlled information handling equipment, while modern digital computers developed from the application to electric circuits of the algebra of propositional relations.

We can pick up patterns midway between class and propositional structure by paying selective attention to propositions in respect to their quantity, connective pattern, and type of variable. For example, we can regard "all men are mortal" as a special value of the "propositional matrix" or "function" '(x) [P(x) ⊃ Q(x)]'—"for every individual x, if x has the property P, then x has the property Q." Formal logic develops from this type of generalization beyond study of argument and classification to a general theory of relational pattern and order, of which the numbers, figures, and volumes of Plato's successive "mathematical sciences" can be seen as special cases.

The power shown by our new formal tools is surprising, and no doubt we are far from appreciating it today. But of equal philosophic interest in connection with the comparison of Plato's program and the modern world are certain limitations of formal systems that have been disclosed—limitations which Plato conjectured any such systems would have. The first limitation is that formal systems start with hypotheses, and so, if no contradictions appear, one starting point seems as good as another; there is nothing in the system to tell us which is the "best hypothesis." To make such a judgment, one would have to go to a more general formal system, but that would rest on hypotheses again. The second limitation is that all these tidy formal systems become inconsistent when we try or are forced to make them self-referential: they cannot talk about themselves. This means that these are models suitable for the ordering of objective fact, but not adequate models of method for the Socratic philosopher seeking to *know himself*. (Recent research suggests that if we modify the rule that abstract systems and classes are always sharply exclusive of one another, some of these limitations may be overcome; the suggestion is entirely in the spirit of Plato's conviction that "philosophic hypotheses" are not exclusive, but rather that they form a single ordered whole.)

CHAPTER XVII

Structure and Process: Modern
Philosophies of Flow

DEVELOPMENTS IN THE nineteenth century initiated the interest in time which is characteristic of our twentieth-century science, art, and philosophy. The most important factors in this change were the theory of evolution and the special and general theories of relativity. Evolution extends the notion of a developmental growth to species as well as individuals; it finds new data which make it necessary to interpret the Aristotelian view of the invariance and eternity of species as holding only over relatively short stretches of time. In longer intervals, new species appear, with a constant tendency among those that survive and reproduce toward more complex organization and more effective consciousness. Relativity theory introduces a new close association of space and time: if there are any laws of nature invariant for all observers, "distance" must be measured not in two separate systems, one for three spatial, the other for one temporal "dimension," but in a four-dimensional space-time system. Arguments for and against "operational" definitions increase our awareness of the different ways in which "time" might be measured, and raise a problem of what we mean by "congruent intervals of duration" which finally reintroduces the subjective time sense of some human observer just when we had thought we were rid of him. Literature begins to explore and exploit the interpenetration of past, present, and future (as in Faulkner), or the mystery of passage (as in Proust). Technology changes the elementary tempo of our common-sense careers, and discovers new types of periodicity which have unsuspectedly accurate regularity.

Philosophy would indeed be out of touch with the rest of the world if it were unaffected by these developments. The effect takes several forms. On the one hand, Henri Bergson initiated a line of development that culminates in the modern existentialist notion that to exist is exactly to be in time. Bergson pointed out that "time" as the value of "t" in physical equations, is a high order abstraction; science and mathematics use static concepts to treat the temporal. He went back to Zeno's arrow to show that real experienced time cannot be built by mere adjoining of static snapshots; pure duration, as we experience it intuitively, is radically continuous and dynamic. Further, science allows observation only of closed "facts"; but our normal experience includes an awareness of the future as something not yet wholly determinate, but partially determined in its possible nature. A scientist talking about future events, said Bergson, imagines them as they will look once they are over; in other words, he still thinks of the future as it will look after it has become past. Bergson also doubted whether the mechanistic explanations of evolution by natural selection and random variation will explain the constant direction toward consciousness and complex organization. The exact data he uses to support his case are now somewhat out of date; but we find an eminent biochemist wondering, no longer ago than last week, whether some new law of nature is not needed to explain why there seems a drive toward formation of amino-acid molecules which will be self-replicating—and the problem is the same.

Existentialism combines Bergson's line of criticism with more acknowledgment of aesthetics as philosophically relevant, and insists that human existence is radically individual (categories falsify it), radically temporal, and (contrary to the deterministic view of physics) radically free. (I say contrary to the deterministic view of physics with full awareness of "quantum theory" and "indeterminacy"; but it is by no means clear or necessary that these involve any relaxation of

the determinability, in principle, of such large-scale phenomena as human thought and choice.) The fascinating recent extension of this to psychoanalytic theory rests on the
recognition—which scientists and philosophers had been evad-
ing or denying from Aristotle's *De Generatione et Corruptione*
on—that each person has his own world of "life-space" and
"life-time," and that to "understand" someone else, we must
be able to take a stand for ourselves in his particular spatio-
temporal situation.

Pragmatism, with its emphasis on consequences as tests of
truth and criteria of meaning, emphasizes the role of the
future, much as Bergson had accused "science" of overem-
phasis on the past.

The most speculatively audacious and comprehensive development of a philosophy of flow remains Whitehead's philosophic work, culminating in the brilliant but impenetrable
Process and Reality. Whitehead speaks of himself as a "Platonist," trying to bring together the abstract laws of physics,
the techniques of common sense, and the subjective feelings
and sensitivities of aesthetics. The reason *Process* is so baffling,
or at least *a* reason, is that all of the laws and relations of
science are re-stated in the vocabulary of art—"feelings, feelings of feelings, lures, harmonies," etc. His work offers a high
point in modern Platonism, bringing into focus the changes in
Plato that Whitehead believes we need to adapt the great
Greek philosopher's ideas to the modern world.

The most important modification Whitehead makes in Plato
is to re-interpret the "forms" as "eternal objects." "Eternal
objects" exist only as possibilities, until they become concrete
through "ingression" into an occasion in space and time. As
purely possible, such abstract entities have no "value"; apart
from three limiting conditions, they stand to each other in
"all [logically] possible relations"—a sharp contrast with Plato's
notion of the determinate order of his world of form (in the
strictest senses of "form"). In a restless universe, where
novelty is part of the creative advance of life and nature,
Whitehead insists that objective, actual forms would be a
strait-jacket that does not fit in with what we actually experi-

ence. This has the corollary that ethical decisions cannot be made by reference to objective norms, but must depend on individual sensitivity to the choices which will, and those which will not, create more harmony and value. Such sensitivity is hard to appraise objectively, and whether it can be taught, or even shared intersubjectively, remains a question. The result seems a loss of the strongest feature of Plato's original position: that there is such a thing as an objective standard of right and wrong, good and bad, which can be the basis for ethics and law, as well as for logic and, perhaps, art.

It may well be that Plato himself would not have accepted Whitehead's adaptation—indeed, Whitehead himself doubts whether he would have—but instead, would have insisted, that his own program and vision remain right; and that if the modern world cannot appreciate them, it is a result of "becoming dizzy from too much contemplation of appearances in rapid flow."

CHAPTER XVIII

Ethical Sensitivity: An Area of Progress Since Plato's Time

I BELIEVE THAT there has been, in the Western world, a tremendous increase in our intuitive ethical sensitivity since Plato's time. In a society such as Plato's, even with the increasing democracy of Athens, there is a natural tendency to think of slaves and farm hands as a different variety of human beings from ourselves. Their language, way of life, and lack of culture could be interpreted as due either to some difference in nature or to the impact of different convention; and aristocrats have always found it tempting to accept the former as explanation, though increasing class mobility and educational opportunity repeatedly show that the true cause is the latter.

Plato's philosophy, and the example of his Socrates, are causally related to the later developments that have led us beyond them. The Platonic theory of forms, for example, leads to the conclusion that since there is only one form of man, all human beings are essentially akin; and reason requires like treatment for things the same in kind. This plays a role in the Stoic doctrine that we must follow reason, and that reason requires us to treat all men as equal before the law. The Socratic and Platonic reinterpretation of the self were essential conditions for the fusion of Greek thought and early Christianity with its faith in the worth of every individual, and its doctrine of mutual concern.

In some matters of principle, Plato's philosophy had set the stage for extensions beyond his own powers of imagination.

For example, the *Laws* seems to extend the principle of legality to slavery, affording the slave statutory protection in a way the current city-state law did not. But Plato could not imagine an actual colonial city able to function without slave labor. Nevertheless, the ideal state of the *Republic* would not have slaves; presumably its public works would be taken care of by the auxiliaries, combining the duties of civil service and army. Plato extends the principle of legality, but to preserve discipline and social order, draws his class lines tight, and proposes penalties and treatment for the slaves in his city more severe than those in operation in some of the actual states of his time.

The *psyche* is recognized in the *Republic;* an inner self, sensitive to ideals, common to all men; but hereditary difference in native ability is assumed to account for a far larger amount of individual difference than it does in fact. The genetic theories current in Plato's time lent support to this assumption of hereditary difference; the result is that the *Republic*'s class-structure is related to actual societies much as the divine shepherd in the *Statesman* is to the actual human politician. Interestingly enough, there is one moment in the *Republic* itself where the experience of animal breeders is cited to suggest that education may improve human nature (in which case, more men able to rule might have control in rotation), but both the science and common sense of the time were against this notion, and its consequences were never fully followed out.

The limitations of an ancient Greek point of view show in two other ways. Plato simply cannot imagine an economy of abundance, in spite of his Sicilian travels; this belongs to legends of a lost continent or a golden age. The dilemma of time free from work for men generally, which they may use for leisure or for loafing, he locates in a vanished "golden age," another cosmic cycle from our own. Further, the tendency to look at one's fellow-citizens from the outside—an objective, factual view which identifies a person with his body and his overt actions—remains too ingrained to be easily set aside. The result seems to us to be a needless toughness in dealing with deformed infants and chronically ill artisans, and an insensitive dependence on corporeal punishment as a part of normal social operation.

We can congratulate ourselves on this increased sensitivity, provided it does not lead us to forget that the end of life is not simply comfort and avoidance of pain; duty and dignity still have their price, and we still live in the age of iron, where we must fend for ourselves and a life worth living is sometimes painful and hard.

Automation and Intemperance

Although Plato never wrote the projected dialogues that would have given us a clear notion of his ideas on alliances and international relations, so that it would be very conjectural to say what his reaction to our present international situation would be, we can see clearly enough from the comments on Pericles of Plato's Socrates and from the Atlantis story that he would have one urgent message about our domestic affairs, assuming that we would survive to modify them.

The message is this: "technology can be a better thing than anyone realized in my time. But, when it takes a direction that undermines temperance, it can be worse. If a society allows prosperity to make everyone *want more* comfort and commodities, and if an advertising profession has found a way to create new wants, temperance is in jeopardy.

"Temperance, you will recall, is a 'harmony among the "parts of the soul" as to which should rule and which is ruled'; and in particular, reason, with its ideal of due measure, must limit appetite, which left to itself is just a blind desire to have more. If appetite rules, this creates a psychological imbalance not consistent with courage or wisdom.

"At the moment, you seem shortsighted; the technological changes you call 'automation' are beginning, and yet you are not trying to recapture the ideas of nobility and leisure and teach them to your children.

" 'Leisure' meant, in my day, time which a man could devote to his own self-realization and to the improvement of his society. You may quite well criticize our Greek 'leisure class,' but do please realize how different their leisure was from your own. We didn't think of it as play, rest, or conspicuous waste of time: it was devoted to intensive study, to active cultivating of physical fitness in the gymnasium, to active political planning—in short, to such engaged and strenuous activity that you today would call it *work,* and demand time off from it to rest. You talk about 'hobbies' as an energetic use of leisure time: most of these, my age called 'play,' because they did not lead to self-knowledge, social welfare, or the advancement of science—and, in general, we left such games for the children.

"Now, suddenly, your factories are about to produce far more commodities—refrigerators, for example, one hundred times as fast. You must create a demand for them. How will you do it? Clearly, by telling everyone that he needs more than one refrigerator in order to (a) escape discomfort, (b) increase his pleasure, (c) preserve his social status, (d) keep his own sense of dignity and self-esteem.

"I have, after all, a good prophetic imagination, and I can just see the advertisements ten years from now (if there is no war or human race suicide by then):

YOU POOR FELLOW—HOW YOU MUST SUFFER!

BUT—no more going barefoot down cold stairs to get a can of beer from the kitchen—for with Freezo Bedroom Chryostat that night-time refreshment is at your fingertips. Don't be the last family in your neighborhood to take advantage of this new scientific breakthrough!

"Now, as I argued in my *Republic,* wants can increase without limit and harden into 'needs'; and once a society sets about causing everyone to want more, it seems you get what is called an 'unstable feedback'—as wants increase toward infinity, life is too pinned down to their satisfaction to allow any true leisure, and the pursuit of happiness becomes instead the mad life advocated in my *Gorgias* by Callicles.

"Not that I don't prefer a kitchen refrigerator—or a bedroom one—to a relay team of slaves running snow down from the mountains for Alcibiades. But, men of this future world, think and consider that courage and justice may be crushed beneath an endless flow of commodities if you are intemperate in your use of the magic horn of plenty which the gods have given you!"

Conclusion

A final comment may be in order about the relation of Plato and the modern world, a modern world which still admires Plato's work, and to which his programs and ideas offer a relevant contribution.

In addition to the dangers of intemperance latent in our advanced technology (necessarily latent there, since efficiency and absence of friction are technology's only built-in criteria of value), the development of specialization in society as a whole and in our institutions of education and research confronts us with the danger of filling our world so full of understanding that no room is left for reason or wisdom. Specialization has a strong centrifugal effect; as each specialist develops his own vocabulary and frame of reference, and tries to extend these beyond the original boundaries of his field, contradictions between accredited experts become inevitable. As the usefulness of information which is exhaustive and detailed becomes appreciated, this leads to the narrowing of areas of specialization: no one today is a scholar specializing in British poetry; he works instead in one era or century or in even a narrower area. The results are that we begin to look on control of information as the test of the wise man, that communication breaks down between workers in different fields, or when it operates it results in immediate apparent contradiction and misunderstanding.

Unfortunately, the individual soul is pulled apart in the same way as its society: the man who believes that virtue is knowledge confronts many knowledges, and must tend to hold them in schizophrenic separation: it seems that what is legal, what is right, what is expedient, what is pleasant, and what is true are decided by different experts using different criteria, and setting different terms on which we can enter discussion of law, politics, religion, science. This, carried to the limit, would match Plato's picture of the "democratic man," whose life was "governed by no coherent principles or goals, but was lived from day to day"; a personality designed to match the absence of policy and principle that Plato disliked in the town-meeting democracy of his society.

The joint operation of technology and specialization, furthermore, restyle our environment and habits of attention in such a way that we run the risk of being turned into roles or animate abstractions; not turned into Platonic forms, through the actual passionate reaching toward an ideal, but rather into the type characters of comedy, in which each actor plays an assigned role predictably as though his life were, as Bergson said, "something mechanical encrusted on the living." Probably, no age has talked more about "sensitivity to the concrete" and "authenticity," but had less of it, than our own. What we find in Greek poetry and medicine and daily life, an awareness of the world in its full vividness and qualitative complexity, an engagement in politics, art, and ideas, dims because it has so little encouragement in our society. No Greek ever questioned his own existence; even when he was shallow-minded, he was authentic and sensitive; and it is a doubtful gain to have replaced existence by existentialism—which talks about the concrete in terms of such high abstraction. Perhaps the worst of it is, that we begin to think of "the concrete" as whatever is most opposite to the familiar artificial forms of technology, and monorail routes of custom in society. Yet the removal of all representational or classical form does not give a concrete vision, but a confrontation with nothing, which Plato describes as a direct encounter with pure dynamic space and unstable quality. The self which Socrates desired to know, which chooses its outer roles but is still different from them, atrophies and only the outer role and inner chaos remain.

Besides, we are in a position where only bewilderment and vertigo result from the attempt to know one's self. Psychology, psychiatry, medicine, biochemistry, religion and education reflect us to ourselves in kaleidoscopic gaiety from many mirrors, but each set gives a different pattern of different shapes and colors.

Appendixes

APPENDIX A

PLATO'S WORKS AS ARRANGED BY THRASYLLUS IN TETRALOGIES

Tet. No.	Number Within Tetralogy			
	1	2	3	4
I	EUTHYPHRO	APOLOGY	CRITO	PHAEDO
II	CRATYLUS	THEAETETUS	SOPHIST	STATESMAN
III	PARMENIDES	PHILEBUS	SYMPOSIUM	PHAEDRUS
IV	ALCIBIADES Ia	ALCIBIADES IIb	HIPPARCHUSb	AMATORESb
V	THEAGESb	CHARMIDES	LACHES	LYSIS
VI	EUTHYDEMUS	PROTAGORAS	GORGIAS	MENO
VII	HIPPIAS MAJORb	HIPPIAS MINORa	ION	MENEXENUS
VIII	CLEITOPHONa	REPUBLIC	TIMAEUS	CRITIAS
IX	MINOSa	LAWS	EPINOMISa	LETTERSc

a Authenticity frequently questioned.

b Almost certainly not authentic.

c Varies for each of the 13 letters.

PLATO'S LIFE

427 Birth of Plato
423 Aristophanes' *Clouds*
404 Athens loses war with Sparta;
    rule of "The Thirty"
403 Exiled Athenian democrats drive out "The Thirty"
399 Trial and execution of Socrates
    Young Plato goes to friends in Megara (?)
    Dialogues of group I (see Appendix C) probably written
387 Plato travels to Syracuse and Tarentum
    (? deported to slave market in Aegina by Dionysius I,
    and ransomed by Anniceris of Cyrene?)
    Dialogues of group II in this period
385 Founding of the Academy
    Dialogues of group III and perhaps group IV in this
    period
368 Eudoxus joins, or visits, but certainly exerts a strong
    intellectual influence on the Academy
367 Plato to Syracuse at Dion's invitation to educate
    Dionysius II
    (First two dialogues of group IVA probably written just
    before this journey)
365 Plato returns to Athens
    (Last two dialogues of group IVA?)
361 Plato returns to Syracuse as mediator between
    Dionysius II and Dion
357 Dion's invasion
    Dion's assassination
354 Letters and dialogues of group V in this period
347 Death of Plato

PLATO'S WORKS, BY SEQUENCE AND APPROXIMATE PERIOD

(For the events of each period, and approximate dates, see Appendix B)

I: Lysis-Charmides-Laches; Euthyphro-Apology-Crito (Phadeo envisaged or begun, but completed later).

II: Ion, Hippias Minor, Gorgias, Menexenus, Protagoras, Euthydemus, Cratylus; (perhaps an earlier version of *Republic I*, which would have been called the Thrasymachus).

III: Phaedo, Symposium, Phaedrus, Republic, (Cleitophon?).

IVA: Parmenides-Theaetetus-Sophist-Statesman (as set up, some indications that another final dialogue, The Philosopher, was also projected here).

IVB: Timaeus-Critias (Critias left incomplete; a projected fourth dialogue, the Hermocrates, announced in the Timaeus as part of the program, but never written).

V: Letters VII, VIII; Philebus; Laws; Epinomis (?).

NOTES:

A hyphen between dialogue titles indicates dialogues connected by theme or by internal cross-reference in sequence.

A question mark in parenthesis indicates dialogues of doubted authenticity.

Because of the relatively primitive technique and thought of *Alcibiades I* and *Hippias Major* as compared to· group I, above, if they were genuine they would form a group 0, and we would have to re-locate the *Lysis* sequence at about group III.

Notes to Chapters

CHAPTER I

1. Aristophanes' *Clouds* is available in a number of English translations. In Greek comedy, real people were taken as models for the characters in the plays.

2. The "idea-works" translates *to phronstisterion,* which carries the idea that Socrates is operating a small production-and-retail trade in thoughts.

3. Euripides' *Trojan Women* is also available in many English translations. The description of the Melian affair, and the best account of the Peloponnesian War, come from the *History* of Thucydides. Perhaps Thucydides has slightly edited the history in making the attack on Melos the *exact* turning point of Athenian fortunes of war.

4. As general background in Greek and Athenian culture, see Bibliography. (The new sun-dial, invented by Meton, who appears as a minor character in another of Aristophanes' plays, was described to me by my colleague, Professor Derek J. Price.)

5. For Anaxagoras' teaching, see the books on Pre-Socratic philosophy in the Bibliography. The evidence for Socrates' career as a young scientist is well presented in A. E. Taylor's *Socrates* and John Burnet's notes to his edition of the text of Plato's *Phaedo.*

6. Here we have what are generally accepted as Plato's own *Letters VII* and *VIII* as authority. See editions cited in Bibliography, and R. S. Bluck's book on Plato.

7. The main information we have about the Sophists comes from Plato's dialogues. The actual speeches and quotations still preserved will be found in K. Freeman's book on Pre-Socratic philosophy; see also Untersteiner's book cited in the Bibliography; and see p. 51.

8. Again, Plato's *Letter VII* is the authority for this. In the *Apology,* Plato has Socrates recount his own adventure: "The Thirty" desired to assassinate one Leon, and to implicate as many citizens as they could in their misdeeds, sent a committee to make the arrest. Socrates, who was one of the men appointed for this, simply went home. He was already on bad terms with Critias, who is supposed to have taken him aside and told him not to talk so much; and we can assume that after the Leon affair, he was listed for execution or assassination had "The Thirty" stayed in power.

9. A. N. Whitehead wrote that "science is simply thinking about the world in a Greek way." The early development of physics and mathematics is a fascinating story; a number of books are listed in the Bibliography, under pre-Socratic philosophy, history of philosophy, and history of science; see also p. 115 for a discussion of the synthesis of all science of the time that Plato and his colleagues carried out in the Academy.

10. The story of philosophy and of physics as we know them today begins in the city of Miletus, on the coast of Asia Minor, with a wise man named Thales. Thales of Miletus "predicted" an eclipse which modern astronomers can date as that of May 23, 585 B.C. This date is one of the few facts about him that has any certainty, for Thales became a popular hero, and all sorts of sayings and adventures were later attributed to him. But we can also be relatively certain that he said "all things are made of *hydor*" ("water" *or* "matter in a fluid state"). This is remarkably simple-minded in one way, but profound in another, for it assumes that there is some sense to asking questions about what "all things" are —that there are some common features of reality which will permit us to relate "everything" real in some single ordered system. The choice of a material as the common base of all things was as sharp a break as one can imagine with the notion, then universally held, of nature as inhabited departmentally by unpredictable personal spirits. If all things are transformations of matter, one can look for laws of such transformations that are reasonable and universal in operation. In the process of doing this, one finds progressively more of the details of the world that can be explained "scientifically." Thus Thales' question and his tentative simple answer have gained him the title of the inventor of science and philosophy, in their Western form.

Anaximander, another Milesian, Thales' successor, built (or at least planned the construction of) a primitive mechanical model which would "explain" the apparent motions of the stars and planets by duplicating them mechanically; and he saw that "an indeterminate something" (*to apeiron*) was a better description of matter than Thales' "*hydor*." Anaximines, "third generation" of these Milesian thinkers, advanced another step by suggesting that mechanical changes of density account for the transformation of matter from one state to another. (He seemed to regress a bit, however, in deciding to describe matter as "*aer*"—air *or* matter in a gaseous state *or* smoke—rather than as "an indeterminate something." Only one step remained to complete the application of laws of physics and mechanics to natural phenomena. To answer the question, *why* the world behaves like a mechanism of separate, externally related parts, Leucippus and Democritus formulated an atomic theory, holding that nature is in fact made up of *"atoma,"* small indivisible particles which interact mechanically.

The second line of development begins with the arrival of Pythagoras in Crotona, Italy, in 530 B.C. In addition to being founder and leader of a social-religious Order, Pythagoras can claim the title of being the inventor of pure mathematics: a study of sets and relations in complete abstraction from the things related, so that right triangles or even numbers were studied apart from the peculiarities of any particular set of instances or examples. It is almost impossible for us today to appreciate this jump of abstraction involved in passing from thinking about land-measuring with a knotted cord to thinking about just triangles, right-triangles, etc. The Pythagoreans had two important ideas, which we can express briefly as "numbers are things" and "things are numbers." The first idea directs attention to the fact that in some sense structure and number, as well as water or air, are "real." Numbers have distinct identities, stay the same, and are the same for every observer; the only sense in which they might *not* be called "real" is that they have no extension or location in space and time. The second idea rests on the belief that it is their quantitative structures which give things their identities and explain their behavior. Scientific explanation should, therefore, use the new techniques of pure mathematics as its tools. The "things are numbers" slogan is an overstatement of an important truth; it seemed justified for a time, as applied mathematics led to significant new discoveries, and it re-directed the attention of philosophy to the role of *structure*, away from exclusive attention to *matter*. (For example, it is the *formula* that explains why hydrogen peroxide—HO—differs from water—H_2O—though both have O and H as their component "matter".)

The discipline of abstract generalization, and the development of rigorous proof in mathematics, lie in the background of the emergence of pure formal logic in the city of Elea, where Zeno devised some acute criticisms of the assumptions made by Pythagorean mathematicians.

Parmenides wrote an epic poem in which a goddess reveals new ideas and arguments to him. The most spectacular of these is the truth that "not-being cannot be." It was certainly not until Plato's dialogue, the *Sophist,* which we will discuss later on, that the Greeks became clear that, in some senses, "nothing" is a kind of "something"; Parmenides' goddess seems to hold the more reasonable view. And yet, if everything that "is" has a common essential character, "being," there is no way to see how things can differ, unless Being or Nothing do not exhaust the alternatives. For beings must differ because they have some property other than being (if that were their only characteristic, they would of course be the same); yet the only thing different from "being" is "non-being," a kind of "nothing." There must, then, be lines of "non-being" that hold things apart: but if those lines *are*, they, too, have being; if they *are not*, there is nothing separating the two things. The goddess is an excellent logician; and Parmenides' second major idea is her statement that "it is the same thing that can be thought and can be." In other words, nothing unreasonable can be real: logic gives us a way of eliminating theories simply by examining their "reasonableness," i.e., their logical consistency. This insight was a major positive contribution to Western science and philosophy. The attempts to explain away the vision of "being" as an unchanging absolute whole were of equal importance, but although this same insight, when it appeared in India, was taken as an ultimate religious vision, in Greece it was taken as a challenging problem: how to protect logic and reason, yet preserve science and common sense. We will see the interpretation Plato gave to this insight when we discuss his dialogue, the *Parmenides*, named for our Eleatic philosopher.

Parmenides' younger associate, Zeno (Zeno of Elea, not to be confused with the founder of the Stoic school, who was Zeno of Citium), set out to use Parmenides' logic in defense of the proposition that motion and change are unintelligible, hence must be unreal. He devised four "paradoxes" of motion, apparently directed (certainly effective) against Pythagorean theories. The Pythagoreans tried to build all things out of "monads"—units and points; but they also held that a continuous quantity, such as a line, could be infinitely divided. Since motion with a finite velocity is just passing through points of space during moments (monads or points of time), Zeno could show a contradiction whether the space and time points were assumed to have some finite size, or to have no extension or duration whatever. Suppose, for example, that "motion" comes from adding distance passed through during time; but suppose, too, that points have zero extension, moments zero duration. Then however many points are passed through, no distance has been traversed; and no sum of moments adds up to a finite time that has elapsed. "If we think of a moving arrow as at rest at each point of its flight, when does it move?" is a paraphrase of this argument. If the definition of motion says that a series of zeros add to a finite sum, what more proof can one want that Parmenides was right, and motion cannot be reasonably defined, hence cannot be? This type of simple problem was not resolved to the satisfaction of mathematicians until the nineteenth century, and philosophers are still discussing the difficulties this early logician raised.

These were not the only significant developments that had gone on before Athens became a center of thought, and there were strong dissenting voices to some of the central ideas we have seen

Wilamowitz' judgment that "life is no sickness, nor is Aesculapius a healer of ills of the soul." But throughout the earlier discussion, the aim of the philosopher has been to escape from the pleasures and pains of life, which prevent his soul from being pure; death is a *katharsis* (*Phaedo* 67C: *"Katharsis de einai . . ."* and cp. 59B, 61B, 62D, 64B, 65A, etc.). And *katharsis* has medical connotations that are very strong; cf. Liddell and Scott's, or any other, Greek Lexicon. The hemlock is a medicine for Socrates' body, though it is a healing of soul that it effects; and the debt to the god for services rendered need not be argued further.

3. For a comparable case of this transfiguration motif, see B. M. W. Knox's study of Sophocles' play, *Oedipus at Colonus,* in his *Oedipus at Thebes* (New Haven, 1957), esp. pp. 159 ff. Many of Plato's admirers have reported this reaction; A. E. Taylor and J. B. Skemp (in his *Theory of Motion . . .*) among them.

4. The more we look at this, the clearer it becomes that the legal case is complex; see, for example, Burnet's notes to his edition, cited in the Bibliography. Probably a case very like this actually occurred, though Plato may well have edited the facts to make a decision more difficult. The notion of "piety" (*to hosion*) included reverence for parents; the city courts took cognizance of murder only insofar as it brought religious pollution to the murderer's city; and for these reasons, the case is a peculiarly appropriate one for a dialogue on "piety."

5. My confidence in the principle that their self-referential structure is intentional and holds up under detailed analysis has been strengthened by a number of dissertations and essays written at Yale over the past six years, as yet unpublished. Dr. Paul Desjardins had independently developed this theme, and illustrated it by analyses of the *Charmides* and *Republic* I-III in his dissertation, "The Form of Platonic Inquiry" (1959). Dr. Philip S. Bashor used this approach as a key to what is certainly one of the most detailed and reasonable studies of the *Lysis* that has been made, "The Structure and Function of Plato's *Lysis*" (1954). Dr. Erazim Kohak treated the *Laches* as a dialogue about education, educational in different ways for its participants, in an unpublished Jacob Cooper Prize Paper, Yale, 1957.

6. And this point holds just as truly for the twentieth century reader as it did for the Athenian of Plato's time. The history of Western philosophy has as one of its continuing interests and problems that of "Know thyself."

7. *Epistle VII* 342A ff.; *Phaedrus* 275B ff.; *Phaedo* 102D.

8. For the dramatic dates, see A. E. Taylor, *Plato;* for a table of approximate chronological dates, W. D. Ross, *Plato's Theory of Ideas.*

CHAPTER III

1. Various translations of the *Gorgias* are listed in the Bibliography. Two ideas of special interest for the modern reader are A. E. Taylor's comparison (in his *Plato*) of the theoretical ethical issue between Socrates and the others with the contemporary debates between views of ethics based on calculation of pleasure and utility (deriving primarily from Bentham and Mill), and theories based on a sense of dignity and duty (deriving from Kant); and E. R. Dodds' comparison, in an Appendix to his recent new edition of this dialogue, of the ethical position of Callicles (the good is pleasure and power) and the "Superman" of Nietzsche's philosophy.

2. The argument in the *Protagoras* presents two interesting problems: the logic Socrates uses seems fallacious, and the assumption he introduces that ethics is a science of calculating maximum pleasure seems un-Socratic and un-Platonic. On the first point, see Vlastos' introduction to the Liberal Arts edition, cited below.

On the second, there is considerable evidence that Socrates (and Plato) would both have held that the best life is also pleasantest, and discussions of relative pleasure are relevant enough to ethics; the central divergence between Platonists and hedonists has usually been over the question "is a life good *because* it is pleasant, or is its pleasantness to be set aside in judging whether it is truly good?"

For the discussion of rhetoric as itself a rhetorical contest, in which the audience's identifications is subtly shifted to Socrates, a case is made out in detail by Dr. Adele Spitzer, in her dissertation, "A Platonic Philosophy of Art" (Yale, 1961), Chap. III.

3. Taylor and Dodds have valuable comments and insights in their treatments of this oration. And, of course, these evident excesses of "interpretation" over evidence in our surroundings explain why responsible scholars have become wary of *any* "interpretations" that add ideas to itemized sets of fact; though adding ideas is a risk philosophers must take, the wariness should be a good corrective for temptations to let fact go.

4. The modern reader who wants to appreciate the irony of the *Euthydemus* should concentrate first on the legal tactics of "answer yes or no" by which the contentious brothers refute *every* proposition. Reading some cases of American jury trials or Congressional Committee Hearings makes the relevance come out all too pointedly. But the brothers (Euthydemus & Dionysiodorus—the "dual number" in Greek makes it possible for Plato to talk about their two-man team as a single unit) are going to do the same thing for philosophy; and they mince up Plato's favorite ideas, too. A new translation of this is in progress by my colleague, Robert

Neville, whose dramatic adaptation as a one-act play was presented
to the American Philosophical Association, Eastern Division Meeting, in 1960. On a more serious side, the dialogue makes one
wonder whether very sharp formal logic is an ideal tool for very
un-sharp problems in politics and law (by "very sharp," I mean
cutting always into only two exclusive alternatives, where in fact
there may be overlap or an indefinite number).

5. This time, Plato's central objection is to Achilles being set
up as the ideal of a gentleman, as the conventional Greek high-
school teacher or literary critic did. The hysterical and inconsistent behavior of Homer's high-strung hero comes in for rather
more detailed analysis in Book II of Plato's *Republic*. In development of the theme, however, Plato presses his technique of "concrete self-reference" further than in any other dialogue: the result
is fascinating, but he never repeats this degree of involution. What
inspired him was, no doubt, the wonderful logical discovery of "the
Liar" paradox: "Epimenides the Cretan says all Cretans are liars,"
the truth or falsity of which statement baffled the logicians of the
time.

6. Just how these dialogues relate in time to Plato's trip to
Sicily and Italy is unclear; but it is evident that a new interest in
both Pythagorean-Orphic myth and in mathematics as relevant to
ethical inquiry appear in the *Gorgias, Protagoras,* and *Meno*. This
suggests contact with and interest in the ideas of Archytas; see
p. 77.

7. The reader will find the two treatments of the *Meno* in R. S.
Bluck's impressive new edition and Koyré's perceptive interpretation particularly helpful.

8. How literally Plato took, or intends Socrates to take, this
theory is an interesting question; Bluck summarizes much of the
evidence in his edition, though my own judgment would be that
Koyré, who thinks it pure myth or metaphor, is right. But the
question does not matter very much for the main theme of the
dialogue itself: it is the moral of the myth that counts, and Socrates at least is sure of that.

9. See Fig. III for the figures Socrates uses in this special example of the method. Bluck's Appendix on the subject does not
question his assumption, which is unsupported, that Meno is a
good mathematician. See B. L. van der Waerden, in *Philosophische
Rundschau*, V (1955), p. 122: "Es könnte also sein, dass Sokrates
zwar an das allgemeine Problem gedacht, aber Menon nur den
speziellen Fall vorgelegt hat."

10. My argument here is drawn primarily from Book I of the
Republic. In particular, I have tried to apply the argument that
pleonexia ("having more") cannot be a tenable goal for any sensible man. This is the argument in *Republic I* that F. M. Cornford

omitted as "archaic" in his translation; my interpretation may give teachers a suggestion of how to add it when they are working from Cornford's very fine book.

11. The literature bearing on this topic in current thought is so extensive that no attempt will be made to list it; but a particularly clear and important contribution is C. W. Morris' *Foundations of the Theory of Signs* (Chicago, 1938), which uses the same three "dimensions of sign-functioning" that I find as "specialized types of language" in the *Cratylus*.

12. The peculiar pleasure Plato takes in the many plays on words reminds us that the study of language was still in its infancy, and the Greeks felt a certain amount of "name-magic" in it which we do not. However, reference to other thinkers in the dialogue also indicates that Plato's Socrates is parodying "inspired etymologists" on the scene: Euthyphro is mentioned as one, Heraclitus and his followers as another group. The device is not hopeless if the modern reader will notice *who* gives the various names discussed, and what sort of meanings these "name-givers" are supposed to have in mind.

CHAPTER IV

1. Archytas is difficult to reconstruct because the evidence is so scattered. Field's more technical book on Plato, cited below, is helpful; Freeman's translations of the Pre-Socratics are good; there is an (unreliable, but interesting) "Life" in Diogenes Laertius' *Lives and Opinions;* Bury's *History of Greece* discusses the political career of Tarentum; Heath's work on the history of mathematics records his most famous proofs; Aristotle, in passing, is our authority for the invention of the new baby-rattle. See Bibliography, esp. numbers 59, 60, 112.

2. E. von Sybel, *Platons Symposion: ein Programm der Akademie,* Marburg, 1880.

CHAPTER V

1. There are two arguments here. The first is that the logical consistency of the *Republic* requires such education for all. Education in music and gymnastic is necessary for temperance; and the artisans must be temperate. The second is that the best genetic theories in Plato's time showed that heredity did not determine social fitness or talent; on this point, see Levinson and my *PMI*.

2. On Plato's mysticism, see the discussion in Friedländer's *Plato* (Bibliography, below).

3. *Phaedrus,* Jowett's trans. (*The Dialogues of Plato,* trans. B. Jowett, 4th ed., Oxford, 1953, IV, p. 184.) Quoted by permission of The Clarendon Press. See Bibliography (#14).

4. Compare Whitehead's definition of an "abstractive hierarchy" in Chap. 10 of *Science and the Modern World*.

CHAPTER VI

1. See my article cited in Bibliography, and Professor Price's articles there discussed.

CHAPTER VII

1. We know the end of the Atlantis story, even though the *Critias* is incomplete, since the *Timaeus* opens with a summary of the complete legend Critias will tell after Timaeus finishes speaking.

CHAPTER VIII

1. Relevant sources for getting a complete picture of Eudoxus are collected in my *Plato on the One*, n. 2,. p. 19. Compare P.-M. Schuhl, *L'Oeuvre de Platon* (Paris, 1954), esp. p. 209.

2. For the tradition of treatises "On the Sphere" (Autolycus, Euclid, Theodosius, and an earlier common source from which these drew), see Heath's *History of Greek Mathematics*, I, pp. 348-54.

CHAPTER IX

1. This conclusion was the one Bertrand Russell came to in his earlier investigation of whether an empiricist could dispense with all Platonic forms.

2. For the mathematical example in the *Theaetetus* see my *PMI;* also R. C. Taliaferro's comments in his review, *New Scholasticism*, 1957, 256-60; E. Stamatis, in *Praktika Akad. Athenon*, 1956, 10-16. For this, as for all other technical problems and passages, Professor Cherniss' "Survey" is indispensable; studies of the present passage are cited and discussed on pp. 201-202.

CHAPTER X

1. The primary sources for this account are Plato's *Letters VII* and *VIII*, and Plutarch's "Life of Dion"; a modern historian's appraisal will be found in Bury's *History of Greece*.

CHAPTER XI

1. See Part Six; the development of an algebra suited to this formal treatment was first published in the nineteenth century by George Boole.

2. Here I am indebted for a number of ideas about the self-reference of the *Statesman* to discussion with my colleague, Mr. John Brentlinger.

CHAPTER XII

1. In addition to works of Stenzel (*Number and Form* . . .), Cherniss (*Aristotle's Criticism* . . .), and Merlan (*From Plato to Neo-Platonism*), Robin's *La Théorie platonicienne des Idées et des Nombres d'après Aristote*, Paris, 1908, is a classic. See also Aristotle, *Fragments*, in Oxford trans., vol. XII.

2. For the *Philebus*, in addition to works cited in Bibliography, see Dr. Carol M. Bosche, "Plato's Doctrine of Quality: a Metaphysical Interpretation of *Philebus* 11A-16A," (Ph.D. dissertation, New Haven, 1960). Dr. Bosche does in fact untangle and "unpack" these five Stephanus pages in her commentary; but to do this adequately requires, as her work shows, almost two hundred closely written pages of English prose.

CHAPTER XIII

1. Aristotle, *Politics II* (1265, a-11).

2. Philip of Opus copied Plato's *Laws* from the wax tablets of Plato's unpolished draft, and certainly had something to do with the *Epinomis*. But more likely he was its editor than author; see for example, the Introd. to A. E. Taylor's trans. (*Philebus and Epinomis* . . .), cited in Bibliography.

CHAPTER XIV

1. Here detailed citation is too complex. For the major outlines, see the histories of philosophy and the Academy cited in the Bibliography.

2. For the *Hippias Major*, see A. Croiset, "Notice," in his Budé edition, (Platon, *Oeuvres Complètes*, II, Paris, 1956, 1-7; *First Alcibiades*, Notice of M. Croiset in the Budé edition, vol. I, 7th edn., Paris, 1959, 49-59.

3. Again, for this historical section, detailed annotation is too complex to attempt; see histories of philosophy cited in the Bibliography.

CHAPTER XV

1. In addition to Alline (cited below), some accounts of recent work on Plato's text are given in Dodds' *Gorgias*, Bluck's *Meno*, and my *Plato on the One;* see also my account of some of R. Klibanky and C. Labowsky's textual work, in the article "A Latin Translation. . . ," cited below.

Annotated Bibliography

This is an annotated list of some of the books and articles in English that came to mind as informative or interesting or both. By following the order of topics as I have, the list may make locating exactly what the reader wants require more looking than other arrangements would; but I myself find it interesting to see what sorts of books there are in a field before I pick out a particular one to read, and as a supplementary chapter on current English studies of Plato, I think the list has some interest in its own right.

With the exceptions of Greek texts and one French work which is the only general survey to date of the history of Plato's text, I have limited this to books in English, and where possible books inexpensively available. The best things to read to understand Plato are Plato's *Works* themselves. For the reader who wants to follow philosophic speculation apart from its historical tradition, but has difficulty in seeing for himself how Plato's *Dialogues* would translate into the language, and apply to the problems of, a modern world, Whitehead's philosophic works are the recommended bridge between ourselves and Plato; at the outset, *The Function of Reason, Religion in the Making, Science and the Modern World,* or *Adventures of Ideas* are recommended rather than Whitehead's earlier technical writings, or his very difficult *Process and Reality.* Excellent bibliographies where the reader will find nearly exhaustive coverage of Platonic studies in all languages are listed in Section II.

I. *Text and Reference*

1. *Platonis Opera,* ed. Manutius, Aldine Press, Venice, 1498. The first printed edition of the text.
2. *Platonis Opera,* ed. J. Stephanus, Paris, 1573. This has become the standard edition for citation (by page, a letter indicating section of column from A to E, and line number).
3. *Platonis Opera,* ed. J. Burnet, 5 vols., Oxford, 1899-1907. An excellent and compact critical edition of the text.
4. Platon, *Oeuvres Complètes,* various eds.; Société Édition "Les Belles Lettres" (the Budé edition), 13 vols., Paris, 1920-1959. Texts with valuable French introductions, translations, and notes. Some new collations supplement Burnet; a careful scholar will use both this and his editions.

5. *Plato's Works*, various translations, including H. N. Fowler and W. Lamb, Loeb Classical Library; Greek text and English on facing pages. An excellent text for the reader to get in the habit of using, if he has any Greek, however rudimentary.
   5a. For such a reader, A. N. Fobes, *Philosophical Greek*, Chicago, 1957, will be both interesting and useful.
6. *Republic*, ed. and trans. P. Shorey, Loeb Classical Library, 2 vols., New York and London, 1930.
7. *Timaeus, Critias, Letters*, etc., ed. and trans. R. G. Bury (Loeb Classical Library), N.Y. and London, 1929.
   Some texts of specific dialogues include valuable English notes and commentary:
8. *Republic*, ed. J. Adam, 2 vols., Cambridge, 1902.
9. *Republic*, ed. B. Jowett and L. Campbell, 3 vols., Oxford, 1894.
10. *Symposium*, ed. R. G. Bury, revised edition, Cambridge, 1932.
11. *Euthyphro, Apology, Crito*, ed. J. Burnet, Oxford, 1924.
12. *Phaedo, Ibid.*, Oxford, 1911. Extensive and excellent notes supplement the austere text alone of Burnet's edition cited above (3).
13. *Gorgias*, ed. E. R. Dodds, Oxford, 1960. Among other excellent notes, a fine appendix on the relation of Plato's Callicles to Nietzsche's Superman.
14. *Plato's Dialogues*, translated with introductory notes by B. Jowett, translation alone of 3rd edition, 2 vols., Random House, N.Y., 1937; 4th ed., revised, 4 vols., Oxford, 1952. Still the standard English translation. Jowett's version should be supplemented by later, more literal or more technically precise, versions of other translators for certain dialogues. The marginal summarizing notes, in the third but not the fourth edition, are an aid to finding a given passage or topic, or to getting a quick review of a line of argument. Jowett does not include the *Letters*.
14a. Plato, *The Complete Dialogues, including the Letters*, in English translation by various translators, ed. by Edith Hamilton and Huntington Cairns (New York, Pantheon Books, 1961). For the later dialogues, particularly, the translations are more exact and contemporary than Jowett's, though for the *Timaeus* Jowett's translation is used and this must be supplemented by Bury or Cornford. Having different translators has both gains and losses; the inclusion of the *Letters* is a clear gain. Ideally, I suppose this would be the book to use for second readings of various dialogues in translation, after a preliminary reading of Jowett.

The Library of Liberal Arts series has published a number of translations and commentaries on individual dialogues, some with new and interesting introductions. These include (New York, 1950-1961):

15. *Euthyphro, Apology, Crito*, trans. F. J. Church, revised and with introduction by R. Cumming. Very good introduction.

16. *Gorgias*, trans. with introduction by W. C. Helmbold. Very good translation, philosophically useless introduction.

17. *Meno*. trans. B. Jowett, with introduction by F. H. Anderson.

18. *Phaedo*, trans. with running commentary and notes by R. S. Bluck (reprint of Bluck's *Phaedo*, London, 1955).

19. *Phaedrus*, trans. W. C. Helmbold and W. G. Rabinowitz.

20. *Phaedrus*, trans. with commentary by R. Hackforth (reprint of *Phaedrus*, Cambridge, 1952).

21. *Protagoras*, trans. B. Jowett, revised by M. Ostwald, with introduction by G. Vlastos. Interesting introduction, including some analysis of Plato's logic.

22. *Statesman*, trans. J. B. Skemp (reprinted from *Plato's Statesman*, trans. with commentary and notes, New Haven, 1954; see below).

23. *Theaetetus* and *Sophist*. trans. with running commentary by F. M. Cornford (reprint of *Plato's Theory of Knowledge*, London, 1935).

24. *Theaetetus*, trans. B. Jowett, with introduction by I. Copi.

25. (*Timaeus*) *Plato's Cosmology*, the *Timaeus* trans. with running commentary by F. M. Cornford (reprint of edition, London, 1937).

26. *Timaeus*, trans. with notes and introduction by F. M. Cornford. Since the text is cut up and hard to follow in C.'s "running commentary" format (#25), there is an advantage to having this consecutive version of his trans. alone.

27. *Parmenides*, trans. with running commentary by F. M. Cornford (reprint of *Plato and Parmenides*, N.Y. and London, 1939). Also contains translation of Parmenides' own poem which inspired the dialogue, and a good chapter on Pythagoreanism.

28. *Philebus*, trans. with notes and commentary by R. Hackforth (reprint of *Plato's Examination of Pleasure*, Cambridge, 1945).

Other English translations include:

29. *The Last Days of Socrates* (*Phaedo*), trans. H. Tredennick (Penguin), Harmondsworth, 1954.

30. *Portrait of Socrates* (*Euthyphro, Apology, Crito*), trans. Sir R. Livingstone, Oxford, 1950.

31. *Great Dialogues of Plato*, trans. W. H. D. Rouse (Mentor Books), N.Y., 1956. Lively colloquial versions giving a notion of right tempo and style for the dialogues as literature. Usually, we are too stately, reverent, or dryly technical in translating and read-

ing to get this dimension. A further corrective to over-slowness and literalness is:

31a. *Plato's Euthydemus,* Jowett's translation revised and adapted as a one-act play by R. Neville, mimeographed, New Haven (Yale University Dept. of Philosophy), 1960.

32. *Republic,* trans. F. M. Cornford (now paperbound); Oxford, 1947. Very clear but misses point of "always wanting to have more" (*pleonexia*) argument in I; perhaps wisely omits "nuptial number" in Bk. VIII.

33. *Republic,* trans. H. D. P. Lee (Penguin), Harmondsworth, 1955. This and Cornford are both good; different teachers and readers vary in preference; my own is slightly for Cornford.

34. *Philebus and Epinomis,* trans. and with an introduction by A. E. Taylor, posthumously published, edited by R. Klibansky with the assistance of G. Calogero and A. C. Lloyd, London and N.Y., 1956. Among other excellent notes and insights, the Introduction has a treatment of the relation of this dialogue to Eudoxus' hedonism.

35. *Sophist and Statesman,* trans. with introduction and notes by A. E. Taylor, edited by R. Klibansky and G. E. M. Anscombe, London and N.Y., 1960. Later versions of Cornford (#25) and Skemp (original of reprint cited above, #22) add touches that are needed; but the translation and introduction, as well as the editors' notes, are excellent; something is gained in the introduction from the fact that Taylor was writing when "classification" was a much more viable philosophic topic than it has been since 1930.

37. *Parmenides,* the "hypotheses" of Parmenides' demonstration of method (137A-end), text, translation, commentary by R. S. Brumbaugh (*Plato on the One,* New Haven, 1960). Also contains some non-technical discussion of the history of the text.

38. *The Thirteen Platonic Epistles,* trans. L. A. Post, Oxford, 1925.

39. *Studies in the Platonic Epistles,* trans. with commentary by G. R. Morrow (Illinois Studies . . .), Urbana, 1935. See also R. S. Bluck's translation of *Epistle VII* (#49, below), and R. G. Bury (above, #7). Bury's very brief notes are a good introduction to the reader as a guide to problems of authenticity.

40. *Epinomis,* trans. with notes by R. Harward, Oxford, 1928.

II. *Reference and Bibliography*

41. (Ancient lives and summaries):·Plato, *Works,* Vol. vi, trans. G. Burges (Bohn's Classical Library), London, includes the lives and summaries of Albinus, "Alcinous' Summary . . ." (really also Albinus), Olympiodorus, Apuleius; the "Lexicon" of one Timaeus

the Sophist; and several inauthentic "Platonic" works. For Diogenes' Laertius' "Life," #42, below, is better.

42. "Life of Plato," Bk. V in Diogenes Laertius, *Lives and Opinions of Eminent Philosophers,* ed. and trans. R. D. Hicks (Loeb), 2 vols., N.Y., 1925.

43. "Selected Bibliography" in N. P. Stallknecht and R. S. Brumbaugh, *The Spirit of Western Philosophy,* N.Y., 1950, pp. 511-20.

44. "Platonic Scholarship, 1945-1955," by T. G. Rosenmeyer, *Classical Weekly,* L (1957), 173-82, 185-96, 197-201, 209-11. Well organized, briefly annotated; important items are starred.

45. H. F. Cherniss, "Plato Studies, 1950-57," *Lustrum,* 1959/4, 1960/5. An exhaustive bibliography of books and articles abstracted and cross-referenced by topic and passage.

45a. F. Ueberweg-K. Praechter, *Grundriss der geschichte der philosophie,* I, *Das Alterthum,* 12th edition, Berlin, 1926. Exhaustive bibliography of older studies, many of which are now out of date. See also Section III, below.

45b. W. C. Greene, ed., *Scholia Platonica,* Haverford, 1929. An edition of the scholia (ancient marginal notes and diagrams in the Plato MSS). Some plates supplementing Greene's line drawings for some figures are published in:

45c. R. S. Brumbaugh, "Logical and Mathematical Symbolism in the Plato Scholia," *Journal of the Warburg Institute,* XXIV (1961), 45-58.

45d. *Lexikon Platonicum,* ed. F. Ast, 3 vols., Leipzig, 1835; repr. in 2 vols., Bonn., 1956. Still the standard Plato lexicon. For textual history, see below, Section V.

III. General Works on Plato and Related Themes

PLATO

46. A. E. Taylor, *Plato: the Man and His Work,* N.Y., 1936. Excellent for dramatic dates, leading figures, treatment of individual dialogues, their order and setting.

47. G. M. A. Grube, *Plato's Thought,* London, 1935; reprinted in paper (Beacon). A tracing of major themes in Plato's philosophy.

48. A. Koyré, *Discovering Plato,* trans. from French by L. C. Rosenfield, N.Y., 1945. Good introduction to spirit and form of the Platonic dialogue.

49. R. S. Bluck, *Plato's Life and Thought,* With translation and comments on the Seventh and Eighth Letters.

50. G. C. Field, *Plato and His Contemporaries,* London, 1930. An attractive, well-written study, which adds a good deal to our understanding of Plato.

50a. G. C. Field, *The Philosophy of Plato* (Home University Library), Oxford, 1949. A brief, clear introduction to a limited selection of Platonic themes and their contemporary relevance; much better than many more pretentious studies, a fine book in its own right.

PHILOSOPHY

See N. P. Stallknecht and R. S. Brumbaugh, #43, above; also:
51. B. Russell, *A History of Western Philosophy*, N.Y., 1945. Brilliant, incisive and witty, but should be used in combination with some more pedestrian version of the history of philosophy.
52. B. A. G. Fuller, *A History of Philosophy*, 2 vols. in 1, N.Y., 1938.
53. F. Thilly, *History of Philosophy*, revised with added bibliography and notes by Ledger Wood, N.Y., 1951. Both this and #52 are very good brief treatments. More detailed treatments in Ueberweg, #46, above; also:
54. E. Zeller, *Plato and the Older Academy*, trans. S. F. Alleyne, London, 1876 (N.Y., 1888). Still good, especially for its notes indicating relevant sources.
55. P. Friedländer, *Plato I*, trans. H. Meyerhof, N.Y., 1958 (Pantheon Books, Bollingen Series). The other two volumes of this thorough, carefully documented study will also be available in English translation.

For Early Greek philosophy, see also:
56. E. Zeller, *Pre-Socratic Philosophy*, trans. S. F. Alleyne, 2 vols. (A History of Greek Philosophy from the Earliest Period to the Times of Socrates), London, 1881. Like #54, still good for its documentation; its lack of more recent citations is corrected in:
56a. Zeller, *op. cit.*, Italian trans. R. Mondolfo, 2 vols., Florence, 1932; each section ends with an extended and up-to-date bibliography.
57. J. Burnet, *Early Greek Philosophy*, 4th edition, London, 1930; reprinted in paper (Meridian Books), N.Y., 1960. A standard study with very good translations of most of the extant fragments.
58. G. S. Kirk and J. E. Raven, *Pre-Socratic Philosophy*, reprinted in paper (Cambridge), N.Y., 1960. Up-to-date, very good discussions; much less thorough a coverage of the fragments than Burnet, and the treatment of Heraclitus follows a line that has drawn considerable dissent. Probably a compromise of Plato's *Cratylus*, the present book, and #58a below is advisable.
58a. P. Wheelwright, *Heraclitus*, Princeton, 1960.
The standard source for this period is H. Diels and W. Kranz,

Fragmente der Vorsokratiker, 10th edition, 3 vols., Berlin, 1952. This is translated into English in #59 and 60.

59. *Ancilla to Diels,* trans. K. Freeman, Oxford, 1948. English translation with notes of all the extant fragments (i.e., direct quotations) which are section A of each part of Diels.

60. *Companion to Pre-Socratic Philosophy,* trans. K. Freeman, Oxford, 1949; a translation, with notes and running comment, of the anecdotes and paraphrases of each early Greek thinker; the B sections of Diels' edition.

THE GREEK WORLD AND ITS HISTORY

61. K. Freeman, *Greek City-States,* N.Y., 1950. An attractive set of case-studies of life in a selected set of the Greek cities.

62. H. Kitto, *The Greeks* (Penguin Books), Harmondsworth, 1951. Particularly good on the role of the *polis* (the word we usually translate—Kitto thinks inexactly—as "city-state") in the life of ancient Greece.

63. Edith Hamilton, *The Greek Way to Western Civilization* (Mentor), N.Y., 1948. Fine sensitivity to the tension and interpenetration of ancient Greek senses of flamboyance and form.

64. W. Jaeger, *Paedeia,* trans. G. Highet, 3 vols., N.Y., 1949. A wealth of source material and perceptive comment on the Greek ideal of culture and the road to its attainment.

The Greeks had their own dramatists and historians; a careful brief modern source on history is:

65. J. B. Bury, *History of Greece* (Modern Library), N.Y., 1937.

There are so many histories and reproductions of Greek art—particularly sculpture and architecture—that no specific ones seem needed here. As a footnote on an elegant minor art see:

65a. C. Seltman, *A Book of Greek Coins* (King Penguin), London, 1952. Unusually attractively illustrated and selected.

More specialized studies include works on the Sophists, Socrates, and the Academy, among them the few cited here:

66. M. Untersteiner, *The Sophists,* trans. K. Freeman, N.Y., 1954. A very interesting book, but the account is frequently criticized as too imaginative; statements should perhaps be checked against their basis in sources.

67. [Aristotle] (i.e., a work attributed to Aristotle but really by some later member of the Lyceum) *On Xenophanes, Melissus, and Gorgias,* translated in Loeb (Aristotle, *Minor Works*) and "Oxford translation" (so cited hereafter: *The Works of Aristotle translated into English,* under general editorship W. D. Ross, 13 vols., Oxford, 1908-1959), VI. A garbled account, but with discernible

outline intact, of Gorgias' ironic and notorious speech demolishing speculative philosophy.

67a. [Aristotle] *On Things Heard; On Marvelous Things Heard,* translated in same vols. as #67. Two notebooks of the sort of thing a Greek scholar (?) found odd enough to be worth recording. Many of Miss Freeman's effective details of life in Greek towns (in #61) come from these collections.

68. Aristotle (really Aristotle, this time), *On Sophistical Refutations,* Oxford trans., vol. I. A. treats Sophistry as misuse of language rather than bad metaphysics, as Plato had treated it.

See also Plato's portraits of Gorgias, Protagoras, Hippias, Cleitophon, Euthydemus & Brother, *et al.*

ON SOCRATES

69. A. E. Taylor, *Socrates,* Oxford, 1933; reprinted in paper (Anchor), Boston, 1951. A standard study, particularly suggestive in its treatment of S.'s early career as scientist (to *ca.* 423).

70. Xenophon, *Memorabilia,* various translations (including Loeb). Socrates' trial seen by a non-philosophical friend; compare also:

70a. Xenophon, *Symposium,* various trans.

71. Aristophanes, *The Clouds,* various trans.

72. Babette Deutsch, *The Mask of Silenus,* N.Y., 1933. A novel about Socrates, seen sympathetically, if highly imaginatively, by an American poetess.

73. Radhakrishnan, ed., *History of Philosophy, East and West,* 2 vols., N.Y., 1952, "Socrates" in Vol. ii. Socrates as seen by an Indian philosopher, who thinks the West has misunderstood him.

74. E. Zeller, *Socrates and the Socratic Schools,* trans. O. J. Reichel, London, 1885. Still a good work, with useful notes, on the four "schools" claiming to carry on Socrates' ideas. See also Diogenes Laertius, #42, above, lives of Aristippus, Euclides of Megara, Antisthenes, and the picturesque Diogenes of Sinope.

ON THE ACADEMY

75. H. F. Cherniss, *Aristotle's Criticism of Plato and the Academy,* I, Baltimore, 1949. A thorough, masterly examination of relevant materials and passages; in the absence of Vol. ii, to deal with the vexed criticisms of Academic mathematics by Aristotle, of possible interest are:

75a. H. Apostle, *Aristotle's Philosophy of Mathematics,* Chicago, 1952.

75b. R. S. Brumbaugh, "Aristotle as a Mathematician," *Review of Metaphysics,* VIII (1955), 381-393.

76. P. Merlan, *From Platonism to Neo-Platonism,* The Hague, 1959.

On specific periods or dialogues, the following are among useful works (in addition to those cited in Sections I and II above).
77. M. Fox, "The Trials of Socrates," *Archiv für geschichte der philosophie,* 6 (1956), 226-261. Sensitive account of the interrelation of Plato's "life of Socrates" trilogy.
78. A. N. Whitehead, "Immortality," in *Essays in Science and Philosophy,* N.Y., 1947. Parallels the sense and proofs of immortality developed in the *Phaedo,* quite independently and as corollaries of W.'s own philosophy.
79. R. Robinson, *Plato's Earlier Dialectic,* 2nd. revised edition, Oxford, 1953. A very unimaginative book; Robinson refuses to credit any writer who uses a method with understanding what he is doing, unless the text specifically says "I am here using method. . . ."; with this canon, Plato looks unmethodical, and so would any classical philosopher. On the other hand, Plato's specific passages on method are meticulously translated and analyzed in the study.
80. R. Robinson, "A Criticism of Plato's *Cratylus,*" *Philosophical Review,* LXV (1956), 324-41. Compare R. Levinson's rejoinder:
81. R. B. Levinson, "Language and the *Cratylus:* Four Questions," *Review of Metaphysics,* XI (1957), 28-41. See also my footnote to this article:
81a. R. S. Brumbaugh, "The Order of Etymologies in Plato's *Cratylus,*" *Rev. of Met.,* XI (1958), 502-10.
82. R. E. Allen, "Anamnesis and Chorismos," *Rev. of Met.,* XIII (Sept., 1959), pp. 165-174. Argues that we should take "recollection" and the "separateness" of the forms more literally than modern scholars tend to. A good counterweight to my treatment of these themes, above.
83. *Idem,* "Participation and Predication in Plato's Middle Dialogues," *Phil. Review,* LXIX (1960), 147-64. Argues that since Plato's "forms" are described as wholly unlike the "ideas," "abstractions," and "universals" of later British philosophy, Plato may not have been trying (singularly ineptly) to make the forms anticipate the latter concepts.
84. M. Isenberg, *The Order of Discourses in Plato's Symposium,* Diss., Chicago, 1942. An excellent reference or starting-point for the reader of the Middle Dialogues, as an example of the sort of organization he should look for. One might find the exclusive stress on method narrower than need be, but H. F. Cherniss (in #45, above) seems to be tendentious in his abstract and appraisal.
85. G. K. Plochmann, "Socrates, the Stranger from Elea, and

some Others," *Classical Philology*, XL (1954), 223-31. A perceptive treatment of the reasons and effect of Plato's decision to have main characters other than Socrates in the later dialogues. Again, Cherniss' appraisal seems to me tendentious, and should not discourage the interested reader.

86. *Symposium*, trans. P. B. Shelley—various editions (1895, 1908, 1928). Interesting as showing how one major poet understood another.

87. R. P. McKeon, "Symposia," in *Proceedings of the American Philosophical Association for 1951-52*, pp. 18-41. A brilliant speech on Plato's *Symposium* and the subsequent tradition of symposia in Western literature and philosophy.

88. T. G. Rosenmeyer, "Plato's Hypothesis and the Upward Path," *American Journal of Philology*, LXXXI (1960), 393-407. Careful study of two metaphors: are "hypotheses" higher than the subject-matter they explain, or lower underpinnings for the principles they support? Plato seems to make them be both, in different contexts.

89. E. Barker, *Greek Political Theory*, London, 1918 (reprinted in University Paperbacks Series, N.Y., 1960). A standard and judicious work.

90. Aristotle, *Politics*, esp. Bk. II. Various translations; McKeon's "Introduction" in *Basic Works of Aristotle* (the Oxford translation, edited with introduction by R. McKeon, Random House, N.Y., 1941) is recommended introductory reading. A practical student of Plato's finds a good many objections to the *Republic* and the *Laws*, and to a "Utopian" approach to politics in general. See also:

90a. Aristophanes, *The Birds*, various trans. The conservative comedian this time aims attacks at city planning and all such unrealistic political Utopianism.

91. K. Popper, *The Open Society and Its Enemies*, London, 1945. This and #92, below, are attacks on Plato answered conclusively in R. Levinson's defense (#93, below). Before accepting either translation or interpretation of Plato the student is advised to compare Levinson's work. Many readers and reviewers have agreed that the theory Popper attacks deserves demolition, but deny that it resembles Plato's.

92. R. H. S. Crossman, *Plato Today*, 2nd edition, N.Y., 1959. Particularly interesting criticisms by an active politician; whether the *Republic* is not taken too literally is a fair question, and whether, again, the political scheme Crossman criticizes is Plato's has been doubted. As with #91, this should be used with Levinson for balance and to avoid being misled.

93. R. B. Levinson, *In Defense of Plato*, Cambridge, Mass., 1950. A careful, moderate, and on most points conclusive book,

showing where and how Plato's critics and detractors have mis-
represented or misread him; Popper's work is treated in most detail, as a case-study.

94. N. R. P. Murphy, *An Interpretation of Plato's Republic*,
Oxford, 1952. Has been charged with missing half of Plato's metaphysics and muddling the other half; in my opinion, quite justly;
but Murphy clearly traces the argument that noble lives are also
pleasantest, which most metaphysicians have tended to miss.

95. H. W. B. Joseph, *The Form of the Good in Plato's Republic*,
London, 1948. An illuminating brief lecture on a crucial philosophic concept; see also A. E. Taylor, #16, above.

96. J. E. Raven, "Sun, Divided Line, and Cave," *Classical Quarterly* III (1953), 22-32. A repeatedly cited article on Bks. VI and
VII of the *Republic*.

97. R. S. Brumbaugh, "Plato's Divided Line," *Review of Metaphysics*, V (1952), 529-34. An attempt to interpret the equality of
segments ii and iii in Plato's figure as neither sheer ignorance (as
W. Fite did) nor intricate epistemological symbolism (as N. R. P.
Murphy does—see #94, above).

98. M. E. Hirst, "The Choice of Odysseus (Plato, *Republic*
620C-D)," *Classical Philology*, XXXV (1940), 67-8. A nice note
on the "choice of lives" in the Myth that conclude the *Republic*.

SCIENCE IN THE ACADEMY

This topic has had strange fortunes. The histories of science of
Sarton, Farrington, and others of this type are incorrect and in-
adequate; see, e.g.:

98a. J. Haden, "The Challenge of the History of Science, Part
I," *Review of Metaphysics*, VII (1953), 74-88. A critical study of
Sarton. Perhaps A. N. Whitehead exaggerates the positive claims,
but his admiration offers some balance. G. de Santillana's recent
work has more appreciation, but not very great precision. A brief
but more balanced and sharper treatment than these is:

98b. M. Claggett, *Greek Science in Antiquity*, N.Y., 1955.

But the interested reader is still faced with reading histories of
individual sciences—astronomy, medicine, psychology, physics—
for himself as context, then reading Plato's *Timaeus* (with help
from the commentaries and notes to translations listed below) and
drawing his own conclusion.

99. A. E. Taylor, *A Commentary on Plato's Timaeus*, Oxford,
1928. Brings to bear a wealth of detail from the scientific background at the Academy's disposal. Taylor treats the *Timaeus* itself
as an attempt to recreate the science of the century before the
dialogue was written, largely because he thinks Plato's own "science" should be closer to Taylor's nineteenth century idea of what

science ought to be. But this anomalous interpretation is now generally rejected; some reasons are given in #100, below.

100. F. M. Cornford, *Plato's Cosmology* (including his translation of the *Timaeus* cited above, ##75, 76); reprinted, N.Y., 1957. The criticisms of Taylor are important

101. Proclus, *Commentary on Plato's Timaeus,* trans. Thomas Taylor, 2 vols., London, 1803. Both the translator ("Tom Taylor the Platonist," whose English Plato was standard until Jowett) and the author (scholar and head of the Academy, *ca.* 450 B.C.) were enthusiastic Neo-Platonists. Still, in spite of lapses into unintelligibility and jargon collaboratively, this is an important book. Modern scholars read it, but underestimate it.

101a. *Plato's Timaeus and Atlanticus,* in the translation of Thomas Taylor, reprinted with introduction by R. C. Taliaferro, (Pantheon), New York, 1944. Of value primarily as showing how Neo-Platonists read these dialogues.

102. E. Rohde, *Psyche,* trans. W. B. Hillis, London and N.Y., 1925.

103. W. H. S. Jones and E. T. Withington, *Hippocrates' Works,* 4 vols. (Loeb), London. A source book for medicine; the reader should note carefully the probable dates and orientation of the individual treatises, which range over some extended time and through several points of view.

103a. Sir William Osler, "Plato on Medicine and Physicians," in *Aequanimitas,* 3rd edition, Philadelphia, 1932. One of England's most distinguished modern doctors comments on Plato's contemporaries in his field. K. Freeman's chapter "Abdera," in #61, above, gives a clear and interesting summary of a doctor's case-book from that town.

104. R. S. Brumbaugh, "Plato and the History of Science," *Studium Generale,* IX (1961), 520-22. Some recent findings in the history of science suggest that Plato and his school did not limit their "science" to pencil-and-paper alone work in some ivory tower.

105. M. Jammer, *Concepts of Space,* with introduction by A. Einstein, Cambridge (Mass.), 1954. Clear presentation of various classical and modern views; compare with Whitehead on this theme, in *Adventures of Ideas.*

106. H. Sigerist, *History of Medicine,* N.Y., 1961.

ATLANTIS

Over the years, "Atlantis" has been variously rediscovered in Egypt, Spain, Helgoland, Cornwall, and Yucatan. A sample of these identifications, and the sort of evidence on which they rest (and a very good sample), is:

106a. E. H. Bjorkman, *The Search for Atlantis,* N.Y., 1927.

Any map of the North Atlantic floor (for example, *Life's Pic-* *torial Atlas of the World,* N.Y., 1961, pp. 260-61) will show the "Plato Seamounts" and "Atlantis Seamounts" there. For maps of Plato's Atlantis, see the Loeb edition, *Timaeus,* etc., trans. and ed. R. G. Bury (#7, above).

For the unwritten "Hermocrates," our only clue is Plato's choice of the Sicilian general as main character; see Thucydides, *History,* IV.58, VI.72.

107. J. B. Skemp, *The Theory of Motion in Plato's Later Dialogues,* Cambridge, 1942. How does a "formalist" explain and analyze change? A perceptive study.

108. G. Morrow, *Plato's Cretan City,* Princeton, 1961. An extended study of the context and background of the *Laws,* which seem to Morrow at least not inconsistent with the principles of the *Statesman* and *Republic.*

109. L. Versenyi, "The Cretan Plato," *Review of Metaphysics,* XV (1961), 67-80. Some questions for Morrow; V. cites some half-dozen important points where he does find Plato inconsistent, and is dissatisfied with M.'s explanation.

110. *Laws,* trans. A. E. Taylor, 2 vols. (Loeb), London, 1934.

111. R. B. England, *The Laws of Plato,* 2 vols., Manchester, 1921. Detailed notes and comments; remains standard, though #108 above is more up-to-date.

A few works of interest on more specialized topics are:

MATHEMATICS

112. Sir Thomas L. Heath, *History of Greek Mathematics,* 2 vols., Oxford, 1921. The standard work; Vol. I includes "Eudoxus," "Archytas," "Theaetetus," "Theodorus," in addition to "Plato."

113. I. Thomas, ed. and trans., *Greek Mathematics, I: Thales to Plato* (Loeb), Cambridge (Mass.), 1939. Texts and translations of important passages.

114. Euclid, *Elements of Geometry,* trans. with notes by Sir T. L. Heath, reprinted in paper (Dover Books), N.Y., 1960, 3 vols. See especially Bks. I-V, X, XI, XIII.

115. J. Stenzel, *Number and Form in Plato and Aristotle,* trans. D. J. Allan, Oxford, 1940. A study now recognized as a classic treating this very controversial problem.

116. R. S. Brumbaugh, *Plato's Mathematical Imagination,* Bloomington, 1954. An attempt to see how Plato used mathematical theorems, diagrams, and concepts as parts of his dialectic.

117. A. Wedberg, *Plato's Philosophy of Mathematics,* Stockholm, 1955. Raises several important questions, in particular the question of self-inclusion among the forms.

118. H. D. P. Lee, "Geometrical Method and Aristotle's Ac-

count of First Principles," *Classical Quarterly,* **XXIX** (1935), 113-24.

119. J. Gow, *Short History of Greek Mathematics,* Cambridge, 1884. This follows, and should be read as a paraphrase of, Proclus' *Commentary on Euclid, Elements Bk. I,* a most important ancient source for the history of mathematics.

GENETICS

This special area is important because of its bearing on whether the "equality of opportunity" in the *Republic* is popular science, pure fabrication, or astrological superstition (the "Nuptial Number" passage, *Rep.* VIII, 546A). See Popper, Levinson, Adam's *Rep.* II, cited above; also my discussion, in #116, above.

THE THEORY OF FORMS, AND SOME OF ITS LOGICAL PROBLEMS

120. Sir D. Ross, *Plato's Theory of Ideas,* Oxford, 1957. Collects evidence clearly, but leaves many problems unresolved.

121. W. F. Lynch, S.J., *An Introduction to the Metaphysics of Plato through the Parmenides,* Princeton, 1959. Suggestive, well-presented study, which has been criticized both for taking the *Parmenides* too imaginatively and too literally.

One of the really awkward problems is Platonic language, which suggests that the form is an instance of itself, and has the same "form" as the things that fall under it. See:

122. G. Vlastos, "The Third Man Argument in the Parmenides," *Philosophical Review,* LXIII (1954), 319-49.

123. W. S. Sellars, "Vlastos and the 'Third Man,'" *Philosophical Review,* LXIC (1955), 405-37.

ASTRONOMY

124. Sir T. L. Heath, *Aristarchus of Samos,* Oxford, 1913. A clear and authoritative standard work.

AESTHETICS

125. R. C. Lodge, *Plato's Theory of Art,* London, 1953 (N.Y., Humanities Press, 1953).

A modification or interpretation that may or may not be consistent with Plato's view, but has proven fruitful in Western aesthetics, is Plotinus' Neo-Platonic doctrine of semblance.

126. R. P. McKeon, "Imitation and Poetry," *Thought, Action, and Passion,* Chicago, 1954, pp. 102-222.

EDUCATION

See Jaeger, above, #65, Vol. II.

127. R. Nettleship, *The Theory of Education in Plato's Republic,* Oxford, 1935.

128. R. C. Lodge, *Plato's Theory of Education,* London, 1947.

And, to see how the "high-school" curriculum of mathematics looks in mediaeval and modern dress, see:

128a. P. Abelson, *The Seven Liberal Arts* (Teachers College Contribs. to Education, N.Y., 1906).

128b. A. N. Whitehead, *Introduction to Mathematics,* reprinted in paper (Galaxy Books), N.Y., 1961. Compare the four main ideas here with the subject-matters of the Quadrivium and *Republic* VII.

ETHICS

In addition to works cited:

129. J. Gould, *The Development of Plato's Ethics,* Cambridge, 1955. A stress on "changes" in position with which many readers and scholars do not agree; compare, for example,

129a. A. Boyce Gibson, "Change and Continuity in Plato's Thought," *Review of Metaphysics,* XI (1957), 237-55.

MYTH AND RELIGION

130. J. A. Stewart, *The Myths of Plato,* London, 1905.

131. P. E. More, *The Religion of Plato,* Princeton, 1921.

132. F. E. Solmsen, *Plato's Theology,* Ithaca, 1942.

133. F. M. Cornford, *From Religion to Philosophy,* reprinted in paper (Harper), N.Y., 1960.

134. G. Murray, *Five Stages of Greek Religion,* 3rd edition, reprinted in paper (Anchor), N.Y., 1955.

135. E. R. Dodds, *The Greeks and the Irrational,* reprinted in paper (Anchor), Berkeley, 1951.

IV. *History: Platonism and the Academy*

136. H. Alline, *Histoire du texte de Platon,* Paris, 1889. The one exception to my rule of citing only works in Greek or English; we have no translation or comparable general study.

137. R. S. Brumbaugh, "A Latin Translation of Plato's *Parmenides*," *Review of Metaphysics,* XIV (1960), 91-109. Includes a brief summary of some of the material in #136.

PLATONISM

138. J. Burnet, *Plato and Platonism*, Berkeley, Calif., 1928.
139. W. Pater, *Plato and Platonism*, N.Y., 1893.
140. R. Klibansky, *The Continuity of the Platonic Tradition in the Middle Ages*, 2nd printing, London, 1939. See the histories of philosophy, cited above.

PLATONISM TODAY

141. R. Demos, *The Philosophy of Plato*, Chicago, 1939.
141a. *Idem*, "Introduction," in *Plato: Selections*, ed. with introduction by R. Demos (Scribners Mod. Schol. Library), Chicago, 1927. A philosophically interesting interpretation of Plato's philosophy and its contemporary significance by a student and admirer of A. N. Whitehead.
142. A. N. Whitehead, *Adventures of Ideas*, reprinted in paper (Pelican Books), Harmondsworth, 1933.
143. *Idem, Science and the Modern World*, New York, 1925; reprinted in paper (Mentor), New York, 1948.
144. *Idem, The Function of Reason* (Beacon Paperbacks), Boston, 1959.
145. *Idem, Essays in Science and Philosophy*, New York, 1948. (In particular, "Immortality" and "Mathematics and the Good.")
For Whitehead's *Introduction to Mathematics*, see above, #128b.

Index

253

appear. Hippocrates of Cos, the "father of medicine," and his school had stressed caution in theory building, careful observation and records, and controlled comparison of case histories. (The Greek poets shared with these doctors sharp observation and awareness of detail in nature, and so much so that we are still not always sure when we are dealing with an account of a controlled experiment and when with poetic imagery.)

And, in Asia Minor, Heraclitus, a misanthropic oracular character, rejected the speculations of his mathematical and scientific contemporaries as too abstract and static. The truth is that "all things flow." Writing in a compact, epigrammatic style, Heraclitus tried to communicate his sense of the restless fluidity and paradoxical tension of concrete existence directly to his hearers. If we are looking for someone we can call "the first Western existentialist," it seems that Heraclitus would be the man.

11. The general public were inclined to pooh-pooh any notion of "stones up in the sky"; but the fall of a large meteorite gave them some pause.

CHAPTER II

1. Plato himself continued to look for a "myth" that would bring together the findings of science as to fact and some ordering principles of value, which would show that the universe is reasonable.

2. The debt to Aesculapius reminds one at once of Socrates' remarks early in the dialogue that the body's pleasures and pains are distractions, release from which would, therefore, presumably be a "healing." Scholars have interpreted this remark in infinite and grotesque ways: Socrates *may* have just remembered some unpaid bill to a physician who had treated his son for measles; he *may* be wandering mentally and making a delirious remark (with due solemnity, however, a learned article points out that aconitine does not make the victim's mind wander); he *may* be healed because his death removes a guilt created by the court's conviction of him (though there is no indication anywhere that he felt such a guilt); but such suggestions are mere free association rather than responsible literary and philosophical interpretation.

The dialogue is from the standpoint of a Socrates whose human life is over; he has become immortal, in effect, already; and from this standpoint, the pleasures and pains of mortality do indeed seem an unimportant thing. The reader, scholar or not, who fails to see this will have trouble interpreting even the literal sense of Plato's text. Dr. Bluck, for example, whose new edition of the *Meno* is excellent, appears to me to forget this over-all orientation for a moment in treating the debt to Aesculapius. He rejects the notion that it is payment for the hemlock, quoting with approval